# THE ULTIMATE

# GOURMIA

# Air Fryer

# COOKBOOK

## 250 AMAZINGLY EASY AIR FRYER RECIPES

## FOR SMART PEOPLE ON A BUDGET

## LESLIE HICKOX

# CONTENTS

## Vegetarians Recipes ..................................................................................................**104**

## Sandwiches And Burgers Recipes.................................................................**123**

# INTRODUCTION

**Getting to Know the Gourmia Air Fryer**

Deep-frying your food may taste amazing, but it's certainly not beneficial for your health. Air fryers perform convective heat transfer, or convection: A heating element heats the surrounding air and then an internal fan rapidly circulates that heated air. Because the heated air is circulated, it makes contact with every bit of surface area on the food, crisping your food and creating a nice crust without the use of excessive oil and grease. In an air fryer, food typically sits in a perforated basket or on a wire rack inside the air fryer, which also facilitates contact between heated air and every surface of the food.

**Seeing the Benefits of the Gourmia Air Fryer**

**1.      Healthier Cooking**

Air fryers are a great option if you're looking for a healthy alternative to typically fatty foods. With an air fryer, you can cook all your favorite fried dishes without the unhealthy amount of oil present in their deep-fried versions. Air fryers are specifically designed to cook with less oil, producing food with up to 80% less fat than traditional fryers. You can cook without any oil at all, or you can toss your food in a small amount of oil before cooking for an extra crunch.

**2.      Quick Meals**

Since they're smaller than an oven and circulate air more rapidly, air fryers cook food faster than other appliances. Air fryers can achieve high temperatures within minutes (or seconds), a process that usually takes at least 10 minutes with a traditional oven. An air fryer is a great option for you if you don't have a lot of time to cook meals. However, keep in mind that most air fryers can only cook so fast because of their small size, so if you have a large family, it may be hard for you to cook for everyone at once.

**3.      Adaptability**

Air fryers are known for their extreme versatility. When we say they can cook almost anything, we mean it. You can cook fresh foods as well as frozen foods and even reheat leftovers. Remember, if you're looking for a frying effect, breaded foods do better than battered foods. Look for different accessories and attachments, such as additional fry baskets, baking racks, and cooking pans, to increase your air fryer's functionality even more!

**4.      Easy Cleanup**

Cleanup – the dreaded process at the end of cooking. Air fryers make cleaning simpler at the end of meals. Most of their internal components are removable for easy cleaning. For added convenience, many are even dishwasher-safe. Easy cleanup can cut down on the amount of time you spend in the kitchen and encourage you to cook more often.

## Tips and Tricks on How to Use the Gourmia Air Fryer

Don't be intimated by the air fryer! Once you get the hang of it, you'll never know how you lived without it before. Try these tips to cook with your air fryer like a pro:

(1)      Always Preheat Before Cooking – Think of your air fryer like a little oven. If yours doesn't have a preheat feature, allow it to warm up for 3-5 minutes before you begin cooking.

(2)      Spray the Basket – Even if your recipe doesn't call for oil, be sure to spray the basket's bottom for best results! You can use cooking spray, butter, or grease it with a little olive oil.

(3)      Don't Overfill the Basket – Cook in batches if you need to! It's important not to let your food overlap. If you try to squeeze too much in, you may end up with a soggy, undercooked mess. Easy does it!

(4)      Flip or Shake Foods You Want Crispy – If you're cooking french fries or chicken wings, flip them halfway through or remove the basket and shake. This helps them crisp evenly.

(5)      Invest in Baking Pans & Accessories – These air fryer accessories will make life so much easier and cleaning a breeze!

(6)      Have Fun & Experiment – We think this tip is the most important! Once you get the hang of cooking with your air fryer, have some fun with it. Branch out and try new things! You'll get used to the cooking times, breading methods, and more, so use your knowledge to create new recipes.

## Hints on Cleaning the Gourmia Air Fryer

Cleaning and preserving are the most important factors to decide the durability of an appliance. The best time to clean an air fryer is immediately after use, which will ensure that food particles do not stick to the sides and become hard to remove. However, do not rush and let the machine cool down about 30 minutes before cleaning.

Air fryers usually come with an instruction manual; hence, you can also refer to this manual to see how best you can care for your new device to extend the useful lifespan saving you money in the long term.

# 1 . Clean the frying basket

1.      The bottom frying basket is where lots of grease and gunk falls, so cleaning it properly to prevent grease build-up and bacteria growth that could foul the foods and make you sick. You can proceed to clean the basket according to the following instructions:

2.      Make sure that the device is unplugged from the power source and wait until it's cool to start cleaning. You can remove the air fryer basket and either set it in the sink or on the counter. This will help it cool down even faster.

3.      Use a damp cloth to wipe down the exterior. Wipe away the soap with a clean damp cloth. And repeat this step for the interior.

4.      Remove the basket and tray from the main unit, then use a bit of dish soap with warm water to wash them with a soft sponge or cloth—no abrasives.

5.      If food is stuck on these components, you should soak them in hot soapy water for at least 10 minutes before scrubbing with a non-abrasive sponge.

6.      Don't forget to dry it completely before you put it back in the air fryer!

7.      It's a good idea to clean the frying basket after each use to ensure to remove all old foods and grease causes to smell and effects to the taste of food.

## 2. Clean the Crumb Basket

1.      Take the crumb basket out and throw away any loose pieces of food leftover in it. Wipe it out with a damp cloth.
2.      Make sure you clean all the crevices and both the outside and inside of the basket. It might help to use a dish brush or toothbrush to clean all the slats.
3.      Dry it completely. Make sure it completely dry before replacing them in the air fryer.

## Note:

➢      The crumb basket has a non-stick coating on it, so please don't use abrasive brushes (like steel wool) on it or any abrasive cleaners that might erode this coating. This is why we do not recommend using a dishwasher. They operate at high heat which erodes the surface of the nonstick cookware. It can lead to flaking which can be toxic.

➢      We are also against using any strong detergents or things that aren't designed to clean. Often, these can have the opposite effect and actually cause damage instead of cleaning.

# Poultry Recipes

## Chicken Cutlets With Broccoli Rabe And Roasted Peppers

Servings: 2       Cooking Time: 10 Minutes

**Ingredients:**
- ½ bunch broccoli rabe
- olive oil, in a spray bottle
- salt and freshly ground black pepper
- ⅔ cup roasted red pepper strips
- 2 (4-ounce) boneless, skinless chicken breasts
- 2 tablespoons all-purpose flour*
- 1 egg, beaten
- ⅓ cup seasoned breadcrumbs*
- 2 slices aged provolone cheese

**Directions:**
1. Bring a medium saucepot of salted water to a boil on the stovetop. Blanch the broccoli rabe for 3 minutes in the boiling water and then drain. When it has cooled a little, squeeze out as much water as possible, drizzle a little olive oil on top, season with salt and black pepper and set aside. Dry the roasted red peppers with a clean kitchen towel and set them aside as well.
2. Place each chicken breast between 2 pieces of plastic wrap. Use a meat pounder to flatten the chicken breasts to about ½-inch thick. Season the chicken on both sides with salt and pepper.
3. Preheat the air fryer to 400°F.
4. Set up a dredging station with three shallow dishes. Place the flour in one dish, the egg in a second dish and the breadcrumbs in a third dish. Coat the chicken on all sides with the flour. Shake off any excess flour and dip the chicken into the egg. Let the excess egg drip off and coat both sides of the chicken in the breadcrumbs.

Spray the chicken with olive oil on both sides and transfer to the air fryer basket.
5. Air-fry the chicken at 400°F for 5 minutes. Turn the chicken over and air-fry for another minute. Then, top the chicken breast with the broccoli rabe and roasted peppers. Place a slice of the provolone cheese on top and secure it with a toothpick or two.
6. Air-fry at 360° for 3 to 4 minutes to melt the cheese and warm everything together.

## Chicken Chunks

Servings: 4       Cooking Time: 10 Minutes

**Ingredients:**
- 1 pound chicken tenders cut in large chunks, about 1½ inches
- salt and pepper
- ½ cup cornstarch
- 2 eggs, beaten
- 1 cup panko breadcrumbs
- oil for misting or cooking spray

**Directions:**
1. Season chicken chunks to your liking with salt and pepper.
2. Dip chicken chunks in cornstarch. Then dip in egg and shake off excess. Then roll in panko crumbs to coat well.
3. Spray all sides of chicken chunks with oil or cooking spray.
4. Place chicken in air fryer basket in single layer and cook at 390°F for 5minutes. Spray with oil, turn chunks over, and spray other side.
5. Cook for an additional 5minutes or until chicken juices run clear and outside is golden brown.

6. Repeat steps 4 and 5 to cook remaining chicken.

## Honey Lemon Thyme Glazed Cornish Hen

Servings: 2
Cooking Time: 20 Minutes

**Ingredients:**
- 1 (2-pound) Cornish game hen, split in half
- olive oil
- salt and freshly ground black pepper
- ¼ teaspoon dried thyme
- ¼ cup honey
- 1 tablespoon lemon zest
- juice of 1 lemon
- 1½ teaspoons chopped fresh thyme leaves
- ½ teaspoon soy sauce
- freshly ground black pepper

**Directions:**
1. Split the game hen in half by cutting down each side of the backbone and then cutting through the breast. Brush or spray both halves of the game hen with the olive oil and then season with the salt, pepper and dried thyme.
2. Preheat the air fryer to 390°F.
3. Place the game hen, skin side down, into the air fryer and air-fry for 5 minutes. Turn the hen halves over and air-fry for 10 minutes.
4. While the hen is cooking, combine the honey, lemon zest and juice, fresh thyme, soy sauce and pepper in a small bowl.
5. When the air fryer timer rings, brush the honey glaze onto the game hen and continue to air-fry for another 3 to 5 minutes, just until the hen is nicely glazed, browned and has an internal temperature of 165°F.
6. Let the hen rest for 5 minutes and serve warm.

## Chicken Adobo

Servings: 6
Cooking Time: 12 Minutes

**Ingredients:**
- 6 boneless chicken thighs
- ¼ cup soy sauce or tamari
- ½ cup rice wine vinegar
- 4 cloves garlic, minced
- ⅛ teaspoon crushed red pepper flakes
- ½ teaspoon black pepper

**Directions:**
1. Place the chicken thighs into a resealable plastic bag with the soy sauce or tamari, the rice wine vinegar, the garlic, and the crushed red pepper flakes. Seal the bag and let the chicken marinate at least 1 hour in the refrigerator.
2. Preheat the air fryer to 400°F.
3. Drain the chicken and pat dry with a paper towel. Season the chicken with black pepper and liberally spray with cooking spray.
4. Place the chicken in the air fryer basket and cook for 9 minutes, turn over at 9 minutes and check for an internal temperature of 165°F, and cook another 3 minutes.

## Crispy Duck With Cherry Sauce

Servings: 2
Cooking Time: 33 Minutes

**Ingredients:**
- 1 whole duck (up to 5 pounds), split in half, back and rib bones removed
- 1 teaspoon olive oil
- salt and freshly ground black pepper
- Cherry Sauce:
- 1 tablespoon butter
- 1 shallot, minced
- ½ cup sherry
- ¾ cup cherry preserves 1 cup chicken stock

- 1 teaspoon white wine vinegar
- 1 teaspoon fresh thyme leaves
- salt and freshly ground black pepper

**Directions:**
1. Preheat the air fryer to 400°F.
2. Trim some of the fat from the duck. Rub olive oil on the duck and season with salt and pepper. Place the duck halves in the air fryer basket, breast side up and facing the center of the basket.
3. Air-fry the duck for 20 minutes. Turn the duck over and air-fry for another 6 minutes.
4. While duck is air-frying, make the cherry sauce. Melt the butter in a large sauté pan. Add the shallot and sauté until it is just starting to brown – about 2 to 3 minutes. Add the sherry and deglaze the pan by scraping up any brown bits from the bottom of the pan. Simmer the liquid for a few minutes, until it has reduced by half. Add the cherry preserves, chicken stock and white wine vinegar. Whisk well to combine all the ingredients. Simmer the sauce until it thickens and coats the back of a spoon – about 5 to 7 minutes. Season with salt and pepper and stir in the fresh thyme leaves.
5. When the air fryer timer goes off, spoon some cherry sauce over the duck and continue to air-fry at 400°F for 4 more minutes. Then, turn the duck halves back over so that the breast side is facing up. Spoon more cherry sauce over the top of the duck, covering the skin completely. Air-fry for 3 more minutes and then remove the duck to a plate to rest for a few minutes.
6. Serve the duck in halves, or cut each piece in half again for a smaller serving. Spoon any additional sauce over the duck or serve it on the side.

# Peanut Butter-barbeque Chicken

Servings: 4
Cooking Time: 20 Minutes

**Ingredients:**
- 1 pound boneless, skinless chicken thighs
- salt and pepper
- 1 large orange
- ½ cup barbeque sauce
- 2 tablespoons smooth peanut butter
- 2 tablespoons chopped peanuts for garnish (optional)
- cooking spray

**Directions:**
1. Season chicken with salt and pepper to taste. Place in a shallow dish or plastic bag.
2. Grate orange peel, squeeze orange and reserve 1 tablespoon of juice for the sauce.
3. Pour remaining juice over chicken and marinate for 30minutes.
4. Mix together the reserved 1 tablespoon of orange juice, barbeque sauce, peanut butter, and 1 teaspoon grated orange peel.
5. Place ¼ cup of sauce mixture in a small bowl for basting. Set remaining sauce aside to serve with cooked chicken.
6. Preheat air fryer to 360°F. Spray basket with nonstick cooking spray.
7. Remove chicken from marinade, letting excess drip off. Place in air fryer basket and cook for 5minutes. Turn chicken over and cook 5minutes longer.
8. Brush both sides of chicken lightly with sauce.
9. Cook chicken 5minutes, then turn thighs one more time, again brushing both sides lightly with sauce. Cook for 5 moreminutes or until chicken is done and juices run clear.
10. Serve chicken with remaining sauce on the side and garnish with chopped peanuts if you like.

# Sweet Chili Spiced Chicken

Servings: 4
Cooking Time: 43 Minutes

**Ingredients:**
- Spice Rub:
- 2 tablespoons brown sugar
- 2 tablespoons paprika
- 1 teaspoon dry mustard powder
- 1 teaspoon chili powder
- 2 tablespoons coarse sea salt or kosher salt
- 2 teaspoons coarsely ground black pepper
- 1 tablespoon vegetable oil
- 1 (3½-pound) chicken, cut into 8 pieces

**Directions:**
1. Prepare the spice rub by combining the brown sugar, paprika, mustard powder, chili powder, salt and pepper. Rub the oil all over the chicken pieces and then rub the spice mix onto the chicken, covering completely. This is done very easily in a zipper sealable bag. You can do this ahead of time and let the chicken marinate in the refrigerator, or just proceed with cooking right away.
2. Preheat the air fryer to 370°F.
3. Air-fry the chicken in two batches. Place the two chicken thighs and two drumsticks into the air fryer basket. Air-fry at 370°F for 10 minutes. Then, gently turn the chicken pieces over and air-fry for another 10 minutes. Remove the chicken pieces and let them rest on a plate while you cook the chicken breasts. Air-fry the chicken breasts, skin side down for 8 minutes. Turn the chicken breasts over and air-fry for another 12 minutes.
4. Lower the temperature of the air fryer to 340°F. Place the first batch of chicken on top of the second batch already in the basket and air-fry for a final 3 minutes.

5. Let the chicken rest for 5 minutes and serve warm with some mashed potatoes and a green salad or vegetables.

# Quick Chicken For Filling

Servings: 2
Cooking Time: 8 Minutes

**Ingredients:**
- 1 pound chicken tenders, skinless and boneless
- ½ teaspoon ground cumin
- ½ teaspoon garlic powder
- cooking spray

**Directions:**
1. Sprinkle raw chicken tenders with seasonings.
2. Spray air fryer basket lightly with cooking spray to prevent sticking.
3. Place chicken in air fryer basket in single layer.
4. Cook at 390°F for 4minutes, turn chicken strips over, and cook for an additional 4minutes.
5. Test for doneness. Thick tenders may require an additional minute or two.

# Chicken Rochambeau

Servings: 4
Cooking Time: 20 Minutes

**Ingredients:**
- 1 tablespoon butter
- 4 chicken tenders, cut in half crosswise
- salt and pepper
- ¼ cup flour
- oil for misting
- 4 slices ham, ¼- to ⅜-inches thick and large enough to cover an English muffin
- 2 English muffins, split
- Sauce
- 2 tablespoons butter
- ½ cup chopped green onions

- ½ cup chopped mushrooms
- 2 tablespoons flour
- 1 cup chicken broth
- ¼ teaspoon garlic powder
- 1½ teaspoons Worcestershire sauce

**Directions:**

1. Place 1 tablespoon of butter in air fryer baking pan and cook at 390°F for 2minutes to melt.

2. Sprinkle chicken tenders with salt and pepper to taste, then roll in the ¼ cup of flour.

3. Place chicken in baking pan, turning pieces to coat with melted butter.

4. Cook at 390°F for 5minutes. Turn chicken pieces over, and spray tops lightly with olive oil. Cook 5minutes longer or until juices run clear. The chicken will not brown.

5. While chicken is cooking, make the sauce: In a medium saucepan, melt the 2 tablespoons of butter.

6. Add onions and mushrooms and sauté until tender, about 3minutes.

7. Stir in the flour. Gradually add broth, stirring constantly until you have a smooth gravy.

8. Add garlic powder and Worcestershire sauce and simmer on low heat until sauce thickens, about 5minutes.

9. When chicken is cooked, remove baking pan from air fryer and set aside.

10. Place ham slices directly into air fryer basket and cook at 390°F for 5minutes or until hot and beginning to sizzle a little. Remove and set aside on top of the chicken for now.

11. Place the English muffin halves in air fryer basket and cook at 390°F for 1 minute.

12. Open air fryer and place a ham slice on top of each English muffin half. Stack 2 pieces of chicken on top of each ham slice. Cook at 390°F for 1 to 2minutes to heat through.

13. Place each English muffin stack on a serving plate and top with plenty of sauce.

# Jerk Turkey Meatballs

Servings: 7
Cooking Time: 8 Minutes

**Ingredients:**

- 1 pound lean ground turkey
- ¼ cup chopped onion
- 1 teaspoon minced garlic
- ½ teaspoon dried thyme
- ¼ teaspoon ground cinnamon
- 1 teaspoon cayenne pepper
- ½ teaspoon paprika
- ½ teaspoon salt
- ⅛ teaspoon black pepper
- ¼ teaspoon red pepper flakes
- 2 teaspoons brown sugar
- 1 large egg, whisked
- ⅓ cup panko breadcrumbs
- 2⅓ cups cooked brown Jasmine rice
- 2 green onions, chopped
- ¾ cup sweet onion dressing

**Directions:**

1. Preheat the air fryer to 350°F.

2. In a medium bowl, mix the ground turkey with the onion, garlic, thyme, cinnamon, cayenne pepper, paprika, salt, pepper, red pepper flakes, and brown sugar. Add the whisked egg and stir in the breadcrumbs until the turkey starts to hold together.

3. Using a 1-ounce scoop, portion the turkey into meatballs. You should get about 28 meatballs.

4. Spray the air fryer basket with olive oil spray.

5. Place the meatballs into the air fryer basket and cook for 5 minutes, shake the basket, and cook another 2 to 4 minutes (or until the internal temperature of the meatballs reaches 165°F).

6. Remove the meatballs from the basket and repeat for the remaining meatballs.

7. Serve warm over a bed of rice with chopped green onions and spicy Caribbean jerk dressing.

# Southwest Gluten-free Turkey Meatloaf

Servings: 8
Cooking Time: 35 Minutes

**Ingredients:**
- 1 pound lean ground turkey
- ¼ cup corn grits
- ¼ cup diced onion
- 1 teaspoon minced garlic
- ½ teaspoon black pepper
- ½ teaspoon salt
- 1 large egg
- ½ cup ketchup
- 4 teaspoons chipotle hot sauce
- ⅓ cup shredded cheddar cheese

**Directions:**
1. Preheat the air fryer to 350°F.
2. In a large bowl, mix together the ground turkey, corn grits, onion, garlic, black pepper, and salt.
3. In a small bowl, whisk the egg. Add the egg to the turkey mixture and combine.
4. In a small bowl, mix the ketchup and hot sauce. Set aside.
5. Liberally spray a 9-x-4-inch loaf pan with olive oil spray. Depending on the size of your air fryer, you may need to use 2 or 3 mini loaf pans.
6. Spoon the ground turkey mixture into the loaf pan and evenly top with half of the ketchup mixture. Cover with foil and place the meatloaf into the air fryer. Cook for 30 minutes; remove the foil and discard. Check the internal temperature (it should be nearing 165°F).
7. Coat the top of the meatloaf with the remaining ketchup mixture, and sprinkle the cheese over the top. Place the meatloaf back in the air fryer for the remaining 5 minutes (or until the internal temperature reaches 165°F).
8. Remove from the oven and let cool 5 minutes before serving. Serve warm with desired sides.

# Fiesta Chicken Plate

Servings: 4
Cooking Time: 15 Minutes

**Ingredients:**
- 1 pound boneless, skinless chicken breasts (2 large breasts)
- 2 tablespoons lime juice
- 1 teaspoon cumin
- ½ teaspoon salt
- ½ cup grated Pepper Jack cheese
- 1 16-ounce can refried beans
- ½ cup salsa
- 2 cups shredded lettuce
- 1 medium tomato, chopped
- 2 avocados, peeled and sliced
- 1 small onion, sliced into thin rings
- sour cream
- tortilla chips (optional)

**Directions:**
1. Split each chicken breast in half lengthwise.
2. Mix lime juice, cumin, and salt together and brush on all surfaces of chicken breasts.
3. Place in air fryer basket and cook at 390°F for 15 minutes, until well done.
4. Divide the cheese evenly over chicken breasts and cook for an additional minute to melt cheese.
5. While chicken is cooking, heat refried beans on stovetop or in microwave.
6. When ready to serve, divide beans among 4 plates. Place chicken breasts on top of beans and spoon salsa over. Arrange the lettuce, tomatoes, and avocados artfully on each plate and scatter with the onion rings.
7. Pass sour cream at the table and serve with tortilla chips if desired.

# Jerk Chicken Drumsticks

Servings: 2
Cooking Time: 20 Minutes

**Ingredients:**
* 1 or 2 cloves garlic
* 1 inch of fresh ginger
* 2 serrano peppers, (with seeds if you like it spicy, seeds removed for less heat)
* 1 teaspoon ground allspice
* 1 teaspoon ground nutmeg
* 1 teaspoon chili powder
* ½ teaspoon dried thyme
* ½ teaspoon ground cinnamon
* ½ teaspoon paprika
* 1 tablespoon brown sugar
* 1 teaspoon soy sauce
* 2 tablespoons vegetable oil
* 6 skinless chicken drumsticks

**Directions:**
1. Combine all the ingredients except the chicken in a small chopper or blender and blend to a paste. Make slashes into the meat of the chicken drumsticks and rub the spice blend all over the chicken (a pair of plastic gloves makes this really easy). Transfer the rubbed chicken to a non-reactive covered container and let the chicken marinate for at least 30 minutes or overnight in the refrigerator.
2. Preheat the air fryer to 400°F.
3. Transfer the drumsticks to the air fryer basket. Air-fry for 10 minutes. Turn the drumsticks over and air-fry for another 10 minutes. Serve warm with some rice and vegetables or a green salad.

# Chicken Nuggets

Servings: 20
Cooking Time: 14 Minutes Per Batch

**Ingredients:**
* 1 pound boneless, skinless chicken thighs, cut into 1-inch chunks
* ¾ teaspoon salt
* ½ teaspoon black pepper
* ½ teaspoon garlic powder
* ½ teaspoon onion powder
* ½ cup flour
* 2 eggs, beaten
* ½ cup panko breadcrumbs
* 3 tablespoons plain breadcrumbs
* oil for misting or cooking spray

**Directions:**
1. In the bowl of a food processor, combine chicken, ½ teaspoon salt, pepper, garlic powder, and onion powder. Process in short pulses until chicken is very finely chopped and well blended.
2. Place flour in one shallow dish and beaten eggs in another. In a third dish or plastic bag, mix together the panko crumbs, plain breadcrumbs, and ¼ teaspoon salt.
3. Shape chicken mixture into small nuggets. Dip nuggets in flour, then eggs, then panko crumb mixture.
4. Spray nuggets on both sides with oil or cooking spray and place in air fryer basket in a single layer, close but not overlapping.
5. Cook at 360°F for 10minutes. Spray with oil and cook 4 minutes, until chicken is done and coating is golden brown.
6. Repeat step 5 to cook remaining nuggets.

# Chicken Strips

Servings: 4
Cooking Time: 8 Minutes

**Ingredients:**
- 1 pound chicken tenders
- Marinade
- ¼ cup olive oil
- 2 tablespoons water
- 2 tablespoons honey
- 2 tablespoons white vinegar
- ½ teaspoon salt
- ½ teaspoon crushed red pepper
- 1 teaspoon garlic powder
- 1 teaspoon onion powder
- ½ teaspoon paprika

**Directions:**
1. Combine all marinade ingredients and mix well.
2. Add chicken and stir to coat. Cover tightly and let marinate in refrigerator for 30minutes.
3. Remove tenders from marinade and place them in a single layer in the air fryer basket.
4. Cook at 390°F for 3minutes. Turn tenders over and cook for 5 minutes longer or until chicken is done and juices run clear.
5. Repeat step 4 to cook remaining tenders.

# Chicken Wellington

Servings: 2
Cooking Time: 31 Minutes

**Ingredients:**
- 2 (5-ounce) boneless, skinless chicken breasts
- ½ cup White Worcestershire sauce
- 3 tablespoons butter
- ½ cup finely diced onion (about ½ onion)
- 8 ounces button mushrooms, finely chopped
- ¼ cup chicken stock
- 2 tablespoons White Worcestershire sauce (or white wine)
- salt and freshly ground black pepper
- 1 tablespoon chopped fresh tarragon
- 2 sheets puff pastry, thawed
- 1 egg, beaten
- vegetable oil

**Directions:**
1. Place the chicken breasts in a shallow dish. Pour the White Worcestershire sauce over the chicken coating both sides and marinate for 30 minutes.
2. While the chicken is marinating, melt the butter in a large skillet over medium-high heat on the stovetop. Add the onion and sauté for a few minutes, until it starts to soften. Add the mushrooms and sauté for 5 minutes until the vegetables are brown and soft. Deglaze the skillet with the chicken stock, scraping up any bits from the bottom of the pan. Add the White Worcestershire sauce and simmer for 3 minutes until the mixture reduces and starts to thicken. Season with salt and freshly ground black pepper. Remove the mushroom mixture from the heat and stir in the fresh tarragon. Let the mushroom mixture cool.
3. Preheat the air fryer to 360°F.
4. Remove the chicken from the marinade and transfer it to the air fryer basket. Tuck the small end of the chicken breast under the thicker part to shape it into a circle rather than an oval. Pour the marinade over the chicken and air-fry for 10 minutes.
5. Roll out the puff pastry and cut out two 6-inch squares. Brush the perimeter of each square with the egg wash. Place half of the mushroom mixture in the center of each puff pastry square. Place the chicken breasts, top side down on the mushroom mixture. Starting with one corner of puff pastry and working in one direction, pull the

pastry up over the chicken to enclose it and press the ends of the pastry together in the middle. Brush the pastry with the egg wash to seal the edges. Turn the Wellingtons over and set aside.

6. To make a decorative design with the remaining puff pastry, cut out four 10-inch strips. For each Wellington, twist two of the strips together, place them over the chicken breast wrapped in puff pastry, and tuck the ends underneath to seal it. Brush the entire top and sides of the Wellingtons with the egg wash.

7. Preheat the air fryer to 350°F.

8. Spray or brush the air fryer basket with vegetable oil. Air-fry the chicken Wellingtons for 13 minutes. Carefully turn the Wellingtons over. Air-fry for another 8 minutes. Transfer to serving plates, light a candle and enjoy!

# Pecan Turkey Cutlets

Servings: 4
Cooking Time: 12 Minutes

**Ingredients:**
- ¾ cup panko breadcrumbs
- ¼ teaspoon salt
- ¼ teaspoon pepper
- ¼ teaspoon dry mustard
- ¼ teaspoon poultry seasoning
- ½ cup pecans
- ¼ cup cornstarch
- 1 egg, beaten
- 1 pound turkey cutlets, ½-inch thick
- salt and pepper
- oil for misting or cooking spray

**Directions:**
1. Place the panko crumbs, ¼ teaspoon salt, ¼ teaspoon pepper, mustard, and poultry seasoning in food processor. Process until crumbs are finely crushed. Add pecans and process in short pulses

just until nuts are finely chopped. Go easy so you don't overdo it!

2. Preheat air fryer to 360°F.

3. Place cornstarch in one shallow dish and beaten egg in another. Transfer coating mixture from food processor into a third shallow dish.

4. Sprinkle turkey cutlets with salt and pepper to taste.

5. Dip cutlets in cornstarch and shake off excess. Then dip in beaten egg and roll in crumbs, pressing to coat well. Spray both sides with oil or cooking spray.

6. Place 2 cutlets in air fryer basket in a single layer and cook for 12 minutes or until juices run clear.

7. Repeat step 6 to cook remaining cutlets.

# Nashville Hot Chicken

Servings: 4
Cooking Time: 27 Minutes

**Ingredients:**
- 1 (4-pound) chicken, cut into 6 pieces (2 breasts, 2 thighs and 2 drumsticks)
- 2 eggs
- 1 cup buttermilk
- 2 cups all-purpose flour
- 2 tablespoons paprika
- 1 teaspoon garlic powder
- 1 teaspoon onion powder
- 2 teaspoons salt
- 1 teaspoon freshly ground black pepper
- vegetable oil, in a spray bottle
- Nashville Hot Sauce:
- 1 tablespoon cayenne pepper
- 1 teaspoon salt
- ¼ cup vegetable oil
- 4 slices white bread
- dill pickle slices

**Directions:**

1. Cut the chicken breasts into 2 pieces so that you have a total of 8 pieces of chicken.
2. Set up a two-stage dredging station. Whisk the eggs and buttermilk together in a bowl. Combine the flour, paprika, garlic powder, onion powder, salt and black pepper in a zipper-sealable plastic bag. Dip the chicken pieces into the egg-buttermilk mixture, then toss them in the seasoned flour, coating all sides. Repeat this procedure (egg mixture and then flour mixture) one more time. This can be a little messy, but make sure all sides of the chicken are completely covered. Spray the chicken with vegetable oil and set aside.
3. Preheat the air fryer to 370°F. Spray or brush the bottom of the air-fryer basket with a little vegetable oil.
4. Air-fry the chicken in two batches at 370°F for 20 minutes, flipping the pieces over halfway through the cooking process. Transfer the chicken to a plate, but do not cover. Repeat with the second batch of chicken.
5. Lower the temperature on the air fryer to 340°F. Flip the chicken back over and place the first batch of chicken on top of the second batch already in the basket. Air-fry for another 7 minutes.
6. While the chicken is air-frying, combine the cayenne pepper and salt in a bowl. Heat the vegetable oil in a small saucepan and when it is very hot, add it to the spice mix, whisking until smooth. It will sizzle briefly when you add it to the spices. Place the fried chicken on top of the white bread slices and brush the hot sauce all over chicken. Top with the pickle slices and serve warm. Enjoy the heat and the flavor!

## Teriyaki Chicken Drumsticks

Servings: 2
Cooking Time: 17 Minutes

**Ingredients:**
- 2 tablespoons soy sauce*
- ¼ cup dry sherry
- 1 tablespoon brown sugar
- 2 tablespoons water
- 1 tablespoon rice wine vinegar
- 1 clove garlic, crushed
- 1-inch fresh ginger, peeled and sliced
- pinch crushed red pepper flakes
- 4 to 6 bone-in, skin-on chicken drumsticks
- 1 tablespoon cornstarch
- fresh cilantro leaves

**Directions:**
1. Make the marinade by combining the soy sauce, dry sherry, brown sugar, water, rice vinegar, garlic, ginger and crushed red pepper flakes. Pour the marinade over the chicken legs, cover and let the chicken marinate for 1 to 4 hours in the refrigerator.
2. Preheat the air fryer to 380°F.
3. Transfer the chicken from the marinade to the air fryer basket, transferring any extra marinade to a small saucepan. Air-fry at 380°F for 8 minutes. Flip the chicken over and continue to air-fry for another 6 minutes, watching to make sure it doesn't brown too much.
4. While the chicken is cooking, bring the reserved marinade to a simmer on the stovetop. Dissolve the cornstarch in 2 tablespoons of water and stir this into the saucepan. Bring to a boil to thicken the sauce. Remove the garlic clove and slices of ginger from the sauce and set aside.
5. When the time is up on the air fryer, brush the thickened sauce on the chicken and air-fry for 3 more minutes. Remove the chicken from the air fryer and brush with the remaining sauce.
6. Serve over rice and sprinkle the cilantro leaves on top.

# Asian Meatball Tacos

Servings: 4
Cooking Time: 10 Minutes

**Ingredients:**
- 1 pound lean ground turkey
- 3 tablespoons soy sauce
- 1 tablespoon brown sugar
- ½ teaspoon onion powder
- ½ teaspoon garlic powder
- 1 tablespoon sesame seeds
- 1 English cucumber
- 4 radishes
- 2 tablespoons white wine vinegar
- 1 lime, juiced and divided
- 1 tablespoon avocado oil
- Salt, to taste
- ½ cup Greek yogurt
- 1 to 3 teaspoons Sriracha, based on desired spiciness
- 1 cup shredded cabbage
- ¼ cup chopped cilantro
- Eight 6-inch flour tortillas

**Directions:**
1. Preheat the air fryer to 360°F.
2. In a large bowl, mix the ground turkey, soy sauce, brown sugar, onion powder, garlic powder, and sesame seeds. Form the meat into 1-inch meatballs and place in the air fryer basket. Cook for 5 minutes, shake the basket, and cook another 5 minutes. Using a food thermometer, make sure the internal temperature of the meatballs is 165°F.
3. Meanwhile, dice the cucumber and radishes and place in a medium bowl. Add the white wine vinegar, 1 teaspoon of the lime juice, and the avocado oil, and stir to coat. Season with salt to desired taste.
4. In a large bowl, mix the Greek yogurt, Sriracha, and the remaining lime juice, and stir.

Add in the cabbage and cilantro; toss well to create a slaw.
5. In a heavy skillet, heat the tortillas over medium heat for 1 to 2 minutes on each side, or until warmed.
6. To serve, place a tortilla on a plate, top with 5 meatballs, then with cucumber and radish salad, and finish with 2 tablespoons of cabbage slaw.

# Buttermilk-fried Drumsticks

Servings: 2
Cooking Time: 25 Minutes

**Ingredients:**
- 1 egg
- ½ cup buttermilk
- ¾ cup self-rising flour
- ¾ cup seasoned panko breadcrumbs
- 1 teaspoon salt
- ¼ teaspoon ground black pepper (to mix into coating)
- 4 chicken drumsticks, skin on
- oil for misting or cooking spray

**Directions:**
1. Beat together egg and buttermilk in shallow dish.
2. In a second shallow dish, combine the flour, panko crumbs, salt, and pepper.
3. Sprinkle chicken legs with additional salt and pepper to taste.
4. Dip legs in buttermilk mixture, then roll in panko mixture, pressing in crumbs to make coating stick. Mist with oil or cooking spray.
5. Spray air fryer basket with cooking spray.
6. Cook drumsticks at 360°F for 10minutes. Turn pieces over and cook an additional 10minutes.
7. Turn pieces to check for browning. If you have any white spots that haven't begun to brown, spritz them with oil or cooking spray. Continue

cooking for 5 more minutes or until crust is golden brown and juices run clear. Larger, meatier drumsticks will take longer to cook than small ones.

## Parmesan Crusted Chicken Cordon Bleu

Servings: 2
Cooking Time: 14 Minutes

**Ingredients:**
- 2 (6-ounce) boneless, skinless chicken breasts
- salt and freshly ground black pepper
- 1 tablespoon Dijon mustard
- 4 slices Swiss cheese
- 4 slices deli-sliced ham
- ¼ cup all-purpose flour*
- 1 egg, beaten
- ¾ cup panko breadcrumbs*
- ⅓ cup grated Parmesan cheese
- olive oil, in a spray bottle

**Directions:**
1. Butterfly the chicken breasts. Place the chicken breast on a cutting board and press down on the breast with the palm of your hand. Slice into the long side of the chicken breast, parallel to the cutting board, but not all the way through to the other side. Open the chicken breast like a "book". Place a piece of plastic wrap over the chicken breast and gently pound it with a meat mallet to make it evenly thick.
2. Season the chicken with salt and pepper. Spread the Dijon mustard on the inside of each chicken breast. Layer one slice of cheese on top of the mustard, then top with the 2 slices of ham and the other slice of cheese.
3. Starting with the long edge of the chicken breast, roll the chicken up to the other side. Secure it shut with 1 or 2 toothpicks.
4. Preheat the air fryer to 350°F.

5. Set up a dredging station with three shallow dishes. Place the flour in the first dish. Place the beaten egg in the second shallow dish. Combine the panko breadcrumbs and Parmesan cheese together in the third shallow dish. Dip the stuffed and rolled chicken breasts in the flour, then the beaten egg and then roll in the breadcrumb-cheese mixture to cover on all sides. Press the crumbs onto the chicken breasts with your hands to make sure they are well adhered. Spray the chicken breasts with olive oil and transfer to the air fryer basket.
6. Air-fry at 350°F for 14 minutes, flipping the breasts over halfway through the cooking time. Let the chicken rest for a few minutes before removing the toothpicks, slicing and serving.

## Tandoori Chicken Legs

Servings: 2
Cooking Time: 30 Minutes

**Ingredients:**
- 1 cup plain yogurt
- 2 cloves garlic, minced
- 1 tablespoon grated fresh ginger
- 2 teaspoons paprika
- 2 teaspoons ground coriander
- 1 teaspoon ground turmeric
- 1 teaspoon salt
- ¼ teaspoon ground cayenne pepper
- juice of 1 lime
- 2 bone-in, skin-on chicken legs
- fresh cilantro leaves

**Directions:**
1. Make the marinade by combining the yogurt, garlic, ginger, spices and lime juice. Make slashes into the chicken legs to help the marinade penetrate the meat. Pour the marinade over the chicken legs, cover and let the chicken marinate for at least an hour or overnight in the refrigerator.

2.  Preheat the air fryer to 380°F.

3.  Transfer the chicken legs from the marinade to the air fryer basket, reserving any extra marinade. Air-fry for 15 minutes. Flip the chicken over and pour the remaining marinade over the top. Air-fry for another 15 minutes, watching to make sure it doesn't brown too much. If it does start to get too brown, you can loosely tent the chicken with aluminum foil, tucking the ends of the foil under the chicken to stop it from blowing around.

4.  Serve over rice with some fresh cilantro on top.

# Appetizers And Snacks

## Crunchy Lobster Bites

Servings: 3
Cooking Time: 6 Minutes

**Ingredients:**
- 1 Large egg white(s)
- 2 tablespoons Water
- ½ cup All-purpose flour or gluten-free all-purpose flour
- ½ cup Yellow cornmeal
- 1 teaspoon Mild paprika
- 1 teaspoon Garlic powder
- 1 teaspoon Onion powder
- 1 teaspoon Table salt
- 4 Small (3- to 4-ounce) lobster tails
- Vegetable oil spray

**Directions:**
1. Preheat the air fryer to 400°F.
2. Whisk the egg white(s) and water in a shallow soup plate or small pie plate until foamy.
3. Stir the flour, cornmeal, paprika, garlic powder, onion powder, and salt in a large bowl until uniform.
4. Slice each lobster tail (shell and all) in half lengthwise, then pull the meat out of each half of the tail shell. Cut each strip of meat into 1-inch segments (2 or 3 segments per strip).
5. Dip a piece of lobster meat in the egg white mixture to coat it on all sides, letting any excess egg white slip back into the rest. Drop the piece of lobster meat into the bowl with the flour mixture. Continue on with the remaining pieces of lobster meat, getting them all in that bowl. Gently toss them all in the flour mixture until well coated.

6. Use two flatware forks to transfer the lobster pieces to a cutting board with the coating intact. Coat them on all sides with vegetable oil spray.
7. Set the lobster pieces in the basket in one layer. Air-fry undisturbed for 6 minutes, or until golden brown and crunchy. Gently dump the contents of the basket onto a wire rack and cool for 2 or 3 minutes before serving.

## Fried Brie With Cherry Tomatoes

Servings: 8
Cooking Time: 15 Minutes

**Ingredients:**
- 1 baguette*
- 2 pints red and yellow cherry tomatoes
- 1 tablespoon olive oil
- salt and freshly ground black pepper
- 1 teaspoon balsamic vinegar
- 1 tablespoon chopped fresh parsley
- 1 (8-ounce) wheel of Brie cheese
- olive oil
- ½ teaspoon Italian seasoning (optional)
- 1 tablespoon chopped fresh basil

**Directions:**
1. Preheat the air fryer to 350°F.
2. Start by making the crostini. Slice the baguette diagonally into ½-inch slices and brush the slices with olive oil on both sides. Air-fry the baguette slices at 350°F in batches for 6 minutes or until lightly browned on all sides. Set the bread aside on your serving platter.
3. Toss the cherry tomatoes in a bowl with the olive oil, salt and pepper. Air-fry the cherry tomatoes for 3 to 5 minutes, shaking the basket a few times during the cooking process. The tomatoes should be soft and some of them will

burst open. Toss the warm tomatoes with the balsamic vinegar and fresh parsley and set aside.

4. Cut a circle of parchment paper the same size as your wheel of Brie cheese. Brush both sides of the Brie wheel with olive oil and sprinkle with Italian seasoning, if using. Place the circle of parchment paper on one side of the Brie and transfer the Brie to the air fryer basket, parchment side down. Air-fry at 350°F for 8 to 10 minutes, or until the Brie is slightly puffed and soft to the touch.

5. Watch carefully and remove the Brie before the rind cracks and the cheese starts to leak out. Transfer the wheel to your serving platter and top with the roasted tomatoes. Sprinkle with basil and serve with the toasted bread slices.

# Shrimp Toasts

Servings: 4
Cooking Time: 8 Minutes

**Ingredients:**
- ½ pound raw shrimp, peeled and de-veined
- 1 egg (or 2 egg whites)
- 2 scallions, plus more for garnish
- 2 teaspoons grated fresh ginger
- 1 teaspoon soy sauce
- ½ teaspoon toasted sesame oil
- 2 tablespoons chopped fresh cilantro or parsley
- 1 to 2 teaspoons sriracha sauce
- 6 slices thinly-sliced white sandwich bread (Pepperidge Farm®)
- ½ cup sesame seeds
- Thai chili sauce

**Directions:**
1. Combine the shrimp, egg, scallions, fresh ginger, soy sauce, sesame oil, cilantro (or parsley) and sriracha sauce in a food processor and process into a chunky paste, scraping down the sides of the food processor bowl as necessary.

2. Cut the crusts off the sandwich bread and generously spread the shrimp paste onto each slice of bread. Place the sesame seeds on a plate and invert each shrimp toast into the sesame seeds to coat, pressing down gently. Cut each slice of bread into 4 triangles.

3. Preheat the air fryer to 400°F.

4. Transfer one layer of shrimp toast triangles to the air fryer and air-fry at 400°F for 8 minutes, or until the sesame seeds are toasted on top.

5. Serve warm with a little Thai chili sauce and some sliced scallions as garnish.

# String Bean Fries

Servings: 4
Cooking Time: 6 Minutes

**Ingredients:**
- ½ pound fresh string beans
- 2 eggs
- 4 teaspoons water
- ½ cup white flour
- ½ cup breadcrumbs
- ¼ teaspoon salt
- ¼ teaspoon ground black pepper
- ¼ teaspoon dry mustard (optional)
- oil for misting or cooking spray

**Directions:**
1. Preheat air fryer to 360°F.
2. Trim stem ends from string beans, wash, and pat dry.
3. In a shallow dish, beat eggs and water together until well blended.
4. Place flour in a second shallow dish.
5. In a third shallow dish, stir together the breadcrumbs, salt, pepper, and dry mustard if using.

6. Dip each string bean in egg mixture, flour, egg mixture again, then breadcrumbs.

7. When you finish coating all the string beans, open air fryer and place them in basket.

8. Cook for 3minutes.

9. Stop and mist string beans with oil or cooking spray.

10. Cook for 3 more minutes or until string beans are crispy and nicely browned.

# Cheese Straws

Servings: 8
Cooking Time: 7 Minutes

**Ingredients:**
- For dusting All-purpose flour
- Two quarters of one thawed sheet (that is, a half of the sheet cut into two even pieces; wrap and refreeze the remainder) A 17.25-ounce box frozen puff pastry
- 1 Large egg(s)
- 2 tablespoons Water
- ¼ cup (about ¾ ounce) Finely grated Parmesan cheese
- up to 1 teaspoon Ground black pepper

**Directions:**
1. Preheat the air fryer to 400°F.

2. Dust a clean, dry work surface with flour. Set one of the pieces of puff pastry on top, dust the pastry lightly with flour, and roll with a rolling pin to a 6-inch square.

3. Whisk the egg(s) and water in a small or medium bowl until uniform. Brush the pastry square(s) generously with this mixture. Sprinkle each square with 2 tablespoons grated cheese and up to ½ teaspoon ground black pepper.

4. Cut each square into 4 even strips. Grasp each end of 1 strip with clean, dry hands; twist it into a cheese straw. Place the twisted straws on a baking sheet.

5. Lay as many straws as will fit in the air-fryer basket—as a general rule, 4 of them in a small machine, 5 in a medium model, or 6 in a large. There should be space for air to circulate around the straws. Set the baking sheet with any remaining straws in the fridge.

6. Air-fry undisturbed for 7 minutes, or until puffed and crisp. Use tongs to transfer the cheese straws to a wire rack, then make subsequent batches in the same way (keeping the baking sheet with the remaining straws in the fridge as each batch cooks). Serve warm.

# Tempura Fried Veggies

Servings: 4
Cooking Time: 6 Minutes

**Ingredients:**
- ½ cup all-purpose flour
- ½ teaspoon black pepper
- ¼ teaspoon salt
- 2 large eggs
- 1¼ cups panko breadcrumbs
- 1 tablespoon extra-virgin olive oil
- 1 cup white button mushrooms, cleaned
- 1 medium zucchini, skinned and sliced
- 1 medium carrot, skinned sliced

**Directions:**
1. Preheat the air fryer to 400°F.

2. In a small bowl, mix the flour, pepper, and salt.

3. In a separate bowl, whisk the eggs.

4. In a third bowl, mix together the breadcrumbs and olive oil.

5. Begin to batter the vegetables by placing them one at a time into the flour, then dipping them in the eggs, and coating them in breadcrumbs. When you've prepared enough to begin air frying, liberally spray the air fryer basket with olive oil and place the vegetables inside.

6. Cook for 6 minutes, or until the breadcrumb coating on the outside appears golden brown. Repeat coating the other vegetables while the first batch is cooking.

7. When the cooking completes, carefully remove the vegetables and keep them warm. Repeat cooking for the remaining vegetables until all are cooked.

8. Serve warm.

# Roasted Red Pepper Dip

Servings: 2
Cooking Time: 15 Minutes

**Ingredients:**
- 2 Medium-size red bell pepper(s)
- 1¾ cups (one 15-ounce can) Canned white beans, drained and rinsed
- 1 tablespoon Fresh oregano leaves, packed
- 3 tablespoons Olive oil
- 1 tablespoon Lemon juice
- ½ teaspoon Table salt
- ½ teaspoon Ground black pepper

**Directions:**
1. Preheat the air fryer to 400°F.

2. Set the pepper(s) in the basket and air-fry undisturbed for 15 minutes, until blistered and even blackened.

3. Use kitchen tongs to transfer the pepper(s) to a zip-closed plastic bag or small bowl. Seal the bag or cover the bowl with plastic wrap. Set aside for 20 minutes.

4. Peel each pepper, then stem it, cut it in half, and remove all its seeds and their white membranes.

5. Set the pieces of the pepper in a food processor. Add the beans, oregano, olive oil, lemon juice, salt, and pepper. Cover and process until smooth, stopping the machine at least once to scrape down the inside of the canister. Scrape the dip into a bowl and serve warm, or cover and refrigerate for up to 3 days (although the dip tastes best if it's allowed to come back to room temperature).

# Cauliflower "tater" Tots

Servings: 6
Cooking Time: 10 Minutes

**Ingredients:**
- 1 head of cauliflower
- 2 eggs
- ¼ cup all-purpose flour*
- ½ cup grated Parmesan cheese
- 1 teaspoon salt
- freshly ground black pepper
- vegetable or olive oil, in a spray bottle

**Directions:**
1. Grate the head of cauliflower with a box grater or finely chop it in a food processor. You should have about 3½ cups. Place the chopped cauliflower in the center of a clean kitchen towel and twist the towel tightly to squeeze all the water out of the cauliflower. (This can be done in two batches to make it easier to drain all the water from the cauliflower.)

2. Place the squeezed cauliflower in a large bowl. Add the eggs, flour, Parmesan cheese, salt and freshly ground black pepper. Shape the cauliflower into small cylinders or "tater tot" shapes, rolling roughly one tablespoon of the mixture at a time. Place the tots on a cookie sheet lined with paper towel to absorb any residual moisture. Spray the cauliflower tots all over with oil.

3. Preheat the air fryer to 400°F.

4. Air-fry the tots at 400°F, one layer at a time for 10 minutes, turning them over for the last few minutes of the cooking process for even browning.

Season with salt and black pepper. Serve hot with your favorite dipping sauce.

# Cinnamon Apple Crisps

Servings: 1
Cooking Time: 22 Minutes

**Ingredients:**
- 1 large apple
- ½ teaspoon ground cinnamon
- 2 teaspoons avocado oil or coconut oil

**Directions:**
1. Preheat the air fryer to 300°F.
2. Using a mandolin or knife, slice the apples to ¼-inch thickness. Pat the apples dry with a paper towel or kitchen cloth. Sprinkle the apple slices with ground cinnamon. Spray or drizzle the oil over the top of the apple slices and toss to coat.
3. Place the apple slices in the air fryer basket. To allow for even cooking, don't overlap the slices; cook in batches if necessary.
4. Cook for 20 minutes, shaking the basket every 5 minutes. After 20 minutes, increase the air fryer temperature to 330°F and cook another 2 minutes, shaking the basket every 30 seconds. Remove the apples from the basket before they get too dark.
5. Spread the chips out onto paper towels to cool completely, at least 5 minutes. Repeat with the remaining apple slices until they're all cooked.

# Fried Mozzarella Sticks

Servings: 7
Cooking Time: 5 Minutes

**Ingredients:**
- 7 1-ounce string cheese sticks, unwrapped
- ½ cup All-purpose flour or tapioca flour
- 2 Large egg(s), well beaten
- 2¼ cups Seasoned Italian-style dried bread crumbs (gluten-free, if a concern)

- Olive oil spray

**Directions:**
1. Unwrap the string cheese and place the pieces in the freezer for 20 minutes (but not longer, or they will be too frozen to soften in the time given in the air fryer).
2. Preheat the air fryer to 400°F.
3. Set up and fill three shallow soup plates or small pie plates on your counter: one for the flour, one for the egg(s), and one for the bread crumbs.
4. Dip a piece of cold string cheese in the flour until well coated (keep the others in the freezer). Gently tap off any excess flour, then set the stick in the egg(s). Roll it around to coat, let any excess egg mixture slip back into the rest, and set the stick in the bread crumbs. Gently roll it around to coat it evenly, even the ends. Now dip it back in the egg(s), then again in the bread crumbs, rolling it to coat well and evenly. Set the stick aside on a cutting board and coat the remaining pieces of string cheese in the same way.
5. Lightly coat the sticks all over with olive oil spray. Place them in the basket in one layer and air-fry undisturbed for 5 minutes, or until golden brown and crisp.
6. Remove the basket from the machine and cool for 5 minutes. Use a nonstick-safe spatula to transfer the mozzarella sticks to a serving platter. Serve hot.

# Corn Dog Muffins

Servings: 8
Cooking Time: 10 Minutes

**Ingredients:**
- 1¼ cups sliced kosher hotdogs (3 or 4, depending on size)
- ½ cup flour
- ½ cup yellow cornmeal
- 2 teaspoons baking powder

- ½ cup skim milk
- 1 egg
- 2 tablespoons canola oil
- 8 foil muffin cups, paper liners removed
- cooking spray
- mustard or your favorite dipping sauce

**Directions:**

1. Slice each hot dog in half lengthwise, then cut in ¼-inch half-moon slices. Set aside.
2. Preheat air fryer to 390°F.
3. In a large bowl, stir together flour, cornmeal, and baking powder.
4. In a small bowl, beat together the milk, egg, and oil until just blended.
5. Pour egg mixture into dry ingredients and stir with a spoon to mix well.
6. Stir in sliced hot dogs.
7. Spray the foil cups lightly with cooking spray.
8. Divide mixture evenly into muffin cups.
9. Place 4 muffin cups in the air fryer basket and cook for 5 minutes.
10. Reduce temperature to 360°F and cook 5 minutes or until toothpick inserted in center of muffin comes out clean.
11. Repeat steps 9 and 10 to bake remaining corn dog muffins.
12. Serve with mustard or other sauces for dipping.

# Antipasto-stuffed Cherry Tomatoes

Servings: 12
Cooking Time: 9 Minutes

**Ingredients:**

- 12 Large cherry tomatoes, preferably Campari tomatoes (about 1½ ounces each and the size of golf balls)
- ½ cup Seasoned Italian-style dried bread crumbs (gluten-free, if a concern)
- ¼ cup (about ¾ ounce) Finely grated Parmesan cheese
- ¼ cup Finely chopped pitted black olives
- ¼ cup Finely chopped marinated artichoke hearts
- 2 tablespoons Marinade from the artichokes
- 4 Sun-dried tomatoes (dry, not packed in oil), finely chopped
- Olive oil spray

**Directions:**

1. Preheat the air fryer to 400°F.
2. Cut the top off of each fresh tomato, exposing the seeds and pulp. (The tops can be saved for a snack, sprinkled with some kosher salt, to tide you over while the stuffed tomatoes cook.) Cut a very small slice off the bottom of each tomato (no cutting into the pulp) so it will stand up flat on your work surface. Use a melon baller to remove and discard the seeds and pulp from each tomato.
3. Mix the bread crumbs, cheese, olives, artichoke hearts, marinade, and sun-dried tomatoes in a bowl until well combined. Stuff this mixture into each prepared tomato, about 1½ tablespoons in each. Generously coat the tops of the tomatoes with olive oil spray.
4. Set the tomatoes stuffing side up in the basket. Air-fry undisturbed for 9 minutes, or until the stuffing has browned a bit and the tomatoes are blistered in places.
5. Remove the basket and cool the tomatoes in it for 5 minutes. Then use kitchen tongs to gently transfer the tomatoes to a serving platter.

# Carrot Chips

Servings: 4
Cooking Time: 10 Minutes

**Ingredients:**
- 1 pound carrots, thinly sliced
- 2 tablespoons extra-virgin olive oil
- ¼ teaspoon garlic powder
- ¼ teaspoon black pepper
- ½ teaspoon salt

**Directions:**
1. Preheat the air fryer to 390°F.
2. In a medium bowl, toss the carrot slices with the olive oil, garlic powder, pepper, and salt.
3. Liberally spray the air fryer basket with olive oil mist.
4. Place the carrot slices in the air fryer basket. To allow for even cooking, don't overlap the carrots; cook in batches if necessary.
5. Cook for 5 minutes, shake the basket, and cook another 5 minutes.
6. Remove from the basket and serve warm. Repeat with the remaining carrot slices until they're all cooked.

# Garlic Wings

Servings: 4
Cooking Time: 15 Minutes

**Ingredients:**
- 2 pounds chicken wings
- oil for misting
- cooking spray
- Marinade
- 1 cup buttermilk
- 2 cloves garlic, mashed flat
- 1 teaspoon Worcestershire sauce
- 1 bay leaf
- Coating
- 1½ cups grated Parmesan cheese
- ¾ cup breadcrumbs
- 1½ tablespoons garlic powder
- ½ teaspoon salt

**Directions:**
1. Mix all marinade ingredients together.
2. Remove wing tips (the third joint) and discard or freeze for stock. Cut the remaining wings at the joint and toss them into the marinade, stirring to coat well. Refrigerate for at least an hour but no more than 8 hours.
3. When ready to cook, combine all coating ingredients in a shallow dish.
4. Remove wings from marinade, shaking off excess, and roll in coating mixture. Press coating into wings so that it sticks well. Spray wings with oil.
5. Spray air fryer basket with cooking spray. Place wings in basket in single layer, close but not touching.
6. Cook at 360°F for 15minutes or until chicken is done and juices run clear.
7. Repeat previous step to cook remaining wings.

# Fried Green Tomatoes

Servings: 4
Cooking Time: 15 Minutes

**Ingredients:**
- 2 eggs
- ¼ cup buttermilk
- ½ cup cornmeal
- ½ cup breadcrumbs
- ¼ teaspoon salt
- 1½ pounds firm green tomatoes, cut in ¼-inch slices
- oil for misting or cooking spray
- Horseradish Drizzle
- ¼ cup mayonnaise
- ¼ cup sour cream
- 2 teaspoons prepared horseradish

- ½ teaspoon Worcestershire sauce
- ½ teaspoon lemon juice
- ⅛ teaspoon black pepper

**Directions:**

1. Mix all ingredients for Horseradish Drizzle together and chill while you prepare the green tomatoes.

2. Preheat air fryer to 390°F.

3. Beat the eggs and buttermilk together in a shallow bowl.

4. Mix cornmeal, breadcrumbs, and salt together in a plate or shallow dish.

5. Dip 4 tomato slices in the egg mixture, then roll in the breadcrumb mixture.

6. Mist one side with oil and place in air fryer basket, oil-side down, in a single layer.

7. Mist the top with oil.

8. Cook for 15minutes, turning once, until brown and crispy.

9. Repeat steps 5 through 8 to cook remaining tomatoes.

10. Drizzle horseradish sauce over tomatoes just before serving.

# Granola Three Ways

Servings: 4
Cooking Time: 10 Minutes

**Ingredients:**

- Nantucket Granola
- ¼ cup maple syrup
- ¼ cup dark brown sugar
- 1 tablespoon butter
- 1 teaspoon vanilla extract
- 1 cup rolled oats
- ½ cup dried cranberries
- ½ cup walnuts, chopped
- ¼ cup pumpkin seeds
- ¼ cup shredded coconut
- Blueberry Delight
- ¼ cup honey
- ¼ cup light brown sugar
- 1 tablespoon butter
- 1 teaspoon lemon extract
- 1 cup rolled oats
- ½ cup sliced almonds
- ½ cup dried blueberries
- ¼ cup pumpkin seeds
- ¼ cup sunflower seeds
- Cherry Black Forest Mix
- ¼ cup honey
- ¼ cup light brown sugar
- 1 tablespoon butter
- 1 teaspoon almond extract
- 1 cup rolled oats
- ½ cup sliced almonds
- ½ cup dried cherries
- ¼ cup shredded coconut
- ¼ cup dark chocolate chips
- oil for misting or cooking spray

**Directions:**

1. Combine the syrup or honey, brown sugar, and butter in a small saucepan or microwave-safe bowl. Heat and stir just until butter melts and sugar dissolves. Stir in the extract.

2. Place all other dry ingredients in a large bowl. (For the Cherry Black Forest Mix, don't add the chocolate chips yet.)

3. Pour melted butter mixture over dry ingredients and stir until oat mixture is well coated.

4. Lightly spray a baking pan with oil or cooking spray.

5. Pour granola into pan and cook at 390°F for 5minutes. Stir. Continue cooking for 5minutes, stirring every minute or two, until golden brown. Watch closely. Once the mixture begins to brown, it will cook quickly.

6. Remove granola from pan and spread on wax paper. It will become crispier as it cools.

7. For the Cherry Black Forest Mix, stir in chocolate chips after granola has cooled completely.

8. Store in an airtight container.

# Barbecue Chicken Nachos

Servings: 3
Cooking Time: 5 Minutes

**Ingredients:**

* 3 heaping cups (a little more than 3 ounces) Corn tortilla chips (gluten-free, if a concern)
* ¾ cup Shredded deboned and skinned rotisserie chicken meat (gluten-free, if a concern)
* 3 tablespoons Canned black beans, drained and rinsed
* 9 rings Pickled jalapeño slices
* 4 Small pickled cocktail onions, halved
* 3 tablespoons Barbecue sauce (any sort)
* ¾ cup (about 3 ounces) Shredded Cheddar cheese

**Directions:**

1. Preheat the air fryer to 400°F.

2. Cut a circle of parchment paper to line a 6-inch round cake pan for a small air fryer, a 7-inch round cake pan for a medium air fryer, or an 8-inch round cake pan for a large machine.

3. Fill the pan with an even layer of about two-thirds of the chips. Sprinkle the chicken evenly over the chips. Set the pan in the basket and air-fry undisturbed for 2 minutes.

4. Remove the basket from the machine. Scatter the beans, jalapeño rings, and pickled onion halves over the chicken. Drizzle the barbecue sauce over everything, then sprinkle the cheese on top.

5. Return the basket to the machine and air-fry undisturbed for 3 minutes, or until the cheese has melted and is bubbly. Remove the pan from the machine and cool for a couple of minutes before serving.

# Indian Cauliflower Tikka Bites

Servings: 6
Cooking Time: 20 Minutes

**Ingredients:**

* 1 cup plain Greek yogurt
* 1 teaspoon fresh ginger
* 1 teaspoon minced garlic
* 1 teaspoon vindaloo
* ½ teaspoon cardamom
* ½ teaspoon paprika
* ½ teaspoon turmeric powder
* ½ teaspoon cumin powder
* 1 large head of cauliflower, washed and cut into medium-size florets
* ½ cup panko breadcrumbs
* 1 lemon, quartered

**Directions:**

1. Preheat the air fryer to 350°F.

2. In a large bowl, mix the yogurt, ginger, garlic, vindaloo, cardamom, paprika, turmeric, and cumin. Add the cauliflower florets to the bowl, and coat them with the yogurt.

3. Remove the cauliflower florets from the bowl and place them on a baking sheet. Sprinkle the panko breadcrumbs over the top. Place the cauliflower bites into the air fryer basket, leaving space between the florets. Depending on the size of your air fryer, you may need to make more than one batch.

4. Cook the cauliflower for 10 minutes, shake the basket, and continue cooking another 10 minutes (or until the florets are lightly browned).

5. Remove from the air fryer and keep warm. Continue to cook until all the florets are done.

6. Before serving, lightly squeeze lemon over the top. Serve warm.

# Okra Chips

Servings: 4        Cooking Time: 16 Minutes

**Ingredients:**
- 1¼ pounds Thin fresh okra pods, cut into 1-inch pieces
- 1½ tablespoons Vegetable or canola oil
- ¾ teaspoon Coarse sea salt or kosher salt

**Directions:**
1. Preheat the air fryer to 400°F.
2. Toss the okra, oil, and salt in a large bowl until the pieces are well and evenly coated.
3. When the machine is at temperature, pour the contents of the bowl into the basket. Air-fry, tossing several times, for 16 minutes, or until crisp and quite brown (maybe even a little blackened on the thin bits).
4. Pour the contents of the basket onto a wire rack. Cool for a couple of minutes before serving.

# Sweet Chili Peanuts

Servings: 6        Cooking Time: 5 Minutes

**Ingredients:**
- 2 cups (10 ounces) Shelled raw peanuts
- 2 tablespoons Granulated white sugar
- 2 teaspoons Hot red pepper sauce, such as Cholula or Tabasco (gluten-free, if a concern)

**Directions:**
1. Preheat the air fryer to 400°F.
2. Toss the peanuts, sugar, and hot pepper sauce in a bowl until the peanuts are well coated.
3. When the machine is at temperature, pour the peanuts into the basket, spreading them into one layer as much as you can. Air-fry undisturbed for 3 minutes.
4. Shake the basket to rearrange the peanuts. Continue air-frying for 2 minutes more, shaking and stirring the peanuts every 30 seconds, until golden brown.

5. Pour the peanuts onto a large lipped baking sheet. Spread them into one layer and cool for 5 minutes before serving.

# Sweet Plantain Chips

Servings: 4        Cooking Time: 11 Minutes

**Ingredients:**
- 2 Very ripe plantain(s), peeled and sliced into 1-inch pieces
- Vegetable oil spray
- 3 tablespoons Maple syrup
- For garnishing Coarse sea salt or kosher salt

**Directions:**
1. Pour about ½ cup water into the bottom of your air fryer basket or into a metal tray on a lower rack in some models. Preheat the air fryer to 400°F.
2. Put the plantain pieces in a bowl, coat them with vegetable oil spray, and toss gently, spraying at least one more time and tossing repeatedly, until the pieces are well coated.
3. When the machine is at temperature, arrange the plantain pieces in the basket in one layer. Air-fry undisturbed for 5 minutes.
4. Remove the basket from the machine and spray the back of a metal spatula with vegetable oil spray. Use the spatula to press down on the plantain pieces, spraying it again as needed, to flatten the pieces to about half their original height. Brush the plantain pieces with maple syrup, then return the basket to the machine and continue air-frying undisturbed for 6 minutes, or until the plantain pieces are soft and caramelized.
5. Use kitchen tongs to transfer the pieces to a serving platter. Sprinkle the pieces with salt and cool for a couple of minutes before serving. Or cool to room temperature before serving, about 1 hour.

# Veggie Cheese Bites

Servings: 4          Cooking Time: 8 Minutes

**Ingredients:**
- 2 cups riced vegetables (see the Note below)
- ½ cup shredded zucchini
- ½ teaspoon garlic powder
- ¼ teaspoon black pepper
- ¼ teaspoon salt
- 1 large egg
- ¾ cup shredded cheddar cheese
- ⅓ cup whole-wheat flour

**Directions:**
1.  Preheat the air fryer to 350°F.
2.  In a large bowl, mix together the riced vegetables, zucchini, garlic powder, pepper, and salt. Mix in the egg. Stir in the shredded cheese and whole-wheat flour until a thick, doughlike consistency forms. If you need to, add 1 teaspoon of flour at a time so you can mold the batter into balls.
3.  Using a 1-inch scoop, portion the batter out into about 12 balls.
4.  Liberally spray the air fryer basket with olive oil spray. Then place the veggie bites inside. Leave enough room between each bite so the air can flow around them.
5.  Cook for 8 minutes, or until the outside is slightly browned. Depending on the size of your air fryer, you may need to cook these in batches.
6.  Remove and let cool slightly before serving.

# Meatball Arancini

Servings: 6
Cooking Time: 10 Minutes

**Ingredients:**
- 1⅓ cups Water
- ⅔ cup Raw white Arborio rice
- 2 teaspoons Butter
- ¼ teaspoon Table salt
- 2 Large egg(s), well beaten
- ¾ cup Seasoned Italian-style dried bread crumbs (gluten-free, if a concern)
- ⅓ cup (about 1 ounce) Finely grated Parmesan cheese
- 6 ½-ounce "bite-size" frozen meatballs (any variety, even vegan and/or gluten-free, if a concern), thawed
- Olive oil spray

**Directions:**
1.  Combine the water, rice, butter, and salt in a small saucepan. Bring to a boil over medium-high heat, stirring occasionally. Cover, reduce the heat to very low, and simmer very slowly for 20 minutes.
2.  Take the saucepan off the heat and let it stand, covered, for 10 minutes. Uncover it and fluff the rice. Cool for 20 minutes. (The rice can be made up to 1 hour in advance; keep it covered in its saucepan.)
3.  Preheat the air fryer to 375°F .
4.  Set up and fill two shallow soup plates or small bowls on your counter: one with the beaten egg(s) and one with the bread crumbs mixed with the grated cheese.
5.  With clean but wet hands, scoop up about 3 tablespoons of the cooked rice and form it into a ball around a mini meatball, forming a sealed casing. Dip the ball in the egg(s) to coat completely, letting any excess egg slip back into the rest. Set the ball in the bread-crumb mixture and roll it gently to coat evenly but lightly all over. Set aside and continue making more rice balls.
6.  Generously spray the balls with olive oil spray, then set them in the basket in one layer. They must not touch. Air-fry undisturbed for 10 minutes, or until crunchy and golden brown. Use kitchen tongs to gently transfer the balls to a wire rack. Cool for at least 5 minutes before serving.

# Beef , Pork & Lamb Recipes

## Lamb Meatballs With Quick Tomato Sauce

Servings: 4
Cooking Time: 8 Minutes

### Ingredients:

- ½ small onion, finely diced
- 1 clove garlic, minced
- 1 pound ground lamb
- 2 tablespoons fresh parsley, finely chopped (plus more for garnish)
- 2 teaspoons fresh oregano, finely chopped
- 2 tablespoons milk
- 1 egg yolk
- salt and freshly ground black pepper
- ½ cup crumbled feta cheese, for garnish
- Tomato Sauce:
- 2 tablespoons butter
- 1 clove garlic, smashed
- pinch crushed red pepper flakes
- ¼ teaspoon ground cinnamon
- 1 (28-ounce) can crushed tomatoes
- salt, to taste

### Directions:

1. Combine all ingredients for the meatballs in a large bowl and mix just until everything is combined. Shape the mixture into 1½-inch balls or shape the meat between two spoons to make quenelles (little three-sided footballs).
2. Preheat the air fryer to 400°F.
3. While the air fryer is Preheating, start the quick tomato sauce. Place the butter, garlic and red pepper flakes in a sauté pan and heat over medium heat on the stovetop. Let the garlic sizzle a little, but before the butter starts to brown, add the cinnamon and tomatoes. Bring to a simmer and simmer for 15 minutes. Season to taste with salt (but not too much as the feta that you will be sprinkling on at the end will be salty).
4. Brush the bottom of the air fryer basket with a little oil and transfer the meatballs to the air fryer basket in one layer, air-frying in batches if necessary.
5. Air-fry at 400°F for 8 minutes, giving the basket a shake once during the cooking process to turn the meatballs over.
6. To serve, spoon a pool of the tomato sauce onto plates and add the meatballs in a decorative manner. Sprinkle the feta cheese on top and garnish with more fresh parsley. Serve immediately.

## Flank Steak With Roasted Peppers And Chimichurri

Servings: 4
Cooking Time: 22 Minutes

### Ingredients:

- 2 cups flat-leaf parsley leaves
- ¼ cup fresh oregano leaves
- 3 cloves garlic
- ½ cup olive oil
- ¼ cup red wine vinegar
- ½ teaspoon salt
- freshly ground black pepper
- ¼ teaspoon crushed red pepper flakes
- ½ teaspoon ground cumin
- 1 pound flank steak
- 1 red bell pepper, cut into strips
- 1 yellow bell pepper, cut into strips

### Directions:

1. Make the chimichurri sauce by chopping the parsley, oregano and garlic in a food processor.

Add the olive oil, vinegar and seasonings and process again. Pour half of the sauce into a shallow dish with the flank steak and set the remaining sauce aside. Pierce the flank steak with a needle-style meat tenderizer or a paring knife and marinate the steak for 2 to 24 hours in the refrigerator. When you are ready to cook, remove the steak from the refrigerator and let it sit at room temperature for 30 minutes.
2.  Preheat the air fryer to 400°F.
3.  Cut the flank steak in half so that it fits more easily into the air fryer and transfer both pieces to the air fryer basket. Air-fry for 14 minutes, depending on how you like your steak cooked (10 minutes will give you medium for a 1-inch thick flank steak). Flip the steak over halfway through the cooking time.
4.  When the flank steak is cooked to your liking, transfer it to a cutting board, loosely tent with foil and let it rest while you cook the peppers.
5.  Toss the peppers in a little olive oil, salt and freshly ground black pepper and transfer them to the air fryer basket. Air-fry at 400°F for 8 minutes, shaking the basket once or twice throughout the cooking process. To serve, slice the flank steak against the grain of the meat and top with the roasted peppers. Drizzle the reserved chimichurri sauce on top, thinning the sauce with another tablespoon of olive oil if desired.

## Mustard And Rosemary Pork Tenderloin With Fried Apples

Servings: 2
Cooking Time: 26 Minutes

**Ingredients:**
- 1 pork tenderloin (about 1-pound)
- 2 tablespoons coarse brown mustard
- salt and freshly ground black pepper

- 1½ teaspoons finely chopped fresh rosemary, plus sprigs for garnish
- 2 apples, cored and cut into 8 wedges
- 1 tablespoon butter, melted
- 1 teaspoon brown sugar

**Directions:**
1.  Preheat the air fryer to 370°F.
2.  Cut the pork tenderloin in half so that you have two pieces that fit into the air fryer basket. Brush the mustard onto both halves of the pork tenderloin and then season with salt, pepper and the fresh rosemary. Place the pork tenderloin halves into the air fryer basket and air-fry for 10 minutes. Turn the pork over and air-fry for an additional 8 minutes or until the internal temperature of the pork registers 155°F on an instant read thermometer. If your pork tenderloin is especially thick, you may need to add a minute or two, but it's better to check the pork and add time, than to overcook it.
3.  Let the pork rest for 5 minutes. In the meantime, toss the apple wedges with the butter and brown sugar and air-fry at 400°F for 8 minutes, shaking the basket once or twice during the cooking process so the apples cook and brown evenly.
4.  Slice the pork on the bias. Serve with the fried apples scattered over the top and a few sprigs of rosemary as garnish.

## Beef Al Carbon (street Taco Meat)

Servings: 6
Cooking Time: 8 Minutes

**Ingredients:**
- 1½ pounds sirloin steak, cut into ½-inch cubes
- ¾ cup lime juice
- ½ cup extra-virgin olive oil
- 1 teaspoon ground cumin

- 2 teaspoons garlic powder
- 1 teaspoon salt

**Directions:**

1. In a large bowl, toss together the steak, lime juice, olive oil, cumin, garlic powder, and salt. Allow the meat to marinate for 30 minutes. Drain off all the marinade and pat the meat dry with paper towels.
2. Preheat the air fryer to 400°F.
3. Place the meat in the air fryer basket and spray with cooking spray. Cook the meat for 5 minutes, toss the meat, and continue cooking another 3 minutes, until slightly crispy.

# Tuscan Chimichangas

Servings: 2
Cooking Time: 8 Minutes

**Ingredients:**

- ¼ pound Thinly sliced deli ham, chopped
- 1 cup Drained and rinsed canned white beans
- ½ cup (about 2 ounces) Shredded semi-firm mozzarella
- ¼ cup Chopped sun-dried tomatoes
- ¼ cup Bottled Italian salad dressing, vinaigrette type
- 2 Burrito-size (12-inch) flour tortilla(s)
- Olive oil spray

**Directions:**

1. Preheat the air fryer to 375°F .
2. Mix the ham, beans, cheese, tomatoes, and salad dressing in a bowl.
3. Lay a tortilla on a clean, dry work surface. Put all of the ham mixture in a narrow oval in the middle of the tortilla, if making one burrito; or half of this mixture, if making two. Fold the parts of the tortilla that are closest to the ends of the filling oval up and over the filling, then roll the tortilla tightly closed, but don't press down hard.

Generously coat the tortilla with olive oil spray. Make a second filled tortilla, if necessary.
4. Set the filled tortilla(s) seam side down in the basket, with at least ½ inch between them, if making two. Air-fry undisturbed for 8 minutes, or until crisp and lightly browned.
5. Use kitchen tongs and a nonstick-safe spatula to transfer the chimichanga(s) to a wire rack. Cool for 5 minutes before serving.

# Perfect Strip Steaks

Servings: 2
Cooking Time: 17 Minutes

**Ingredients:**

- 1½ tablespoons Olive oil
- 1½ tablespoons Minced garlic
- 2 teaspoons Ground black pepper
- 1 teaspoon Table salt
- 2 ¾-pound boneless beef strip steak(s)

**Directions:**

1. Preheat the air fryer to 375°F (or 380°F or 390°F, if one of these is the closest setting).
2. Mix the oil, garlic, pepper, and salt in a small bowl, then smear this mixture over both sides of the steak(s).
3. When the machine is at temperature, put the steak(s) in the basket with as much air space as possible between them for the larger batch. They should not overlap or even touch. That said, even just a ¼-inch between them will work. Air-fry for 12 minutes, turning once, until an instant-read meat thermometer inserted into the thickest part of a steak registers 127°F for rare (not USDA-approved). Or air-fry for 15 minutes, turning once, until an instant-read meat thermometer registers 145°F for medium (USDA-approved). If the machine is at 390°F, the steaks may cook 2 minutes more quickly than the stated timing.

4. Use kitchen tongs to transfer the steak(s) to a wire rack. Cool for 5 minutes before serving.

# Carne Asada

Servings: 4
Cooking Time: 15 Minutes

**Ingredients:**
* 4 cloves garlic, minced
* 3 chipotle peppers in adobo, chopped
* ⅓ cup chopped fresh parsley
* ⅓ cup chopped fresh oregano
* 1 teaspoon ground cumin seed
* juice of 2 limes
* ⅓ cup olive oil
* 1 to 1½ pounds flank steak (depending on your appetites)
* salt
* tortillas and guacamole (optional – for serving)

**Directions:**
1. Make the marinade: Combine the garlic, chipotle, parsley, oregano, cumin, lime juice and olive oil in a non-reactive bowl. Coat the flank steak with the marinade and let it marinate for 30 minutes to 8 hours. (Don't leave the steak out of refrigeration for longer than 2 hours, however.)
2. Preheat the air fryer to 390°F.
3. Remove the steak from the marinade and place it in the air fryer basket. Season the steak with salt and air-fry for 15 minutes, turning the steak over halfway through the cooking time and seasoning again with salt. This should cook the steak to medium. Add or subtract two minutes for medium-well or medium-rare.
4. Remember to let the steak rest before slicing the meat against the grain. Serve with warm tortillas, guacamole and a fresh salsa like the Tomato-Corn Salsa below.

# Barbecue Country-style Pork Ribs

Servings: 3
Cooking Time: 30 Minutes

**Ingredients:**
* 3 8-ounce boneless country-style pork ribs
* 1½ teaspoons Mild smoked paprika
* 1½ teaspoons Light brown sugar
* ¾ teaspoon Onion powder
* ¾ teaspoon Ground black pepper
* ¼ teaspoon Table salt
* Vegetable oil spray

**Directions:**
1. Preheat the air fryer to 350°F . Set the ribs in a bowl on the counter as the machine heats.
2. Mix the smoked paprika, brown sugar, onion powder, pepper, and salt in a small bowl until well combined. Rub this mixture over all the surfaces of the country-style ribs. Generously coat the country-style ribs with vegetable oil spray.
3. Set the ribs in the basket with as much air space between them as possible. Air-fry undisturbed for 30 minutes, or until browned and sizzling and an instant-read meat thermometer inserted into one rib registers at least 145°F.
4. Use kitchen tongs to transfer the country-style ribs to a wire rack. Cool for 5 minutes before serving.

# Crunchy Fried Pork Loin Chops

Servings: 3
Cooking Time: 12 Minutes

**Ingredients:**
* 1 cup All-purpose flour or tapioca flour
* 1 Large egg(s), well beaten
* 1½ cups Seasoned Italian-style dried bread crumbs (gluten-free, if a concern)
* 3 4- to 5-ounce boneless center-cut pork loin chops

- Vegetable oil spray

**Directions:**
1. Preheat the air fryer to 350°F .
2. Set up and fill three shallow soup plates or small pie plates on your counter: one for the flour, one for the beaten egg(s), and one for the bread crumbs.
3. Dredge a pork chop in the flour, coating both sides as well as around the edge. Gently shake off any excess, then dip the chop in the egg(s), again coating both sides and the edge. Let any excess egg slip back into the rest, then set the chop in the bread crumbs, turning it and pressing gently to coat well on both sides and the edge. Coat the pork chop all over with vegetable oil spray and set aside so you can dredge, coat, and spray the additional chop(s).
4. Set the chops in the basket with as much air space between them as possible. Air-fry undisturbed for 12 minutes, or until brown and crunchy and an instant-read meat thermometer inserted into the center of a chop registers 145°F.
5. Use kitchen tongs to transfer the chops to a wire rack. Cool for 5 minutes before serving.

# Balsamic Marinated Rib Eye Steak With Balsamic Fried Cipollini Onions

Servings: 2
Cooking Time: 22-26 Minutes

**Ingredients:**
- 3 tablespoons balsamic vinegar
- 2 cloves garlic, sliced
- 1 tablespoon Dijon mustard
- 1 teaspoon fresh thyme leaves
- 1 (16-ounce) boneless rib eye steak
- coarsely ground black pepper
- salt
- 1 (8-ounce) bag cipollini onions, peeled
- 1 teaspoon balsamic vinegar

**Directions:**
1. Combine the 3 tablespoons of balsamic vinegar, garlic, Dijon mustard and thyme in a small bowl. Pour this marinade over the steak. Pierce the steak several times with a paring knife or
2. a needle-style meat tenderizer and season it generously with coarsely ground black pepper. Flip the steak over and pierce the other side in a similar fashion, seasoning again with the coarsely ground black pepper. Marinate the steak for 2 to 24 hours in the refrigerator. When you are ready to cook, remove the steak from the refrigerator and let it sit at room temperature for 30 minutes.
3. Preheat the air fryer to 400°F.
4. Season the steak with salt and air-fry at 400°F for 12 minutes (medium-rare), 14 minutes (medium), or 16 minutes (well-done), flipping the steak once half way through the cooking time.
5. While the steak is air-frying, toss the onions with 1 teaspoon of balsamic vinegar and season with salt.
6. Remove the steak from the air fryer and let it rest while you fry the onions. Transfer the onions to the air fryer basket and air-fry for 10 minutes, adding a few more minutes if your onions are very large. Then, slice the steak on the bias and serve with the fried onions on top.

# Pesto-rubbed Veal Chops

Servings: 2
Cooking Time: 12-15 Minutes

**Ingredients:**
- ¼ cup Purchased pesto
- 2 10-ounce bone-in veal loin or rib chop(s)
- ½ teaspoon Ground black pepper

**Directions:**

1. Preheat the air fryer to 400°F.

2. Rub the pesto onto both sides of the veal chop(s). Sprinkle one side of the chop(s) with the ground black pepper. Set aside at room temperature as the machine comes up to temperature.

3. Set the chop(s) in the basket. If you're cooking more than one chop, leave as much air space between them as possible. Air-fry undisturbed for 12 minutes for medium-rare, or until an instant-read meat thermometer inserted into the center of a chop (without touching bone) registers 135°F (not USDA-approved). Or air-fry undisturbed for 15 minutes for medium-well, or until an instant-read meat thermometer registers 145°F (USDA-approved).

4. Use kitchen tongs to transfer the chops to a cutting board or a wire rack. Cool for 5 minutes before serving.

# Meatloaf With Tangy Tomato Glaze

Servings: 6
Cooking Time: 50 Minutes

**Ingredients:**
- 1 pound ground beef
- ½ pound ground pork
- ½ pound ground veal (or turkey)
- 1 medium onion, diced
- 1 small clove of garlic, minced
- 2 egg yolks, lightly beaten
- ½ cup tomato ketchup
- 1 tablespoon Worcestershire sauce
- ½ cup plain breadcrumbs*
- 2 teaspoons salt
- freshly ground black pepper
- ½ cup chopped fresh parsley, plus more for garnish
- 6 tablespoons ketchup
- 1 tablespoon balsamic vinegar
- 2 tablespoons brown sugar

**Directions:**
1. Combine the meats, onion, garlic, egg yolks, ketchup, Worcestershire sauce, breadcrumbs, salt, pepper and fresh parsley in a large bowl and mix well.

2. Preheat the air fryer to 350°F and pour a little water into the bottom of the air fryer drawer. (This will help prevent the grease that drips into the bottom drawer from burning and smoking.)

3. Transfer the meatloaf mixture to the air fryer basket, packing it down gently. Run a spatula around the meatloaf to create a space about ½-inch wide between the meat and the side of the air fryer basket.

4. Air-fry at 350°F for 20 minutes. Carefully invert the meatloaf onto a plate (remember to remove the basket from the air fryer drawer so you don't pour all the grease out) and slide it back into the air fryer basket to turn it over. Re-shape the meatloaf with a spatula if necessary. Air-fry for another 20 minutes at 350°F.

5. Combine the ketchup, balsamic vinegar and brown sugar in a bowl and spread the mixture over the meatloaf. Air-fry for another 10 minutes, until an instant read thermometer inserted into the center of the meatloaf registers 160°F.

6. Allow the meatloaf to rest for a few more minutes and then transfer it to a serving platter using a spatula. Slice the meatloaf, sprinkle a little chopped parsley on top if desired, and serve.

# Better-than-chinese-take-out Sesame Beef

Servings: 4
Cooking Time: 14 Minutes

**Ingredients:**
- 1¼ pounds Beef flank steak

- 2½ tablespoons Regular or low-sodium soy sauce or gluten-free tamari sauce
- 2 tablespoons Toasted sesame oil
- 2½ teaspoons Cornstarch
- 1 pound 2 ounces (about 4½ cups) Frozen mixed vegetables for stir-fry, thawed, seasoning packet discarded
- 3 tablespoons Unseasoned rice vinegar (see here)
- 3 tablespoons Thai sweet chili sauce
- 2 tablespoons Light brown sugar
- 2 tablespoons White sesame seeds
- 2 teaspoons Water
- Vegetable oil spray
- 1½ tablespoons Minced peeled fresh ginger
- 1 tablespoon Minced garlic

**Directions:**

1. Set the flank steak on a cutting board and run your clean fingers across it to figure out which way the meat's fibers are running. (Usually, they run the long way from end to end, or perhaps slightly at an angle lengthwise along the cut.) Cut the flank steak into three pieces parallel to the meat's grain. Then cut each of these pieces into ½-inch-wide strips against the grain.

2. Put the meat strips in a large bowl. For a small batch, add 2 teaspoons of the soy or tamari sauce, 2 teaspoons of the sesame oil, and ½ teaspoon of the cornstarch; for a medium batch, add 1 tablespoon of the soy or tamari sauce, 1 tablespoon of the sesame oil, and 1 teaspoon of the cornstarch; and for a large batch, add 1½ tablespoons of the soy or tamari sauce, 1½ tablespoons of the sesame oil, and 1½ teaspoons of the cornstarch. Toss well until the meat is thoroughly coated in the marinade. Set aside at room temperature.

3. Preheat the air fryer to 400°F.

4. When the machine is at temperature, place the beef strips in the basket in as close to one layer as possible. The strips will overlap or even cover each other. Air-fry for 10 minutes, tossing and rearranging the strips three times so that the covered parts get exposed, until browned and even a little crisp. Pour the strips into a clean bowl.

5. Spread the vegetables in the basket and air-fry undisturbed for 4 minutes, just until they are heated through and somewhat softened. Pour these into the bowl with the meat strips. Turn off the air fryer.

6. Whisk the rice vinegar, sweet chili sauce, brown sugar, sesame seeds, the remaining soy sauce, and the remaining sesame oil in a small bowl until well combined. For a small batch, whisk the remaining 1 teaspoon cornstarch with the water in a second small bowl to make a smooth slurry; for medium batch, whisk the remaining 1½ teaspoons cornstarch with the water in a second small bowl to make a smooth slurry; and for a large batch, whisk the remaining 2 teaspoons cornstarch with the water in a second small bowl to make a smooth slurry.

7. Generously coat the inside of a large wok with vegetable oil spray, then set the wok over high heat for a few minutes. Add the ginger and garlic; stir-fry for 10 seconds or so, just until fragrant. Add the meat and vegetables; stir-fry for 1 minute to heat through.

8. Add the rice vinegar mixture and continue stir-frying until the sauce is bubbling, less than 1 minute. Add the cornstarch slurry and stir-fry until the sauce has thickened, just a few seconds. Remove the wok from the heat and serve hot.

# Steak Fingers

Servings: 4
Cooking Time: 8 Minutes

**Ingredients:**

- 4 small beef cube steaks
- salt and pepper
- ½ cup flour
- oil for misting or cooking spray

**Directions:**

1. Cut cube steaks into 1-inch-wide strips.
2. Sprinkle lightly with salt and pepper to taste.
3. Roll in flour to coat all sides.
4. Spray air fryer basket with cooking spray or oil.
5. Place steak strips in air fryer basket in single layer, very close together but not touching. Spray top of steak strips with oil or cooking spray.
6. Cook at 390°F for 4minutes, turn strips over, and spray with oil or cooking spray.
7. Cook 4 more minutes and test with fork for doneness. Steak fingers should be crispy outside with no red juices inside. If needed, cook an additional 4 minutes or until well done. (Don't eat beef cube steak rare.)
8. Repeat steps 5 through 7 to cook remaining strips.

# Calzones South Of The Border

Servings: 8
Cooking Time: 8 Minutes

**Ingredients:**

- Filling
- ¼ pound ground pork sausage
- ½ teaspoon chile powder
- ¼ teaspoon ground cumin
- ⅛ teaspoon garlic powder
- ⅛ teaspoon onion powder
- ⅛ teaspoon oregano
- ½ cup ricotta cheese
- 1 ounce sharp Cheddar cheese, shredded
- 2 ounces Pepper Jack cheese, shredded
- 1 4-ounce can chopped green chiles, drained
- oil for misting or cooking spray
- salsa, sour cream, or guacamole
- Crust
- 2 cups white wheat flour, plus more for kneading and rolling
- 1 package (¼ ounce) RapidRise yeast
- 1 teaspoon salt
- ½ teaspoon chile powder
- ½ teaspoon ground cumin
- 1 cup warm water (115°F to 125°F)
- 2 teaspoons olive oil

**Directions:**

1. Crumble sausage into air fryer baking pan and stir in the filling seasonings: chile powder, cumin, garlic powder, onion powder, and oregano. Cook at 390°F for 2minutes. Stir, breaking apart, and cook for 3 to 4minutes, until well done. Remove and set aside on paper towels to drain.
2. To make dough, combine flour, yeast, salt, chile powder, and cumin. Stir in warm water and oil until soft dough forms. Turn out onto lightly floured board and knead for 3 or 4minutes. Let dough rest for 10minutes.
3. Place the three cheeses in a medium bowl. Add cooked sausage and chiles and stir until well mixed.
4. Cut dough into 8 pieces.
5. Working with 4 pieces of the dough, press each into a circle about 5 inches in diameter. Top each dough circle with 2 heaping tablespoons of filling. Fold over into a half-moon shape and press edges together. Seal edges firmly to prevent leakage. Spray both sides with oil or cooking spray.
6. Place 4 calzones in air fryer basket and cook at 360°F for 5minutes. Mist with oil or spray and

cook for 3minutes, until crust is done and nicely browned.

7. While the first batch is cooking, press out the remaining dough, fill, and shape into calzones.

8. Spray both sides with oil or cooking spray and cook for 5minutes. If needed, mist with oil and continue cooking for 3 minutes longer. This second batch will cook a little faster than the first because your air fryer is already hot.

9. Serve plain or with salsa, sour cream, or guacamole.

# Tuscan Veal Chops

Servings: 2
Cooking Time: 12-15 Minutes

**Ingredients:**
- 4 teaspoons Olive oil
- 2 teaspoons Finely minced garlic
- 2 teaspoons Finely minced fresh rosemary leaves
- 1 teaspoon Finely grated lemon zest
- 1 teaspoon Crushed fennel seeds
- 1 teaspoon Table salt
- Up to ¼ teaspoon Red pepper flakes
- 2 10-ounce bone-in veal loin or rib chop(s), about ½ inch thick

**Directions:**
1. Preheat the air fryer to 400°F.
2. Mix the oil, garlic, rosemary, lemon zest, fennel seeds, salt, and red pepper flakes in a small bowl. Rub this mixture onto both sides of the veal chop(s). Set aside at room temperature as the machine comes to temperature.
3. Set the chop(s) in the basket. If you're cooking more than one chop, leave as much air space between them as possible. Air-fry undisturbed for 12 minutes for medium-rare, or until an instant-read meat thermometer inserted into the center of a chop (without touching bone)

registers 135°F (not USDA-approved). Or air-fry undisturbed for 15 minutes for medium-well, or until an instant-read meat thermometer registers 145°F (USDA-approved).

4. Use kitchen tongs to transfer the chops to a cutting board or a wire rack. Cool for 5 minutes before serving.

# Stuffed Pork Chops

Servings: 4
Cooking Time: 12 Minutes

**Ingredients:**
- 4 boneless pork chops
- ½ teaspoon salt
- ½ teaspoon black pepper
- ¼ teaspoon paprika
- 1 cup frozen spinach, defrosted and squeezed dry
- 2 cloves garlic, minced
- 2 ounces cream cheese
- ¼ cup grated Parmesan cheese
- 1 tablespoon extra-virgin olive oil

**Directions:**
1. Pat the pork chops with a paper towel. Make a slit in the side of each pork chop to create a pouch.
2. Season the pork chops with the salt, pepper, and paprika.
3. In a small bowl, mix together the spinach, garlic, cream cheese, and Parmesan cheese.
4. Divide the mixture into fourths and stuff the pork chop pouches. Secure the pouches with toothpicks.
5. Preheat the air fryer to 400°F.
6. Place the stuffed pork chops in the air fryer basket and spray liberally with cooking spray. Cook for 6 minutes, flip and coat with more cooking spray, and cook another 6 minutes. Check to make sure the meat is cooked to an

internal temperature of 145°F. Cook the pork chops in batches, as needed.

# Smokehouse-style Beef Ribs

Servings: 3
Cooking Time: 25 Minutes

**Ingredients:**
- ¼ teaspoon Mild smoked paprika
- ¼ teaspoon Garlic powder
- ¼ teaspoon Onion powder
- ¼ teaspoon Table salt
- ¼ teaspoon Ground black pepper
- 3 10- to 12-ounce beef back ribs (not beef short ribs)

**Directions:**
1. Preheat the air fryer to 350°F .
2. Mix the smoked paprika, garlic powder, onion powder, salt, and pepper in a small bowl until uniform. Massage and pat this mixture onto the ribs.
3. When the machine is at temperature, set the ribs in the basket in one layer, turning them on their sides if necessary, sort of like they're spooning but with at least ¼ inch air space between them. Air-fry for 25 minutes, turning once, until deep brown and sizzling.
4. Use kitchen tongs to transfer the ribs to a wire rack. Cool for 5 minutes before serving.

# Italian Sausage & Peppers

Servings: 6
Cooking Time: 25 Minutes

**Ingredients:**
- 1 6-ounce can tomato paste
- ⅔ cup water
- 1 8-ounce can tomato sauce
- 1 teaspoon dried parsley flakes
- ½ teaspoon garlic powder
- ⅛ teaspoon oregano
- ½ pound mild Italian bulk sausage
- 1 tablespoon extra virgin olive oil
- ½ large onion, cut in 1-inch chunks
- 4 ounces fresh mushrooms, sliced
- 1 large green bell pepper, cut in 1-inch chunks
- 8 ounces spaghetti, cooked
- Parmesan cheese for serving

**Directions:**
1. In a large saucepan or skillet, stir together the tomato paste, water, tomato sauce, parsley, garlic, and oregano. Heat on stovetop over very low heat while preparing meat and vegetables.
2. Break sausage into small chunks, about ½-inch pieces. Place in air fryer baking pan.
3. Cook at 390°F for 5minutes. Stir. Cook 7 minutes longer or until sausage is well done. Remove from pan, drain on paper towels, and add to the sauce mixture.
4. If any sausage grease remains in baking pan, pour it off or use paper towels to soak it up. (Be careful handling that hot pan!)
5. Place olive oil, onions, and mushrooms in pan and stir. Cook for 5minutes or just until tender. Using a slotted spoon, transfer onions and mushrooms from baking pan into the sauce and sausage mixture.
6. Place bell pepper chunks in air fryer baking pan and cook for 8 minutes or until tender. When done, stir into sauce with sausage and other vegetables.
7. Serve over cooked spaghetti with plenty of Parmesan cheese.

# Apple Cornbread Stuffed Pork Loin With Apple Gravy

Servings: 4
Cooking Time: 61 Minutes

**Ingredients:**
- 4 strips of bacon, chopped
- 1 Granny Smith apple, peeled, cored and finely chopped
- 2 teaspoons fresh thyme leaves
- ¼ cup chopped fresh parsley
- 2 cups cubed cornbread
- ½ cup chicken stock
- salt and freshly ground black pepper
- 1 (2-pound) boneless pork loin
- kitchen twine
- Apple Gravy:
- 2 tablespoons butter
- 1 shallot, minced
- 1 Granny Smith apple, peeled, cored and finely chopped
- 3 sprigs fresh thyme
- 2 tablespoons flour
- 1 cup chicken stock
- ½ cup apple cider
- salt and freshly ground black pepper, to taste

**Directions:**
1. Preheat the air fryer to 400°F.
2. Add the bacon to the air fryer and air-fry for 6 minutes until crispy. While the bacon is cooking, combine the apple, fresh thyme, parsley and cornbread in a bowl and toss well. Moisten the mixture with the chicken stock and season to taste with salt and freshly ground black pepper. Add the cooked bacon to the mixture.
3. Butterfly the pork loin by holding it flat on the cutting board with one hand, while slicing into the pork loin parallel to the cutting board with the other. Slice into the longest side of the pork loin, but stop before you cut all the way through. You should then be able to open the pork loin up like a book, making it twice as wide as it was when you started. Season the inside of the pork with salt and freshly ground black pepper.
4. Spread the cornbread mixture onto the butterflied pork loin, leaving a one-inch border around the edge of the pork. Roll the pork loin up around the stuffing to enclose the stuffing, and tie the rolled pork in several places with kitchen twine or secure with toothpicks. Try to replace any stuffing that falls out of the roast as you roll it, by stuffing it into the ends of the rolled pork. Season the outside of the pork with salt and freshly ground black pepper.
5. Preheat the air fryer to 360°F.
6. Place the stuffed pork loin into the air fryer, seam side down. Air-fry the pork loin for 15 minutes at 360°F. Turn the pork loin over and air-fry for an additional 15 minutes. Turn the pork loin a quarter turn and air-fry for an additional 15 minutes. Turn the pork loin over again to expose the fourth side, and air-fry for an additional 10 minutes. The pork loin should register 155°F on an instant read thermometer when it is finished.
7. While the pork is cooking, make the apple gravy. Preheat a saucepan over medium heat on the stovetop and melt the butter. Add the shallot, apple and thyme sprigs and sauté until the apple starts to soften and brown a little. Add the flour and stir for a minute or two. Whisk in the stock and apple cider vigorously to prevent the flour from forming lumps. Bring the mixture to a boil to thicken and season to taste with salt and pepper.
8. Transfer the pork loin to a resting plate and loosely tent with foil, letting the pork rest for at

least 5 minutes before slicing and serving with the apple gravy poured over the top.

# Pork Schnitzel

Servings: 4
Cooking Time: 14 Minutes

**Ingredients:**
- 4 boneless pork chops, pounded to ¼-inch thickness
- 1 teaspoon salt, divided
- 1 teaspoon black pepper, divided
- ½ cup all-purpose flour
- 2 eggs
- 1 cup breadcrumbs
- ¼ teaspoon paprika
- 1 lemon, cut into wedges

**Directions:**
1. Season both sides of the pork chops with ½ teaspoon of the salt and ½ teaspoon of the pepper.
2. On a plate, place the flour.
3. In a large bowl, whisk the eggs.
4. In another large bowl, place the breadcrumbs.
5. Season the flour with the paprika and season the breadcrumbs with the remaining ½ teaspoon of salt and ½ teaspoon of pepper.
6. To bread the pork, place a pork chop in the flour, then into the whisked eggs, and then into the breadcrumbs. Place the breaded pork onto a plate and finish breading the remaining pork chops.
7. Preheat the air fryer to 390°F.
8. Place the pork chops into the air fryer, not overlapping and working in batches as needed. Spray the pork chops with cooking spray and cook for 8 minutes; flip the pork and cook for another 4 to 6 minutes or until cooked to an internal temperature of 145°F.
9. Serve with lemon wedges.

# Pork Schnitzel With Dill Sauce

Servings: 4
Cooking Time: 4 Minutes

**Ingredients:**
- 6 boneless, center cut pork chops (about 1½ pounds)
- ½ cup flour
- 1½ teaspoons salt
- freshly ground black pepper
- 2 eggs
- ½ cup milk
- 1½ cups toasted fine breadcrumbs
- 1 teaspoon paprika
- 3 tablespoons butter, melted
- 2 tablespoons vegetable or olive oil
- lemon wedges
- Dill Sauce:
- 1 cup chicken stock
- 1½ tablespoons cornstarch
- ⅓ cup sour cream
- 1½ tablespoons chopped fresh dill
- salt and pepper

**Directions:**
1. Trim the excess fat from the pork chops and pound each chop with a meat mallet between two pieces of plastic wrap until they are ½-inch thick.
2. Set up a dredging station. Combine the flour, salt, and black pepper in a shallow dish. Whisk the eggs and milk together in a second shallow dish. Finally, combine the breadcrumbs and paprika in a third shallow dish.
3. Dip each flattened pork chop in the flour. Shake off the excess flour and dip each chop into the egg mixture. Finally dip them into the breadcrumbs and press the breadcrumbs onto the meat firmly. Place each finished chop on a baking sheet until they are all coated.
4. Preheat the air fryer to 400°F.

5. Combine the melted butter and the oil in a small bowl and lightly brush both sides of the coated pork chops. Do not brush the chops too heavily or the breading will not be as crispy.

6. Air-fry one schnitzel at a time for 4 minutes, turning it over halfway through the cooking time. Hold the cooked schnitzels warm on a baking pan in a 170°F oven while you finish air-frying the rest.

7. While the schnitzels are cooking, whisk the chicken stock and cornstarch together in a small saucepan over medium-high heat on the stovetop. Bring the mixture to a boil and simmer for 2 minutes. Remove the saucepan from heat and whisk in the sour cream. Add the chopped fresh dill and season with salt and pepper.

8. Transfer the pork schnitzel to a platter and serve with dill sauce and lemon wedges. For a traditional meal, serve this along side some egg noodles, spätzle or German potato salad.

# Pepper Steak

Servings: 4
Cooking Time: 30 Minutes

**Ingredients:**
- 2 tablespoons cornstarch
- 1 tablespoon sugar
- ¾ cup beef broth
- ¼ cup hoisin sauce
- 3 tablespoons soy sauce
- 1 teaspoon sesame oil
- ½ teaspoon freshly ground black pepper
- 1½ pounds boneless New York strip steaks, sliced into ½-inch strips
- 1 onion, sliced
- 3 small bell peppers, red, yellow and green, sliced

**Directions:**

1. Whisk the cornstarch and sugar together in a large bowl to break up any lumps in the cornstarch. Add the beef broth and whisk until combined and smooth. Stir in the hoisin sauce, soy sauce, sesame oil and freshly ground black pepper. Add the beef, onion and peppers, and toss to coat. Marinate the beef and vegetables at room temperature for 30 minutes, stirring a few times to keep meat and vegetables coated.

2. Preheat the air fryer to 350°F.

3. Transfer the beef, onion, and peppers to the air fryer basket with tongs, reserving the marinade. Air-fry the beef and vegetables for 30 minutes, stirring well two or three times during the cooking process.

4. While the beef is air-frying, bring the reserved marinade to a simmer in a small saucepan over medium heat on the stovetop. Simmer for 5 minutes until the sauce thickens.

5. When the steak and vegetables have finished cooking, transfer them to a serving platter. Pour the hot sauce over the pepper steak and serve with white rice.

# Honey Mesquite Pork Chops

Servings: 2
Cooking Time: 10 Minutes

**Ingredients:**
- 2 tablespoons mesquite seasoning
- ¼ cup honey
- 1 tablespoon olive oil
- 1 tablespoon water
- freshly ground black pepper
- 2 bone-in center cut pork chops (about 1 pound)

**Directions:**

1. Whisk the mesquite seasoning, honey, olive oil, water and freshly ground black pepper together in a shallow glass dish. Pierce the chops

all over and on both sides with a fork or meat tenderizer. Add the pork chops to the marinade and massage the marinade into the chops. Cover and marinate for 30 minutes.

2. Preheat the air fryer to 330°F.

3. Transfer the pork chops to the air fryer basket and pour half of the marinade over the chops, reserving the remaining marinade. Air-fry the pork chops for 6 minutes. Flip the pork chops over and pour the remaining marinade on top. Air-fry for an additional 3 minutes at 330°F. Then, increase the air fryer temperature to 400°F and air-fry the pork chops for an additional minute.

4. Transfer the pork chops to a serving plate, and let them rest for 5 minutes before serving. If you'd like a sauce for these chops, pour the cooked marinade from the bottom of the air fryer over the top.

# Rib Eye Cheesesteaks With Fried Onions

Servings: 2
Cooking Time: 20 Minutes

**Ingredients:**
- 1 (12-ounce) rib eye steak
- 2 tablespoons Worcestershire sauce
- salt and freshly ground black pepper
- ½ onion, sliced
- 2 tablespoons butter, melted
- 4 ounces sliced Cheddar or provolone cheese
- 2 long hoagie rolls, lightly toasted

**Directions:**
1. Place the steak in the freezer for 30 minutes to make it easier to slice. When it is well-chilled, thinly slice the steak against the grain and transfer it to a bowl. Pour the Worcestershire sauce over the steak and season it with salt and pepper. Allow the meat to come to room temperature.

2. Preheat the air fryer to 400°F.

3. Toss the sliced onion with the butter and transfer it to the air fryer basket. Air-fry at 400°F for 12 minutes, shaking the basket a few times during the cooking process. Place the steak on top of the onions and air-fry for another 6 minutes, stirring the meat and onions together halfway through the cooking time.

4. When the air fryer has finished cooking, divide the steak and onions in half in the air fryer basket, pushing each half to one side of the air fryer basket. Place the cheese on top of each half, push the drawer back into the turned off air fryer and let it sit for 2 minutes, until the cheese has melted.

5. Transfer each half of the cheesesteak mixture into a toasted roll with the cheese side up and dig in!

# City "chicken"

Servings: 3
Cooking Time: 10 Minutes

**Ingredients:**
- 1 pound Pork tenderloin, cut into 2-inch cubes
- ½ cup All-purpose flour or tapioca flour
- 1 Large egg(s)
- 1 teaspoon Dried poultry seasoning blend
- 1¼ cups Plain panko bread crumbs (gluten-free, if a concern)
- Vegetable oil spray

**Directions:**
1. Preheat the air fryer to 350°F .

2. Thread 3 or 4 pieces of pork on a 4-inch bamboo skewer. You'll need 2 or 3 skewers for a small batch, 3 or 4 for a medium, and up to 6 for a large batch.

3. Set up and fill three shallow soup plates or small pie plates on your counter: one for the flour;

one for the egg(s), beaten with the poultry seasoning until foamy; and one for the bread crumbs.

4. Dip and roll one skewer into the flour, coating all sides of the meat. Gently shake off any excess flour, then dip and roll the skewer in the egg mixture. Let any excess egg mixture slip back into the rest, then set the skewer in the bread crumbs and roll it around, pressing gently, until the exterior surfaces of the meat are evenly coated. Generously coat the meat on the skewer with vegetable oil spray. Set aside and continue dredging, dipping, coating, and spraying the remaining skewers.

5. Set the skewers in the basket in one layer and air-fry undisturbed for 10 minutes, or until brown and crunchy.

6. Use kitchen tongs to transfer the skewers to a wire rack. Cool for a minute or two before serving.

# Pretzel-coated Pork Tenderloin

Servings: 4
Cooking Time: 10 Minutes

**Ingredients:**

- 1 Large egg white(s)
- 2 teaspoons Dijon mustard (gluten-free, if a concern)
- 1½ cups (about 6 ounces) Crushed pretzel crumbs (see the headnote; gluten-free, if a concern)
- 1 pound (4 sections) Pork tenderloin, cut into ¼-pound (4-ounce) sections
- Vegetable oil spray

**Directions:**

1. Preheat the air fryer to 350°F .

2. Set up and fill two shallow soup plates or small pie plates on your counter: one for the egg white(s), whisked with the mustard until foamy; and one for the pretzel crumbs.

3. Dip a section of pork tenderloin in the egg white mixture and turn it to coat well, even on the ends. Let any excess egg white mixture slip back into the rest, then set the pork in the pretzel crumbs. Roll it several times, pressing gently, until the pork is evenly coated, even on the ends. Generously coat the pork section with vegetable oil spray, set it aside, and continue coating and spraying the remaining sections.

4. Set the pork sections in the basket with at least ¼ inch between them. Air-fry undisturbed for 10 minutes, or until an instant-read meat thermometer inserted into the center of one section registers 145°F.

5. Use kitchen tongs to transfer the pieces to a wire rack. Cool for 3 to 5 minutes before serving.

# Almond And Sun-dried Tomato Crusted Pork Chops

Servings: 4
Cooking Time: 10 Minutes

**Ingredients:**

- ½ cup oil-packed sun-dried tomatoes
- ½ cup toasted almonds
- ¼ cup grated Parmesan cheese
- ½ cup olive oil
- 2 tablespoons water
- ½ teaspoon salt
- freshly ground black pepper
- 4 center-cut boneless pork chops (about 1¼ pounds)

**Directions:**

1. Place the sun-dried tomatoes into a food processor and pulse them until they are coarsely chopped. Add the almonds, Parmesan cheese, olive oil, water, salt and pepper. Process all the ingredients into a smooth paste. Spread most of the paste (leave a little in reserve) onto both sides of the pork chops and then pierce the meat

several times with a needle-style meat tenderizer or a fork. Let the pork chops sit and marinate for at least 1 hour (refrigerate if marinating for longer than 1 hour).

2. Preheat the air fryer to 370°F.

3. Brush a little olive oil on the bottom of the air fryer basket. Transfer the pork chops into the air fryer basket, spooning a little more of the sun-dried tomato paste onto the pork chops if there are any gaps where the paste may have been rubbed off. Air-fry the pork chops at 370°F for 10 minutes, turning the chops over halfway through the cooking process.

4. When the pork chops have finished cooking, transfer them to a serving plate and serve with mashed potatoes and vegetables for a hearty meal.

# Extra Crispy Country-style Pork Riblets

Servings: 3
Cooking Time: 30 Minutes

**Ingredients:**
- ⅓ cup Tapioca flour
- 2½ tablespoons Chile powder
- ¾ teaspoon Table salt (optional)
- 1¼ pounds Boneless country-style pork ribs, cut into 1½-inch chunks
- Vegetable oil spray

**Directions:**
1. Preheat the air fryer to 375°F .

2. Mix the tapioca flour, chile powder, and salt (if using) in a large bowl until well combined. Add the country-style rib chunks and toss well to coat thoroughly.

3. When the machine is at temperature, gently shake off any excess tapioca coating from the chunks. Generously coat them on all sides with vegetable oil spray. Arrange the chunks in the basket in one (admittedly fairly tight) layer. The pieces may touch. Air-fry for 30 minutes, rearranging the pieces at the 10- and 20-minute marks to expose any touching bits, until very crisp and well browned.

4. Gently pour the contents of the basket onto a wire rack. Cool for 5 minutes before serving.

# Barbecue-style Beef Cube Steak

Servings: 2
Cooking Time: 14 Minutes

**Ingredients:**
- 2 4-ounce beef cube steak(s)
- 2 cups (about 8 ounces) Fritos (original flavor) or a generic corn chip equivalent, crushed to crumbs (see here)
- 6 tablespoons Purchased smooth barbecue sauce, any flavor (gluten-free, if a concern)

**Directions:**
1. Preheat the air fryer to 375°F .

2. Spread the Fritos crumbs in a shallow soup plate or a small pie plate. Rub the barbecue sauce onto both sides of the steak(s). Dredge the steak(s) in the Fritos crumbs to coat well and thoroughly, turning several times and pressing down to get the little bits to adhere to the meat.

3. When the machine is at temperature, set the steak(s) in the basket. Leave as much air space between them as possible if you're working with more than one piece of beef. Air-fry undisturbed for 12 minutes, or until lightly brown and crunchy. If the machine is at 360°F, you may need to add 2 minutes to the cooking time.

4. Use kitchen tongs to transfer the steak(s) to a wire rack. Cool for 5 minutes before serving.

# Pork Cutlets With Almond-lemon Crust

Servings: 3
Cooking Time: 14 Minutes

**Ingredients:**
- ¾ cup Almond flour
- ¾ cup Plain dried bread crumbs (gluten-free, if a concern)
- 1½ teaspoons Finely grated lemon zest
- 1¼ teaspoons Table salt
- ¾ teaspoon Garlic powder
- ¾ teaspoon Dried oregano
- 1 Large egg white(s)
- 2 tablespoons Water
- 3 6-ounce center-cut boneless pork loin chops (about ¾ inch thick)
- Olive oil spray

**Directions:**
1. Preheat the air fryer to 375°F .
2. Mix the almond flour, bread crumbs, lemon zest, salt, garlic powder, and dried oregano in a large bowl until well combined.
3. Whisk the egg white(s) and water in a shallow soup plate or small pie plate until uniform.
4. Dip a chop in the egg white mixture, turning it to coat all sides, even the ends. Let any excess egg white mixture slip back into the rest, then set it in the almond flour mixture. Turn it several times, pressing gently to coat it evenly. Generously coat the chop with olive oil spray, then set aside to dip and coat the remaining chop(s).
5. Set the chops in the basket with as much air space between them as possible. Air-fry undisturbed for 12 minutes, or until browned and crunchy. You may need to add 2 minutes to the cooking time if the machine is at 360°F.
6. Use kitchen tongs to transfer the chops to a wire rack. Cool for a few minutes before serving.

# Cinnamon-stick Kofta Skewers

Servings: 8
Cooking Time: 15 Minutes

**Ingredients:**
- 1 pound Lean ground beef
- ½ teaspoon Ground cumin
- ½ teaspoon Onion powder
- ½ teaspoon Ground dried turmeric
- ½ teaspoon Ground cinnamon
- ½ teaspoon Table salt
- Up to a ⅛ teaspoon Cayenne
- 8 3½- to 4-inch-long cinnamon sticks (see the headnote)
- Vegetable oil spray

**Directions:**
1. Preheat the air fryer to 375°F .
2. Gently mix the ground beef, cumin, onion powder, turmeric, cinnamon, salt, and cayenne in a bowl until the meat is evenly mixed with the spices. (Clean, dry hands work best!) Divide this mixture into 2-ounce portions, each about the size of a golf ball.
3. Wrap one portion of the meat mixture around a cinnamon stick, using about three-quarters of the length of the stick, covering one end but leaving a little "handle" of cinnamon stick protruding from the other end. Set aside and continue making more kofta skewers.
4. Generously coat the formed kofta skewers on all sides with vegetable oil spray. Set them in the basket with as much air space between them as possible. Air-fry undisturbed for 13 minutes, or until browned and cooked through. If the machine is at 360°F, you may need to add 2 minutes to the cooking time.

5. Use a nonstick-safe spatula, and perhaps kitchen tongs for balance, to gently transfer the kofta skewers to a wire rack. Cool for at least 5 minutes or up to 20 minutes before serving.

# Boneless Ribeyes

Servings: 2
Cooking Time: 10-15 Minutes

**Ingredients:**
- 2 8-ounce boneless ribeye steaks
- 4 teaspoons Worcestershire sauce
- ½ teaspoon garlic powder
- pepper
- 4 teaspoons extra virgin olive oil
- salt

**Directions:**
1. Season steaks on both sides with Worcestershire sauce. Use the back of a spoon to spread evenly.
2. Sprinkle both sides of steaks with garlic powder and coarsely ground black pepper to taste.
3. Drizzle both sides of steaks with olive oil, again using the back of a spoon to spread evenly over surfaces.
4. Allow steaks to marinate for 30minutes.
5. Place both steaks in air fryer basket and cook at 390°F for 5minutes.
6. Turn steaks over and cook until done:
7. Medium rare: additional 5 minutes
8. Medium: additional 7 minutes
9. Well done: additional 10 minutes
10. Remove steaks from air fryer basket and let sit 5minutes. Salt to taste and serve.

# Meat Loaves

Servings: 4
Cooking Time: 19 Minutes

**Ingredients:**
- Sauce
- ¼ cup white vinegar
- ¼ cup brown sugar
- 2 tablespoons Worcestershire sauce
- ½ cup ketchup
- Meat Loaves
- 1 pound very lean ground beef
- ⅔ cup dry bread (approx. 1 slice torn into small pieces)
- 1 egg
- ⅓ cup minced onion
- 1 teaspoon salt
- 2 tablespoons ketchup

**Directions:**
1. In a small saucepan, combine all sauce ingredients and bring to a boil. Remove from heat and stir to ensure that brown sugar dissolves completely.
2. In a large bowl, combine the beef, bread, egg, onion, salt, and ketchup. Mix well.
3. Divide meat mixture into 4 portions and shape each into a thick, round patty. Patties will be about 3 to 3½ inches in diameter, and all four should fit easily into the air fryer basket at once.
4. Cook at 360°F for 18 minutes, until meat is well done. Baste tops of mini loaves with a small amount of sauce, and cook 1 minute.
5. Serve hot with additional sauce on the side.

# Beef Short Ribs

Servings: 4
Cooking Time: 20 Minutes

**Ingredients:**
- 2 tablespoons soy sauce
- 1 tablespoon sesame oil
- 2 tablespoons brown sugar
- 1 teaspoon ground ginger
- 2 garlic cloves, crushed
- 1 pound beef short ribs

**Directions:**

1. In a small bowl, mix together the soy sauce, sesame oil, brown sugar, and ginger. Transfer the mixture to a large resealable plastic bag, and place the garlic cloves and short ribs into the bag. Secure and place in the refrigerator for an hour (or overnight).

2. When you're ready to prepare the dish, preheat the air fryer to 330°F.

3. Liberally spray the air fryer basket with olive oil mist and set the beef short ribs in the basket.

4. Cook for 10 minutes, flip the short ribs, and then cook another 10 minutes.

5. Remove the short ribs from the air fryer basket, loosely cover with aluminum foil, and let them rest. The short ribs will continue to cook after they're removed from the basket. Check the internal temperature after 5 minutes to make sure it reached 145°F if you prefer a well-done meat. If it didn't reach 145°F and you would like it to be cooked longer, you can put it back into the air fryer basket at 330°F for another 3 minutes.

6. Remove from the basket and let it rest, covered with aluminum foil, for 5 minutes. Serve immediately.

# Vegetable Side Dishes Recipes

## Wilted Brussels Sprout Slaw

Servings: 4
Cooking Time: 18 Minutes

**Ingredients:**
- 2 Thick-cut bacon strip(s), halved widthwise (gluten-free, if a concern)
- 4½ cups (about 1 pound 2 ounces) Bagged shredded Brussels sprouts
- ¼ teaspoon Table salt
- 2 tablespoons White balsamic vinegar (see here)
- 2 teaspoons Worcestershire sauce (gluten-free, if a concern)
- 1 teaspoon Dijon mustard (gluten-free, if a concern)
- ¼ teaspoon Ground black pepper

**Directions:**
1. Preheat the air fryer to 375°F .
2. When the machine is at temperature, lay the bacon strip halves in the basket in one layer and air-fry for 10 minutes, or until crisp.
3. Use kitchen tongs to transfer the bacon pieces to a wire rack. Put the shredded Brussels sprouts in a large bowl. Drain any fat from the basket or the tray under the basket onto the Brussels sprouts. Add the salt and toss well to coat.
4. Put the Brussels sprout shreds in the basket, spreading them out into as close to an even layer as you can. Air-fry for 8 minutes, tossing the basket's contents at least three times, until wilted and lightly browned.
5. Pour the contents of the basket into a serving bowl. Chop the bacon and add it to the Brussels sprouts. Add the vinegar, Worcestershire sauce, mustard, and pepper. Toss well to blend the dressing and coat the Brussels sprout shreds. Serve warm.

## Roasted Belgian Endive With Pistachios And Lemon

Servings: 2
Cooking Time: 7 Minutes

**Ingredients:**
- 2 Medium 3-ounce Belgian endive head(s)
- 2 tablespoons Olive oil
- ½ teaspoon Table salt
- ¼ cup Finely chopped unsalted shelled pistachios
- Up to 2 teaspoons Lemon juice

**Directions:**
1. Preheat the air fryer to 325°F (or 330°F, if that's the closest setting).
2. Trim the Belgian endive head(s), removing the little bit of dried-out stem end but keeping the leaves intact. Quarter the head(s) through the stem (which will hold the leaves intact). Brush the endive quarters with oil, getting it down between the leaves. Sprinkle the quarters with salt.
3. When the machine is at temperature, set the endive quarters cut sides up in the basket with as much air space between them as possible. They should not touch. Air-fry undisturbed for 7 minutes, or until lightly browned along the edges.
4. Use kitchen tongs to transfer the endive quarters to serving plates or a platter. Sprinkle with the pistachios and lemon juice. Serve warm or at room temperature.

# Fried Corn On The Cob

Servings: 2
Cooking Time: 10 Minutes

**Ingredients:**
- 1½ tablespoons Regular or low-fat mayonnaise (not fat-free; gluten-free, if a concern)
- 1½ teaspoons Minced garlic
- ¼ teaspoon Table salt
- ¾ cup Plain panko bread crumbs (gluten-free, if a concern)
- 3 4-inch lengths husked and de-silked corn on the cob
- Vegetable oil spray

**Directions:**
1. Preheat the air fryer to 400°F.
2. Stir the mayonnaise, garlic, and salt in a small bowl until well combined. Spread the panko on a dinner plate.
3. Brush the mayonnaise mixture over the kernels of a piece of corn on the cob. Set the corn in the bread crumbs, then roll, pressing gently, to coat it. Lightly coat with vegetable oil spray. Set it aside, then coat the remaining piece(s) of corn in the same way.
4. Set the coated corn on the cob in the basket with as much air space between the pieces as possible. Air-fry undisturbed for 10 minutes, or until brown and crisp along the coating.
5. Use kitchen tongs to gently transfer the pieces of corn to a wire rack. Cool for 5 minutes before serving.

# Salt And Pepper Baked Potatoes

Servings: 4
Cooking Time: 40 Minutes

**Ingredients:**
- 1 to 2 tablespoons olive oil
- 4 medium russet potatoes (about 9 to 10 ounces each)
- salt and coarsely ground black pepper
- butter, sour cream, chopped fresh chives, scallions or bacon bits (optional)

**Directions:**
1. Preheat the air fryer to 400°F.
2. Rub the olive oil all over the potatoes and season them generously with salt and coarsely ground black pepper. Pierce all sides of the potatoes several times with the tines of a fork.
3. Air-fry for 40 minutes, turning the potatoes over halfway through the cooking time.
4. Serve the potatoes, split open with butter, sour cream, fresh chives, scallions or bacon bits.

# Fried Green Tomatoes With Sriracha Mayo

Servings: 4
Cooking Time: 12 Minutes

**Ingredients:**
- 3 green tomatoes
- salt and freshly ground black pepper
- ⅓ cup all-purpose flour*
- 2 eggs
- ½ cup buttermilk
- 1 cup panko breadcrumbs*
- 1 cup cornmeal
- olive oil, in a spray bottle
- fresh thyme sprigs or chopped fresh chives
- Sriracha Mayo
- ½ cup mayonnaise
- 1 to 2 tablespoons sriracha hot sauce
- 1 tablespoon milk

**Directions:**
1. Cut the tomatoes in ¼-inch slices. Pat them dry with a clean kitchen towel and season generously with salt and pepper.

2.  Set up a dredging station using three shallow dishes. Place the flour in the first shallow dish, whisk the eggs and buttermilk together in the second dish, and combine the panko breadcrumbs and cornmeal in the third dish.

3.  Preheat the air fryer to 400°F.

4.  Dredge the tomato slices in flour to coat on all sides. Then dip them into the egg mixture and finally press them into the breadcrumbs to coat all sides of the tomato.

5.  Spray or brush the air-fryer basket with olive oil. Transfer 3 to 4 tomato slices into the basket and spray the top with olive oil. Air-fry the tomatoes at 400°F for 8 minutes. Flip them over, spray the other side with oil and air-fry for an additional 4 minutes until golden brown.

6.  While the tomatoes are cooking, make the sriracha mayo. Combine the mayonnaise, 1 tablespoon of the sriracha hot sauce and milk in a small bowl. Stir well until the mixture is smooth. Add more sriracha sauce to taste.

7.  When the tomatoes are done, transfer them to a cooling rack or a platter lined with paper towels so the bottom does not get soggy. Before serving, carefully stack the all the tomatoes into air fryer and air-fry at 350°F for 1 to 2 minutes to heat them back up.

8.  Serve the fried green tomatoes hot with the sriracha mayo on the side. Season one last time with salt and freshly ground black pepper and garnish with sprigs of fresh thyme or chopped fresh chives.

# Tuna Platter

Servings: 4
Cooking Time: 9 Minutes

**Ingredients:**
- 4 new potatoes, boiled in their jackets
- ½ cup vinaigrette dressing, plus 2 tablespoons
- ½ pound fresh green beans, cut in half-inch pieces and steamed
- 1 tablespoon Herbes de Provence
- 1 tablespoon minced shallots
- 1½ tablespoons tarragon vinegar
- 4 tuna steaks, each ¾-inch thick, about 1 pound
- salt and pepper
- Salad
- 8 cups chopped romaine lettuce
- 12 grape tomatoes, halved lengthwise
- ½ cup pitted olives (black, green, nicoise, or combination)
- 2 boiled eggs, peeled and halved lengthwise

**Directions:**
1.  Quarter potatoes and toss with 1 tablespoon salad dressing.

2.  Toss the warm beans with the other tablespoon of salad dressing. Set both aside while you prepare the tuna.

3.  Mix together the herbs, shallots, and vinegar and rub into all sides of tuna. Season fish to taste with salt and pepper.

4.  Cook tuna at 390°F for 7minutes and check. If needed, cook 2 minutes longer, until tuna is barely pink in the center.

5.  Spread the lettuce over a large platter.

6.  Slice the tuna steaks in ½-inch pieces and arrange them in the center of the lettuce.

7.  Place the remaining ingredients around the tuna. Diners create their own plates by selecting what they want from the platter. Pass remainder of salad dressing at the table.

# Smashed Fried Baby Potatoes

Servings: 3
Cooking Time: 18 Minutes

**Ingredients:**
- 1½ pounds baby red or baby Yukon gold potatoes
- ¼ cup butter, melted
- 1 teaspoon olive oil
- ½ teaspoon paprika
- 1 teaspoon dried parsley
- salt and freshly ground black pepper
- 2 scallions, finely chopped

**Directions:**
1. Bring a large pot of salted water to a boil. Add the potatoes and boil for 18 minutes or until the potatoes are fork-tender.
2. Drain the potatoes and transfer them to a cutting board to cool slightly. Spray or brush the bottom of a drinking glass with a little oil. Smash or flatten the potatoes by pressing the glass down on each potato slowly. Try not to completely flatten the potato or smash it so hard that it breaks apart.
3. Combine the melted butter, olive oil, paprika, and parsley together.
4. Preheat the air fryer to 400°F.
5. Spray the bottom of the air fryer basket with oil and transfer one layer of the smashed potatoes into the basket. Brush with some of the butter mixture and season generously with salt and freshly ground black pepper.
6. Air-fry at 400°F for 10 minutes. Carefully flip the potatoes over and air-fry for an additional 8 minutes until crispy and lightly browned.
7. Keep the potatoes warm in a 170°F oven or tent with aluminum foil while you cook the second batch. Sprinkle minced scallions over the potatoes and serve warm.

# Butternut Medallions With Honey Butter And Sage

Servings: 2
Cooking Time: 15 Minutes

**Ingredients:**
- 1 butternut squash, peeled
- olive oil, in a spray bottle
- salt and freshly ground black pepper
- 2 tablespoons butter, softened
- 2 tablespoons honey
- pinch ground cinnamon
- pinch ground nutmeg
- chopped fresh sage

**Directions:**
1. Preheat the air fryer to 370°F.
2. Cut the neck of the butternut squash into disks about ½-inch thick. (Use the base of the butternut squash for another use.) Brush or spray the disks with oil and season with salt and freshly ground black pepper.
3. Transfer the butternut disks to the air fryer in one layer (or just ever so slightly overlapping). Air-fry at 370°F for 5 minutes.
4. While the butternut squash is cooking, combine the butter, honey, cinnamon and nutmeg in a small bowl. Brush this mixture on the butternut squash, flip the disks over and brush the other side as well. Continue to air-fry at 370°F for another 5 minutes. Flip the disks once more, brush with more of the honey butter and air-fry for another 5 minutes. The butternut should be browning nicely around the edges.
5. Remove the butternut squash from the air-fryer and repeat with additional batches if necessary. Transfer to a serving platter, sprinkle with the fresh sage and serve.

# Buttery Rolls

Servings: 6
Cooking Time: 14 Minutes

**Ingredients:**

- 6½ tablespoons Room-temperature whole or low-fat milk
- 3 tablespoons plus 1 teaspoon Butter, melted and cooled
- 3 tablespoons plus 1 teaspoon (or 1 medium egg, well beaten) Pasteurized egg substitute, such as Egg Beaters
- 1½ tablespoons Granulated white sugar
- 1¼ teaspoons Instant yeast
- ¼ teaspoon Table salt
- 2 cups, plus more for dusting All-purpose flour
- Vegetable oil
- Additional melted butter, for brushing

**Directions:**

1. Stir the milk, melted butter, pasteurized egg substitute (or whole egg), sugar, yeast, and salt in a medium bowl to combine. Stir in the flour just until the mixture makes a soft dough.
2. Lightly flour a clean, dry work surface. Turn the dough out onto the work surface. Knead the dough for 5 minutes to develop the gluten.
3. Lightly oil the inside of a clean medium bowl. Gather the dough into a compact ball and set it in the bowl. Turn the dough over so that its surface has oil on it all over. Cover the bowl tightly with plastic wrap and set aside in a warm, draft-free place until the dough has doubled in bulk, about 1½ hours.
4. Punch down the dough, then turn it out onto a clean, dry work surface. Divide it into 5 even balls for a small batch, 6 balls for a medium batch, or 8 balls for a large one.
5. For a small batch, lightly oil the inside of a 6-inch round cake pan and set the balls around its perimeter, separating them as much as possible.
6. For a medium batch, lightly oil the inside of a 7-inch round cake pan and set the balls in it with one ball at its center, separating them as much as possible.
7. For a large batch, lightly oil the inside of an 8-inch round cake pan and set the balls in it with one at the center, separating them as much as possible.
8. Cover with plastic wrap and set aside to rise for 30 minutes.
9. Preheat the air fryer to 350°F .
10. Uncover the pan and brush the rolls with a little melted butter, perhaps ½ teaspoon per roll. When the machine is at temperature, set the cake pan in the basket. Air-fry undisturbed for 14 minutes, or until the rolls have risen and browned.
11. Using kitchen tongs and a nonstick-safe spatula, two hot pads, or silicone baking mitts, transfer the cake pan from the basket to a wire rack. Cool the rolls in the pan for a minute or two. Turn the rolls out onto a wire rack, set them top side up again, and cool for at least another couple of minutes before serving warm.

# Brown Rice And Goat Cheese Croquettes

Servings: 3
Cooking Time: 8 Minutes

**Ingredients:**

- ¾ cup Water
- 6 tablespoons Raw medium-grain brown rice, such as brown Arborio
- ½ cup Shredded carrot
- ¼ cup Walnut pieces
- 3 tablespoons (about 1½ ounces) Soft goat cheese

- 1 tablespoon Pasteurized egg substitute, such as Egg Beaters (gluten-free, if a concern)
- ¼ teaspoon Dried thyme
- ¼ teaspoon Table salt
- ¼ teaspoon Ground black pepper
- Olive oil spray

**Directions:**

1. Combine the water, rice, and carrots in a small saucepan set over medium-high heat. Bring to a boil, stirring occasionally. Cover, reduce the heat to very low, and simmer very slowly for 45 minutes, or until the water has been absorbed and the rice is tender. Set aside, covered, for 10 minutes.

2. Scrape the contents of the saucepan into a food processor. Cool for 10 minutes.

3. Preheat the air fryer to 400°F.

4. Put the nuts, cheese, egg substitute, thyme, salt, and pepper into the food processor. Cover and pulse to a coarse paste, stopping the machine at least once to scrape down the inside of the canister.

5. Uncover the food processor; scrape down and remove the blade. Using wet, clean hands, form the mixture into two 4-inch-diameter patties for a small batch, three 4-inch-diameter patties for a medium batch, or four 4-inch-diameter patties for a large one. Generously coat both sides of the patties with olive oil spray.

6. Set the patties in the basket with as much air space between them as possible. Air-fry undisturbed for 8 minutes, or until brown and crisp.

7. Use a nonstick-safe spatula to transfer the croquettes to a wire rack. Cool for 5 minutes before serving.

# Okra

Servings: 4

Cooking Time: 12 Minutes

**Ingredients:**

- 7–8 ounces fresh okra
- 1 egg
- 1 cup milk
- 1 cup breadcrumbs
- ½ teaspoon salt
- oil for misting or cooking spray

**Directions:**

1. Remove stem ends from okra and cut in ½-inch slices.

2. In a medium bowl, beat together egg and milk. Add okra slices and stir to coat.

3. In a sealable plastic bag or container with lid, mix together the breadcrumbs and salt.

4. Remove okra from egg mixture, letting excess drip off, and transfer into bag with breadcrumbs.

5. Shake okra in crumbs to coat well.

6. Place all of the coated okra into the air fryer basket and mist with oil or cooking spray. Okra doesn't need to cook in a single layer, nor is it necessary to spray all sides at this point. A good spritz on top will do.

7. Cook at 390°F for 5minutes. Shake basket to redistribute and give it another spritz as you shake.

8. Cook 5 more minutes. Shake and spray again. Cook for 2 minutes longer or until golden brown and crispy.

# Corn On The Cob

Servings: 4

Cooking Time: 12 Minutes

**Ingredients:**

- 2 large ears fresh corn
- olive oil for misting
- salt (optional)

**Directions:**

1. Shuck corn, remove silks, and wash.

2. Cut or break each ear in half crosswise.

3. Spray corn with olive oil.

4. Cook at 390°F for 12 minutes or until browned as much as you like.

5. Serve plain or with coarsely ground salt.

# Cheesy Potato Pot

Servings: 4
Cooking Time: 13 Minutes

**Ingredients:**

- 3 cups cubed red potatoes (unpeeled, cut into ½-inch cubes)
- ½ teaspoon garlic powder
- salt and pepper
- 1 tablespoon oil
- chopped chives for garnish (optional)
- Sauce
- 2 tablespoons milk
- 1 tablespoon butter
- 2 ounces sharp Cheddar cheese, grated
- 1 tablespoon sour cream

**Directions:**

1. Place potato cubes in large bowl and sprinkle with garlic, salt, and pepper. Add oil and stir to coat well.

2. Cook at 390°F for 13 minutes or until potatoes are tender. Stir every 4 or 5minutes during cooking time.

3. While potatoes are cooking, combine milk and butter in a small saucepan. Warm over medium-low heat to melt butter. Add cheese and stir until it melts. The melted cheese will remain separated from the milk mixture. Remove from heat until potatoes are done.

4. When ready to serve, add sour cream to cheese mixture and stir over medium-low heat just until warmed. Place cooked potatoes in serving bowl. Pour sauce over potatoes and stir to combine.

5. Garnish with chives if desired.

# Perfect Asparagus

Servings: 3
Cooking Time: 10 Minutes

**Ingredients:**

- 1 pound Very thin asparagus spears
- 2 tablespoons Olive oil
- 1 teaspoon Coarse sea salt or kosher salt
- ¾ teaspoon Finely grated lemon zest

**Directions:**

1. Preheat the air fryer to 400°F.

2. Trim just enough off the bottom of the asparagus spears so they'll fit in the basket. Put the spears on a large plate and drizzle them with some of the olive oil. Turn them over and drizzle more olive oil, working to get all the spears coated.

3. When the machine is at temperature, place the spears in one direction in the basket. They may be touching. Air-fry for 10 minutes, tossing and rearranging the spears twice, until tender.

4. Dump the contents of the basket on a serving platter. Spread out the spears. Sprinkle them with the salt and lemon zest while still warm. Serve at once.

# Moroccan Cauliflower

Servings: 6
Cooking Time: 15 Minutes

**Ingredients:**

- 1 tablespoon curry powder
- 2 teaspoons smoky paprika
- ½ teaspoon ground cumin
- ½ teaspoon salt
- 1 head cauliflower, cut into bite-size pieces
- ¼ cup red wine vinegar
- 2 tablespoons extra-virgin olive oil
- 2 tablespoons chopped parsley

**Directions:**
1.   Preheat the air fryer to 370°F.
2.   In a large bowl, mix the curry powder, paprika, cumin, and salt. Add the cauliflower and stir to coat. Pour the red wine vinegar over the top and continue stirring.
3.   Place the cauliflower into the air fryer basket; drizzle olive oil over the top.
4.   Cook the cauliflower for 5 minutes, toss, and cook another 5 minutes. Raise the temperature to 400°F and continue cooking for 4 to 6 minutes, or until crispy.

# Polenta

Servings: 4
Cooking Time: 15 Minutes

**Ingredients:**
*   1 pound polenta
*   ¼ cup flour
*   oil for misting or cooking spray

**Directions:**
1.   Cut polenta into ½-inch slices.
2.   Dip slices in flour to coat well. Spray both sides with oil or cooking spray.
3.   Cook at 390°F for 5minutes. Turn polenta and spray both sides again with oil.
4.   Cook 10 more minutes or until brown and crispy.

# Tomato Candy

Servings: 12
Cooking Time: 120 Minutes

**Ingredients:**
*   6 Small Roma or plum tomatoes, halved lengthwise
*   1½ teaspoons Coarse sea salt or kosher salt

**Directions:**

1.   Before you turn the machine on, set the tomatoes cut side up in a single layer in the basket (or the basket attachment). They can touch each other, but try to leave at least a fraction of an inch between them (depending, of course, on the size of the basket or basket attachment). Sprinkle the cut sides of the tomatoes with the salt.
2.   Set the machine to cook at 225°F (or 230°F, if that's the closest setting). Put the basket in the machine and air-fry for 2 hours, or until the tomatoes are dry but pliable, with a little moisture down in their centers.
3.   Remove the basket from the machine and cool the tomatoes in it for 10 minutes before gently transferring them to a plate for serving, or to a shallow dish that you can cover and store in the refrigerator for up to 1 week.

# Onions

Servings: 4
Cooking Time: 18 Minutes

**Ingredients:**
*   2 yellow onions (Vidalia or 1015 recommended)
*   salt and pepper
*   ¼ teaspoon ground thyme
*   ¼ teaspoon smoked paprika
*   2 teaspoons olive oil
*   1 ounce Gruyère cheese, grated

**Directions:**
1.   Peel onions and halve lengthwise (vertically).
2.   Sprinkle cut sides of onions with salt, pepper, thyme, and paprika.
3.   Place each onion half, cut-surface up, on a large square of aluminum foil. Pull sides of foil up to cup around onion. Drizzle cut surface of onions with oil.
4.   Crimp foil at top to seal closed.

5. Place wrapped onions in air fryer basket and cook at 390°F for 18 minutes. When done, onions should be soft enough to pierce with fork but still slightly firm.

6. Open foil just enough to sprinkle each onion with grated cheese.

7. Cook for 30 seconds to 1 minute to melt cheese.

## Charred Radicchio Salad

Servings: 4
Cooking Time: 5 Minutes

**Ingredients:**
- 2 Small 5- to 6-ounce radicchio head(s)
- 3 tablespoons Olive oil
- ½ teaspoon Table salt
- 2 tablespoons Balsamic vinegar
- Up to ¼ teaspoon Red pepper flakes

**Directions:**
1. Preheat the air fryer to 375°F .

2. Cut the radicchio head(s) into quarters through the stem end. Brush the oil over the heads, particularly getting it between the leaves along the cut sides. Sprinkle the radicchio quarters with the salt.

3. When the machine is at temperature, set the quarters cut sides up in the basket with as much air space between them as possible. They should not touch. Air-fry undisturbed for 5 minutes, watching carefully because they burn quickly, until blackened in bits and soft.

4. Use a nonstick-safe spatula to transfer the quarters to a cutting board. Cool for a minute or two, then cut out the thick stems inside the heads. Discard these tough bits and chop the remaining heads into bite-size bits. Scrape them into a bowl. Add the vinegar and red pepper flakes. Toss well and serve warm.

## Roasted Peppers With Balsamic Vinegar And Basil

Servings: 6
Cooking Time: 12 Minutes

**Ingredients:**
- 4 Small or medium red or yellow bell peppers
- 3 tablespoons Olive oil
- 1 tablespoon Balsamic vinegar
- Up to 6 Fresh basil leaves, torn up

**Directions:**
1. Preheat the air fryer to 400°F.

2. When the machine is at temperature, put the peppers in the basket with at least ¼ inch between them. Air-fry undisturbed for 12 minutes, until blistered, even blackened in places.

3. Use kitchen tongs to transfer the peppers to a medium bowl. Cover the bowl with plastic wrap. Set aside at room temperature for 30 minutes.

4. Uncover the bowl and use kitchen tongs to transfer the peppers to a cutting board or work surface. Peel off the filmy exterior skin. If there are blackened bits under it, these can stay on the peppers. Cut off and remove the stem ends. Split open the peppers and discard any seeds and their spongy membranes. Slice the peppers into ½-inch- to 1-inch-wide strips.

5. Put these in a clean bowl and gently toss them with the oil, vinegar, and basil. Serve at once. Or cover and store at room temperature for up to 4 hours or in the refrigerator for up to 5 days.

## Roasted Cauliflower With Garlic And Capers

Servings: 3
Cooking Time: 10 Minutes

**Ingredients:**

- 3 cups (about 15 ounces) 1-inch cauliflower florets
- 2 tablespoons Olive oil
- 1½ tablespoons Drained and rinsed capers, chopped
- 2 teaspoons Minced garlic
- ¼ teaspoon Table salt
- Up to ¼ teaspoon Red pepper flakes

**Directions:**

1. Preheat the air fryer to 375°F .
2. Stir the cauliflower florets, olive oil, capers, garlic, salt, and red pepper flakes in a large bowl until the florets are evenly coated.
3. When the machine is at temperature, put the florets in the basket, spreading them out to as close to one layer as you can. Air-fry for 10 minutes, tossing once to get any covered pieces exposed to the air currents, until tender and lightly browned.
4. Dump the contents of the basket into a serving bowl or onto a serving platter. Cool for a minute or two before serving.

# Roasted Garlic And Thyme Tomatocs

Servings: 2
Cooking Time: 15 Minutes

**Ingredients:**

- 4 Roma tomatoes
- 1 tablespoon olive oil
- salt and freshly ground black pepper
- 1 clove garlic, minced
- ½ teaspoon dried thyme

**Directions:**

1. Preheat the air fryer to 390°F.
2. Cut the tomatoes in half and scoop out the seeds and any pithy parts with your fingers. Place the tomatoes in a bowl and toss with the olive oil, salt, pepper, garlic and thyme.
3. Transfer the tomatoes to the air fryer, cut side up. Air-fry for 15 minutes. The edges should just start to brown. Let the tomatoes cool to an edible temperature for a few minutes and then use in pastas, on top of crostini, or as an accompaniment to any poultry, meat or fish.

# Sesame Carrots And Sugar Snap Peas

Servings: 4
Cooking Time: 16 Minutes

**Ingredients:**

- 1 pound carrots, peeled sliced on the bias (½-inch slices)
- 1 teaspoon olive oil
- salt and freshly ground black pepper
- ⅓ cup honey
- 1 tablespoon sesame oil
- 1 tablespoon soy sauce
- ½ teaspoon minced fresh ginger
- 4 ounces sugar snap peas (about 1 cup)
- 1½ teaspoons sesame seeds

**Directions:**

1. Preheat the air fryer to 360°F.
2. Toss the carrots with the olive oil, season with salt and pepper and air-fry for 10 minutes, shaking the basket once or twice during the cooking process.
3. Combine the honey, sesame oil, soy sauce and minced ginger in a large bowl. Add the sugar snap peas and the air-fried carrots to the honey mixture, toss to coat and return everything to the air fryer basket.
4. Turn up the temperature to 400°F and air-fry for an additional 6 minutes, shaking the basket once during the cooking process.

5. Transfer the carrots and sugar snap peas to a serving bowl. Pour the sauce from the bottom of the cooker over the vegetables and sprinkle sesame seeds over top. Serve immediately.

# Cheesy Texas Toast

Servings: 2
Cooking Time: 4 Minutes

**Ingredients:**
• 2 1-inch-thick slice(s) Italian bread (each about 4 inches across)
• 4 teaspoons Softened butter
• 2 teaspoons Minced garlic
• ¼ cup (about ¾ ounce) Finely grated Parmesan cheese

**Directions:**
1. Preheat the air fryer to 400°F.
2. Spread one side of a slice of bread with 2 teaspoons butter. Sprinkle with 1 teaspoon minced garlic, followed by 2 tablespoons grated cheese. Repeat this process if you're making one or more additional toasts.
3. When the machine is at temperature, put the bread slice(s) cheese side up in the basket (with as much air space between them as possible if you're making more than one). Air-fry undisturbed for 4 minutes, or until browned and crunchy.
4. Use a nonstick-safe spatula to transfer the toasts cheese side up to a wire rack. Cool for 5 minutes before serving.

# Cheesy Potato Skins

Servings: 6
Cooking Time: 54 Minutes

**Ingredients:**
• 3 6- to 8-ounce small russet potatoes
• 3 Thick-cut bacon strips, halved widthwise (gluten-free, if a concern)
• ¾ teaspoon Mild paprika
• ¼ teaspoon Garlic powder
• ¼ teaspoon Table salt
• ¼ teaspoon Ground black pepper
• ½ cup plus 1 tablespoon (a little over 2 ounces) Shredded Cheddar cheese
• 3 tablespoons Thinly sliced trimmed chives
• 6 tablespoons (a little over 1 ounce) Finely grated Parmesan cheese

**Directions:**
1. Preheat the air fryer to 375°F .
2. Prick each potato in four places with a fork (not four places in a line but four places all around the potato). Set the potatoes in the basket with as much air space between them as possible. Air-fry undisturbed for 45 minutes, or until the potatoes are tender when pricked with a fork.
3. Use kitchen tongs to gently transfer the potatoes to a wire rack. Cool for 15 minutes. Maintain the machine's temperature.
4. Lay the bacon strip halves in the basket in one layer. They may touch but should not overlap. Air-fry undisturbed for 5 minutes, until crisp. Use those same tongs to transfer the bacon pieces to the wire rack. If there's a great deal of rendered bacon fat in the basket's bottom or on a tray under the basket attachment, pour this into a bowl, cool, and discard. Don't throw it down the drain!
5. Cut the potatoes in half lengthwise (not just slit them open but actually cut in half). Use a flatware spoon to scoop the hot, soft middles into a bowl, leaving ½ inch of potato all around the inside of the spud next to the skin. Sprinkle the inside of the potato "shells" evenly with paprika, garlic powder, salt, and pepper.
6. Chop the bacon pieces into small bits. Sprinkle these along with the Cheddar and chives evenly inside the potato shells. Crumble 2 to 3 tablespoons of the soft potato insides over the

filling mixture. Divide the grated Parmesan evenly over the tops of the potatoes.

7. Set the stuffed potatoes in the basket with as much air space between them as possible. Air-fry undisturbed for 4 minutes, until the cheese melts and lightly browns.

8. Use kitchen tongs to gently transfer the stuffed potato halves to a wire rack. Cool for 5 minutes before serving.

# Chicken Eggrolls

Servings: 10
Cooking Time: 17 Minutes

**Ingredients:**
- 1 tablespoon vegetable oil
- ¼ cup chopped onion
- 1 clove garlic, minced
- 1 cup shredded carrot
- ½ cup thinly sliced celery
- 2 cups cooked chicken
- 2 cups shredded white cabbage
- ½ cup teriyaki sauce
- 20 egg roll wrappers
- 1 egg, whisked
- 1 tablespoon water

**Directions:**
1. Preheat the air fryer to 390°F.
2. In a large skillet, heat the oil over medium-high heat. Add in the onion and sauté for 1 minute. Add in the garlic and sauté for 30 seconds. Add in the carrot and celery and cook for 2 minutes. Add in the chicken, cabbage, and teriyaki sauce. Allow the mixture to cook for 1 minute, stirring to combine. Remove from the heat.
3. In a small bowl, whisk together the egg and water for brushing the edges.
4. Lay the eggroll wrappers out at an angle. Place ¼ cup filling in the center. Fold the bottom corner up first and then fold in the corners; roll up to complete eggroll.
5. Place the eggrolls in the air fryer basket, spray with cooking spray, and cook for 8 minutes, turn over, and cook another 2 to 4 minutes.

# Summer Vegetables With Balsamic Drizzle, Goat Cheese And Basil

Servings: 2
Cooking Time: 17 Minutes

**Ingredients:**
- 1 cup balsamic vinegar
- 1 zucchini, sliced
- 1 yellow squash, sliced
- 2 tablespoons olive oil
- 1 clove garlic, minced
- ½ teaspoon Italian seasoning
- salt and freshly ground black pepper
- ½ cup cherry tomatoes, halved
- 2 ounces crumbled goat cheese
- 2 tablespoons chopped fresh basil, plus more leaves for garnish

**Directions:**
1. Place the balsamic vinegar in a small saucepot on the stovetop. Bring the vinegar to a boil, lower the heat and simmer uncovered for 20 minutes, until the mixture reduces and thickens. Set aside to cool.
2. Preheat the air fryer to 390°F.
3. Combine the zucchini and yellow squash in a large bowl. Add the olive oil, minced garlic, Italian seasoning, salt and pepper and toss to coat.
4. Air-fry the vegetables at 390°F for 10 minutes, shaking the basket several times during the cooking process. Add the cherry tomatoes and continue to air-fry for another 5 minutes.

Sprinkle the goat cheese over the vegetables and air-fry for 2 more minutes.

5. Transfer the vegetables to a serving dish, drizzle with the balsamic reduction and season with freshly ground black pepper. Garnish with the fresh basil leaves.

# Roasted Heirloom Carrots With Orange And Thyme

Servings: 2
Cooking Time: 12 Minutes

**Ingredients:**
- 10 to 12 heirloom or rainbow carrots (about 1 pound), scrubbed but not peeled
- 1 teaspoon olive oil
- salt and freshly ground black pepper
- 1 tablespoon butter
- 1 teaspoon fresh orange zest
- 1 teaspoon chopped fresh thyme

**Directions:**
1. Preheat the air fryer to 400°F.
2. Scrub the carrots and halve them lengthwise. Toss them in the olive oil, season with salt and freshly ground black pepper and transfer to the air fryer.
3. Air-fry at 400°F for 12 minutes, shaking the basket every once in a while to rotate the carrots as they cook.
4. As soon as the carrots have finished cooking, add the butter, orange zest and thyme and toss all the ingredients together in the air fryer basket to melt the butter and coat evenly. Serve warm.

# Five-spice Roasted Sweet Potatoes

Servings: 4
Cooking Time: 12 Minutes

**Ingredients:**
- ½ teaspoon ground cinnamon
- ¼ teaspoon ground cumin
- ¼ teaspoon paprika
- 1 teaspoon chile powder
- ⅛ teaspoon turmeric
- ½ teaspoon salt (optional)
- freshly ground black pepper
- 2 large sweet potatoes, peeled and cut into ¾-inch cubes (about 3 cups)
- 1 tablespoon olive oil

**Directions:**
1. In a large bowl, mix together cinnamon, cumin, paprika, chile powder, turmeric, salt, and pepper to taste.
2. Add potatoes and stir well.
3. Drizzle the seasoned potatoes with the olive oil and stir until evenly coated.
4. Place seasoned potatoes in the air fryer baking pan or an ovenproof dish that fits inside your air fryer basket.
5. Cook for 6minutes at 390°F, stop, and stir well.
6. Cook for an additional 6minutes.

# Salmon Salad With Steamboat Dressing

Servings: 4
Cooking Time: 18 Minutes

**Ingredients:**
- ¼ teaspoon salt
- 1½ teaspoons dried dill weed
- 1 tablespoon fresh lemon juice
- 8 ounces fresh or frozen salmon fillet (skin on)
- 8 cups shredded romaine, Boston, or other leaf lettuce
- 8 spears cooked asparagus, cut in 1-inch pieces
- 8 cherry tomatoes, halved or quartered

**Directions:**

1. Mix the salt and dill weed together. Rub the lemon juice over the salmon on both sides and sprinkle the dill and salt all over. Refrigerate for 15 to 20minutes.

2. Make Steamboat Dressing and refrigerate while cooking salmon and preparing salad.

3. Cook salmon in air fryer basket at 330°F for 18 minutes. Cooking time will vary depending on thickness of fillets. When done, salmon should flake with fork but still be moist and tender.

4. Remove salmon from air fryer and cool slightly. At this point, the skin should slide off easily. Cut salmon into 4 pieces and discard skin.

5. Divide the lettuce among 4 plates. Scatter asparagus spears and tomato pieces evenly over the lettuce, allowing roughly 2 whole spears and 2 whole cherry tomatoes per plate.

6. Top each salad with one portion of the salmon and drizzle with a tablespoon of dressing. Serve with additional dressing to pass at the table.

# Panzanella Salad With Crispy Croutons

Servings: 4

Cooking Time: 3 Minutes

**Ingredients:**

- ½ French baguette, sliced in half lengthwise
- 2 large cloves garlic
- 2 large ripe tomatoes, divided
- 2 small Persian cucumbers, quartered and diced
- ¼ cup Kalamata olives
- 1 tablespoon chopped, fresh oregano or 1 teaspoon dried oregano
- ¼ cup chopped fresh basil
- ¼ cup chopped fresh parsley
- ½ cup sliced red onion
- 2 tablespoons red wine vinegar
- ¼ cup extra-virgin olive oil
- Salt and pepper, to taste

**Directions:**

1. Preheat the air fryer to 380°F.

2. Place the baguette into the air fryer and toast for 3 to 5 minutes or until lightly golden brown.

3. Remove the bread from air fryer and immediately rub 1 raw garlic clove firmly onto the inside portion of each piece of bread, scraping the garlic onto the bread.

4. Slice 1 of the tomatoes in half and rub the cut edge of one half of the tomato onto the toasted bread. Season the rubbed bread with sea salt to taste.

5. Cut the bread into cubes and place in a large bowl. Cube the remaining 1½ tomatoes and add to the bowl. Add the cucumbers, olives, oregano, basil, parsley, and onion; stir to mix. Drizzle the red wine vinegar into the bowl, and stir. Drizzle the olive oil over the top, stir, and adjust the seasonings with salt and pepper.

6. Serve immediately or allow to sit at room temperature up to 1 hour before serving.

# Steakhouse Baked Potatoes

Servings: 3

Cooking Time: 55 Minutes

**Ingredients:**

- 3 10-ounce russet potatoes
- 2 tablespoons Olive oil
- 1 teaspoon Table salt

**Directions:**

1. Preheat the air fryer to 375°F .

2. Poke holes all over each potato with a fork. Rub the skin of each potato with 2 teaspoons of the olive oil, then sprinkle ¼ teaspoon salt all over each potato.

3. When the machine is at temperature, set the potatoes in the basket in one layer with as much

air space between them as possible. Air-fry for 50 minutes, turning once, or until soft to the touch but with crunchy skins. If the machine is at 360°F, you may need to add up to 5 minutes to the cooking time.

4.  Use kitchen tongs to gently transfer the baked potatoes to a wire rack. Cool for 5 or 10 minutes before serving.

# Acorn Squash Halves With Maple Butter Glaze

Servings: 2
Cooking Time: 33 Minutes

**Ingredients:**
* 1 medium (1 to 1¼ pounds) Acorn squash
* Vegetable oil spray
* ¼ teaspoon Table salt
* 1½ tablespoons Butter, melted
* 1½ tablespoons Maple syrup

**Directions:**
1.  Preheat the air fryer to 325°F (or 330°F, if that's the closest setting).
2.  Cut a squash in half through the stem end. Use a flatware spoon (preferably, a serrated grapefruit spoon) to scrape out and discard the seeds and membranes in each half. Use a paring knife to make a crisscross pattern of cuts about ½ inch apart and ¼ inch deep across the "meat" of the squash. If working with a second squash, repeat this step for that one.
3.  Generously coat the cut side of the squash halves with vegetable oil spray. Sprinkle the halves with the salt. Set them in the basket cut side up with at least ¼ inch between them. Air-fry undisturbed for 30 minutes.
4.  Increase the machine's temperature to 400°F. Mix the melted butter and syrup in a small bowl until uniform. Brush this mixture over the cut sides of the squash(es), letting it pool in the center. Air-fry undisturbed for 3 minutes, or until the glaze is bubbling.
5.  Use a nonstick-safe spatula and kitchen tongs to transfer the squash halves cut side up to a wire rack. Cool for 5 to 10 minutes before serving.

# Steak Fries

Servings: 4
Cooking Time: 20 Minutes

**Ingredients:**
* 2 russet potatoes, scrubbed and cut into wedges lengthwise
* 1 tablespoon olive oil
* 2 teaspoons seasoning salt (recipe below)

**Directions:**
1.  Preheat the air fryer to 400°F.
2.  Toss the potatoes with the olive oil and the seasoning salt.
3.  Air-fry for 20 minutes (depending on the size of the wedges), turning the potatoes over gently a few times throughout the cooking process to brown and cook them evenly.

# Broccoli Tots

Servings: 24
Cooking Time: 10 Minutes

**Ingredients:**
- 2 cups broccoli florets (about ½ pound broccoli crowns)
- 1 egg, beaten
- ⅛ teaspoon onion powder
- ¼ teaspoon salt
- ⅛ teaspoon pepper
- 2 tablespoons grated Parmesan cheese
- ¼ cup panko breadcrumbs
- oil for misting

**Directions:**
1. Steam broccoli for 2minutes. Rinse in cold water, drain well, and chop finely.
2. In a large bowl, mix broccoli with all other ingredients except the oil.
3. Scoop out small portions of mixture and shape into 24 tots. Lay them on a cookie sheet or wax paper as you work.
4. Spray tots with oil and place in air fryer basket in single layer.
5. Cook at 390°F for 5minutes. Shake basket and spray with oil again. Cook 5minutes longer or until browned and crispy.

# Bread And Breakfast

## Bacon Puff Pastry Pinwheels

Servings: 8
Cooking Time: 10 Minutes

**Ingredients:**
- 1 sheet of puff pastry
- 2 tablespoons maple syrup
- ¼ cup brown sugar
- 8 slices bacon (not thick cut)
- coarsely cracked black pepper
- vegetable oil

**Directions:**
1. On a lightly floured surface, roll the puff pastry out into a square that measures roughly 10 inches wide by however long your bacon strips are (usually about 11 inches). Cut the pastry into eight even strips.
2. Brush the strips of pastry with the maple syrup and sprinkle the brown sugar on top, leaving 1 inch of dough exposed at the far end of each strip. Place a slice of bacon on each strip of puff pastry, letting 1/8-inch of the length of bacon hang over the edge of the pastry. Season generously with coarsely ground black pepper.
3. With the exposed end of the pastry strips away from you, roll the bacon and pastry strips up into pinwheels. Dab a little water on the exposed end of the pastry and pinch it to the pinwheel to seal the pastry shut.
4. Preheat the air fryer to 360°F.
5. Brush or spray the air fryer basket with a little vegetable oil. Place the pinwheels into the basket and air-fry at 360°F for 8 minutes. Turn the pinwheels over and air-fry for another 2 minutes to brown the bottom. Serve warm.

## Southwest Cornbread

Servings: 6
Cooking Time: 18 Minutes

**Ingredients:**
- cooking spray
- ½ cup yellow cornmeal
- ½ cup flour
- 2 teaspoons baking powder
- ½ teaspoon salt
- ½ cup frozen corn kernels, thawed and drained
- ¼ cup finely chopped onion
- 1 or 2 small jalapeño peppers, seeded and chopped
- 1 egg
- ½ cup milk
- 2 tablespoons melted butter
- 2 ounces sharp Cheddar cheese, grated

**Directions:**
1. Preheat air fryer to 360°F.
2. Spray air fryer baking pan with nonstick cooking spray.
3. In a medium bowl, stir together the cornmeal, flour, baking powder, and salt.
4. Stir in the corn, onion, and peppers.
5. In a small bowl, beat together the egg, milk, and butter. Stir into dry ingredients until well combined.
6. Spoon half the batter into prepared baking pan, spreading to edges. Top with grated cheese. Spoon remaining batter on top of cheese and gently spread to edges of pan so it completely covers the cheese.
7. Cook at 360°F for 18 minutes, until cornbread is done and top is crispy brown.

# Cinnamon Rolls With Cream Cheese Glaze

Servings: 8
Cooking Time: 9 Minutes

**Ingredients:**

- 1 pound frozen bread dough, thawed
- ¼ cup butter, melted and cooled
- ¾ cup brown sugar
- 1½ tablespoons ground cinnamon
- Cream Cheese Glaze:
- 4 ounces cream cheese, softened
- 2 tablespoons butter, softened
- 1¼ cups powdered sugar
- ½ teaspoon vanilla

**Directions:**

1. Let the bread dough come to room temperature on the counter. On a lightly floured surface roll the dough into a 13-inch by 11-inch rectangle. Position the rectangle so the 13-inch side is facing you. Brush the melted butter all over the dough, leaving a 1-inch border uncovered along the edge farthest away from you.

2. Combine the brown sugar and cinnamon in a small bowl. Sprinkle the mixture evenly over the buttered dough, keeping the 1-inch border uncovered. Roll the dough into a log starting with the edge closest to you. Roll the dough tightly, making sure to roll evenly and push out any air pockets. When you get to the uncovered edge of the dough, press the dough onto the roll to seal it together.

3. Cut the log into 8 pieces slicing slowly with a sawing motion so you don't flatten the dough. Turn the slices on their sides and cover with a clean kitchen towel. Let the rolls sit in the warmest part of your kitchen for 1½ to 2 hours to rise.

4. To make the glaze, place the cream cheese and butter in a microwave-safe bowl. Soften the mixture in the microwave for 30 seconds at a time until it is easy to stir. Gradually add the powdered sugar and stir to combine. Add the vanilla extract and whisk until smooth. Set aside.

5. When the rolls have risen, Preheat the air fryer to 350°F.

6. Transfer 4 of the rolls to the air fryer basket. Air-fry for 5 minutes. Turn the rolls over and air-fry for another 4 minutes. Repeat with the remaining 4 rolls.

7. Let the rolls cool for a couple of minutes before glazing. Spread large dollops of cream cheese glaze on top of the warm cinnamon rolls, allowing some of the glaze to drip down the side of the rolls. Serve warm and enjoy!

# Pumpkin Loaf

Servings: 6
Cooking Time: 22 Minutes

**Ingredients:**

- cooking spray
- 1 large egg
- ½ cup granulated sugar
- ⅓ cup oil
- ½ cup canned pumpkin (not pie filling)
- ½ teaspoon vanilla
- ⅔ cup flour plus 1 tablespoon
- ½ teaspoon baking powder
- ½ teaspoon baking soda
- ½ teaspoon salt
- 1 teaspoon pumpkin pie spice
- ¼ teaspoon cinnamon

**Directions:**

1. Spray 6 x 6-inch baking dish lightly with cooking spray.

2. Place baking dish in air fryer basket and preheat air fryer to 330°F.

3.  In a large bowl, beat eggs and sugar together with a hand mixer.

4.  Add oil, pumpkin, and vanilla and mix well.

5.  Sift together all dry ingredients. Add to pumpkin mixture and beat well, about 1 minute.

6.  Pour batter in baking dish and cook at 330°F for 22 minutes or until toothpick inserted in center of loaf comes out clean.

## Oat Bran Muffins

Servings: 8
Cooking Time: 12 Minutes

**Ingredients:**
- ⅔ cup oat bran
- ½ cup flour
- ¼ cup brown sugar
- 1 teaspoon baking powder
- ½ teaspoon baking soda
- ⅛ teaspoon salt
- ½ cup buttermilk
- 1 egg
- 2 tablespoons canola oil
- ½ cup chopped dates, raisins, or dried cranberries
- 24 paper muffin cups
- cooking spray

**Directions:**
1.  Preheat air fryer to 330°F.

2.  In a large bowl, combine the oat bran, flour, brown sugar, baking powder, baking soda, and salt.

3.  In a small bowl, beat together the buttermilk, egg, and oil.

4.  Pour buttermilk mixture into bowl with dry ingredients and stir just until moistened. Do not beat.

5.  Gently stir in dried fruit.

6.  Use triple baking cups to help muffins hold shape during baking. Spray them with cooking spray, place 4 sets of cups in air fryer basket at a time, and fill each one ¾ full of batter.

7.  Cook for 12minutes, until top springs back when lightly touched and toothpick inserted in center comes out clean.

8.  Repeat for remaining muffins.

## Bacon, Broccoli And Swiss Cheese Bread Pudding

Servings: 2
Cooking Time: 48 Minutes

**Ingredients:**
- ½ pound thick cut bacon, cut into ¼-inch pieces
- 3 cups brioche bread or rolls, cut into ½-inch cubes
- 3 eggs
- 1 cup milk
- ½ teaspoon salt
- freshly ground black pepper
- 1 cup frozen broccoli florets, thawed and chopped
- 1½ cups grated Swiss cheese

**Directions:**
1.  Preheat the air fryer to 400°F.

2.  Air-fry the bacon for 6 minutes until crispy, shaking the basket a few times while it cooks to help it cook evenly. Remove the bacon and set it aside on a paper towel.

3.  Air-fry the brioche bread cubes for 2 minutes to dry and toast lightly. (If your brioche is a few days old and slightly stale, you can omit this step.)

4.  Butter a 6- or 7-inch cake pan. Combine all the ingredients in a large bowl and toss well. Transfer the mixture to the buttered cake pan, cover with aluminum foil and refrigerate the bread pudding overnight, or for at least 8 hours.

5. Remove the casserole from the refrigerator an hour before you plan to cook, and let it sit on the countertop to come to room temperature.

6. Preheat the air fryer to 330°F. Transfer the covered cake pan, to the basket of the air fryer, lowering the dish into the basket using a sling made of aluminum foil (fold a piece of aluminum foil into a strip about 2-inches wide by 24-inches long). Fold the ends of the aluminum foil over the top of the dish before returning the basket to the air fryer. Air-fry for 20 minutes. Remove the foil and air-fry for an additional 20 minutes. If the top starts to brown a little too much before the custard has set, simply return the foil to the pan. The bread pudding has cooked through when a skewer inserted into the center comes out clean.

# Mediterranean Egg Sandwich

Servings: 1
Cooking Time: 8 Minutes

**Ingredients:**
- 1 large egg
- 5 baby spinach leaves, chopped
- 1 tablespoon roasted bell pepper, chopped
- 1 English muffin
- 1 thin slice prosciutto or Canadian bacon

**Directions:**
1. Spray a ramekin with cooking spray or brush the inside with extra-virgin olive oil.
2. In a small bowl, whisk together the egg, baby spinach, and bell pepper.
3. Split the English muffin in half and spray the inside lightly with cooking spray or brush with extra-virgin olive oil.
4. Preheat the air fryer to 350°F for 2 minutes. Place the egg ramekin and open English muffin into the air fryer basket, and cook at 350°F for 5 minutes. Open the air fryer drawer and add the

prosciutto or bacon; cook for an additional 1 minute.

5. To assemble the sandwich, place the egg on one half of the English muffin, top with prosciutto or bacon, and place the remaining piece of English muffin on top.

# Sweet And Spicy Pumpkin Scones

Servings: 8
Cooking Time: 8 Minutes

**Ingredients:**
- 2 cups all-purpose flour
- 3 tablespoons packed brown sugar
- ½ teaspoon baking powder
- ¼ teaspoon baking soda
- ½ teaspoon kosher salt
- ½ teaspoon ground cinnamon
- ¼ teaspoon ground ginger
- ¼ teaspoon ground cardamom
- 4 tablespoons cold unsalted butter
- ½ cup plus 2 tablespoons pumpkin puree, divided
- 4 tablespoons milk, divided
- 1 large egg
- 1 cup powdered sugar

**Directions:**
1. In a large bowl, mix together the flour, brown sugar, baking powder, baking soda, salt, cinnamon, ginger, and cardamom. Using a pastry blender or two knives, cut in the butter until coarse crumbles appear.
2. In a small bowl, whisk together ½ cup of the pumpkin puree, 2 tablespoons of the milk, and the egg until combined. Pour the wet ingredients into the dry ingredients; stir to combine.
3. Form the dough into a ball and place onto a floured service. Press the dough out or use a rolling pin to roll out the dough until ½ inch thick and in a circle. Cut the dough into 8 wedges.

4. Bake at 360°F for 8 to 10 minutes or until completely cooked through. Cook in batches as needed.

5. In a medium bowl, whisk together the powdered sugar, the remaining 2 tablespoons of pumpkin puree, and the remaining 2 tablespoons of milk. When the pumpkin scones have cooled, drizzle the pumpkin glaze over the top before serving.

# Banana Bread

Servings: 6
Cooking Time: 20 Minutes

**Ingredients:**
- cooking spray
- 1 cup white wheat flour
- ½ teaspoon baking powder
- ¼ teaspoon salt
- ¼ teaspoon baking soda
- 1 egg
- ½ cup mashed ripe banana
- ¼ cup plain yogurt
- ¼ cup pure maple syrup
- 2 tablespoons coconut oil
- ½ teaspoon pure vanilla extract

**Directions:**
1. Preheat air fryer to 330°F.
2. Lightly spray 6 x 6-inch baking dish with cooking spray.
3. In a medium bowl, mix together the flour, baking powder, salt, and soda.
4. In a separate bowl, beat the egg and add the mashed banana, yogurt, syrup, oil, and vanilla. Mix until well combined.
5. Pour liquid mixture into dry ingredients and stir gently to blend. Do not beat. Batter may be slightly lumpy.

6. Pour batter into baking dish and cook at 330°F for 20 minutes or until toothpick inserted in center of loaf comes out clean.

# Country Gravy

Servings: 2
Cooking Time: 7 Minutes

**Ingredients:**
- ¼ pound pork sausage, casings removed
- 1 tablespoon butter
- 2 tablespoons flour
- 2 cups whole milk
- ½ teaspoon salt
- freshly ground black pepper
- 1 teaspoon fresh thyme leaves

**Directions:**
1. Preheat a saucepan over medium heat. Add and brown the sausage, crumbling it into small pieces as it cooks. Add the butter and flour, stirring well to combine. Continue to cook for 2 minutes, stirring constantly.
2. Slowly pour in the milk, whisking as you do, and bring the mixture to a boil to thicken. Season with salt and freshly ground black pepper, lower the heat and simmer until the sauce has thickened to your desired consistency – about 5 minutes. Stir in the fresh thyme, season to taste and serve hot.

# Breakfast Pot Pies

Servings: 4
Cooking Time: 20 Minutes

**Ingredients:**
- 1 refrigerated pie crust
- ½ pound pork breakfast sausage
- ¼ cup diced onion
- 1 garlic clove, minced
- ½ teaspoon ground black pepper

- ¼ teaspoon salt
- 1 cup chopped bell peppers
- 1 cup roasted potatoes
- 2 cups milk
- 2 to 3 tablespoons all-purpose flour

**Directions:**

1. Flatten the store-bought pie crust out on an even surface. Cut 4 equal circles that are slightly larger than the circumference of ramekins (by about ¼ inch). Set aside.

2. In a medium pot, sauté the breakfast sausage with the onion, garlic, black pepper, and salt. When browned, add in the bell peppers and potatoes and cook an additional 3 to 4 minutes to soften the bell peppers. Remove from the heat and portion equally into the ramekins.

3. To the same pot (without washing it), add the milk. Heat over medium-high heat until boiling. Slowly reduce to a simmer and stir in the flour, 1 tablespoon at a time, until the gravy thickens and coats the back of a wooden spoon (about 5 minutes).

4. Remove from the heat and equally portion ½ cup of gravy into each ramekin on top of the sausage and potato mixture.

5. Place the circle pie crusts on top of the ramekins, lightly pressing them down on the perimeter of each ramekin with the prongs of a fork. Gently poke the prongs into the center top of the pie crust a few times to create holes for the steam to escape as the pie cooks.

6. Bake in the air fryer for 6 minutes (or until the tops are golden brown).

7. Remove and let cool 5 minutes before serving.

# Carrot Orange Muffins

Servings: 12
Cooking Time: 12 Minutes

**Ingredients:**

- 1½ cups all-purpose flour
- ½ cup granulated sugar
- ½ teaspoon ground cinnamon
- 2 teaspoons baking powder
- ¼ teaspoon baking soda
- ½ teaspoon salt
- 2 large eggs
- ¼ cup vegetable oil
- ⅓ cup orange marmalade
- 2 cups grated carrots

**Directions:**

1. Preheat the air fryer to 320°F.

2. In a large bowl, whisk together the flour, sugar, cinnamon, baking powder, baking soda, and salt; set aside.

3. In a separate bowl, whisk together the eggs, vegetable oil, orange marmalade, and grated carrots.

4. Make a well in the dry ingredients; then pour the wet ingredients into the well of the dry ingredients. Using a rubber spatula, mix the ingredients for 1 minute or until slightly lumpy.

5. Using silicone muffin liners, fill 6 muffin liners two-thirds full.

6. Carefully place the muffin liners in the air fryer basket and bake for 12 minutes (or until the tops are browned and a toothpick inserted in the center comes out clean). Carefully remove the muffins from the basket and repeat with remaining batter.

7. Serve warm.

# Breakfast Chimichangas

Servings: 4
Cooking Time: 8 Minutes

**Ingredients:**

- Four 8-inch flour tortillas
- ½ cup canned refried beans
- 1 cup scrambled eggs

- ½ cup grated cheddar or Monterey jack cheese
- 1 tablespoon vegetable oil
- 1 cup salsa

**Directions:**

1. Lay the flour tortillas out flat on a cutting board. In the center of each tortilla, spread 2 tablespoons refried beans. Next, add ¼ cup eggs and 2 tablespoons cheese to each tortilla.

2. To fold the tortillas, begin on the left side and fold to the center. Then fold the right side into the center. Next fold the bottom and top down and roll over to completely seal the chimichanga. Using a pastry brush or oil mister, brush the tops of the tortilla packages with oil.

3. Preheat the air fryer to 400°F for 4 minutes. Place the chimichangas into the air fryer basket, seam side down, and air fry for 4 minutes. Using tongs, turn over the chimichangas and cook for an additional 2 to 3 minutes or until light golden brown.

# Crunchy French Toast Sticks

Servings: 2
Cooking Time: 9 Minutes

**Ingredients:**

- 2 eggs, beaten
- ¾ cup milk
- ½ teaspoon vanilla extract
- ½ teaspoon ground cinnamon
- 1½ cups crushed crunchy cinnamon cereal, or any cereal flakes
- 4 slices Texas Toast (or other bread that you can slice into 1-inch thick slices)
- maple syrup, for serving
- vegetable oil or melted butter

**Directions:**

1. Combine the eggs, milk, vanilla and cinnamon in a shallow bowl. Place the crushed cereal in a second shallow bowl.

2. Trim the crusts off the slices of bread and cut each slice into 3 sticks. Dip the sticks of bread into the egg mixture, turning them over to coat all sides. Let the bread sticks absorb the egg mixture for ten seconds or so, but don't let them get too wet. Roll the bread sticks in the cereal crumbs, pressing the cereal gently onto all sides so that it adheres to the bread.

3. Preheat the air fryer to 400°F.

4. Spray or brush the air fryer basket with oil or melted butter. Place the coated sticks in the basket. It's ok to stack a few on top of the others in the opposite direction.

5. Air-fry for 9 minutes. Turn the sticks over a couple of times during the cooking process so that the sticks crisp evenly. Serve warm with the maple syrup or some berries.

# Roasted Tomato And Cheddar Rolls

Servings: 12
Cooking Time: 55 Minutes

**Ingredients:**

- 4 Roma tomatoes
- ½ clove garlic, minced
- 1 tablespoon olive oil
- ¼ teaspoon dried thyme
- salt and freshly ground black pepper
- 4 cups all-purpose flour
- 1 teaspoon active dry yeast
- 2 teaspoons sugar
- 2 teaspoons salt
- 1 tablespoon olive oil
- 1 cup grated Cheddar cheese, plus more for sprinkling at the end
- 1½ cups water

**Directions:**
1.  Cut the Roma tomatoes in half, remove the seeds with your fingers and transfer to a bowl. Add the garlic, olive oil, dried thyme, salt and freshly ground black pepper and toss well.
2.  Preheat the air fryer to 390°F.
3.  Place the tomatoes, cut side up in the air fryer basket and air-fry for 10 minutes. The tomatoes should just start to brown. Shake the basket to redistribute the tomatoes, and air-fry for another 5 to 10 minutes at 330°F until the tomatoes are no longer juicy. Let the tomatoes cool and then rough chop them.
4.  Combine the flour, yeast, sugar and salt in the bowl of a stand mixer. Add the olive oil, chopped roasted tomatoes and Cheddar cheese to the flour mixture and start to mix using the dough hook attachment. As you're mixing, add 1¼ cups of the water, mixing until the dough comes together. Continue to knead the dough with the dough hook for another 10 minutes, adding enough water to the dough to get it to the right consistency.
5.  Transfer the dough to an oiled bowl, cover with a clean kitchen towel and let it rest and rise until it has doubled in volume – about 1 to 2 hours. Then, divide the dough into 12 equal portions. Roll each portion of dough into a ball. Lightly coat each dough ball with oil and let the dough balls rest and rise a second time, covered lightly with plastic wrap for 45 minutes. (Alternately, you can place the rolls in the refrigerator overnight and take them out 2 hours before you bake them.)
6.  Preheat the air fryer to 360°F.
7.  Spray the dough balls and the air fryer basket with a little olive oil. Place three rolls at a time in the basket and bake for 10 minutes. Add a little grated Cheddar cheese on top of the rolls for the last 2 minutes of air frying for an attractive finish.

# Cheddar Cheese Biscuits

Servings: 8
Cooking Time: 22 Minutes

**Ingredients:**
*   2⅓ cups self-rising flour
*   2 tablespoons sugar
*   ½ cup butter (1 stick), frozen for 15 minutes
*   ½ cup grated Cheddar cheese, plus more to melt on top
*   1⅓ cups buttermilk
*   1 cup all-purpose flour, for shaping
*   1 tablespoon butter, melted

**Directions:**
1.  Line a buttered 7-inch metal cake pan with parchment paper or a silicone liner.
2.  Combine the flour and sugar in a large mixing bowl. Grate the butter into the flour. Add the grated cheese and stir to coat the cheese and butter with flour. Then add the buttermilk and stir just until you can no longer see streaks of flour. The dough should be quite wet.
3.  Spread the all-purpose (not self-rising) flour out on a small cookie sheet. With a spoon, scoop 8 evenly sized balls of dough into the flour, making sure they don't touch each other. With floured hands, coat each dough ball with flour and toss them gently from hand to hand to shake off any excess flour. Place each floured dough ball into the prepared pan, right up next to the other. This will help the biscuits rise up, rather than spreading out.
4.  Preheat the air fryer to 380°F.
5.  Transfer the cake pan to the basket of the air fryer, lowering it into the basket using a sling made of aluminum foil (fold a piece of aluminum foil into a strip about 2-inches wide by 24-inches long). Let the ends of the aluminum foil sling hang across the cake pan before returning the basket to the air fryer.

6. Air-fry for 20 minutes. Check the biscuits a couple of times to make sure they are not getting too brown on top. If they are, re-arrange the aluminum foil strips to cover any brown parts. After 20 minutes, check the biscuits by inserting a toothpick into the center of the biscuits. It should come out clean. If it needs a little more time, continue to air-fry for a couple of extra minutes. Brush the tops of the biscuits with some melted butter and sprinkle a little more grated cheese on top if desired. Pop the basket back into the air fryer for another 2 minutes. Remove the cake pan from the air fryer using the aluminum sling. Let the biscuits cool for just a minute or two and then turn them out onto a plate and pull apart. Serve immediately.

## Cheddar-ham-corn Muffins

Servings: 8
Cooking Time: 8 Minutes

**Ingredients:**
- ¾ cup yellow cornmeal
- ¼ cup flour
- 1½ teaspoons baking powder
- ¼ teaspoon salt
- 1 egg, beaten
- 2 tablespoons canola oil
- ½ cup milk
- ½ cup shredded sharp Cheddar cheese
- ½ cup diced ham
- 8 foil muffin cups, liners removed and sprayed with cooking spray

**Directions:**
1. Preheat air fryer to 390°F.
2. In a medium bowl, stir together the cornmeal, flour, baking powder, and salt.
3. Add egg, oil, and milk to dry ingredients and mix well.
4. Stir in shredded cheese and diced ham.

5. Divide batter among the muffin cups.
6. Place 4 filled muffin cups in air fryer basket and bake for 5minutes.
7. Reduce temperature to 330°F and bake for 1 to 2minutes or until toothpick inserted in center of muffin comes out clean.
8. Repeat steps 6 and 7 to cook remaining muffins.

## Apple Fritters

Servings: 6
Cooking Time: 12 Minutes

**Ingredients:**
- 1 cup all-purpose flour
- 1½ teaspoons baking powder
- ¼ teaspoon salt
- 2 tablespoon brown sugar
- 1 teaspoon vanilla extract
- ¾ cup plain Greek yogurt
- 1 tablespoon cinnamon
- 1 large Granny Smith apple, cored, peeled, and finely chopped
- ¼ cup chopped walnuts
- ½ cup powdered sugar
- 1 tablespoon milk

**Directions:**
1. Preheat the air fryer to 320°F.
2. In a medium bowl, combine the flour, baking powder, and salt.
3. In a large bowl, add the brown sugar, vanilla, yogurt, cinnamon, apples, and walnuts. Mix the dry ingredients into the wet, using your hands to combine, until all the ingredients are mixed together. Knead the mixture in the bowl about 4 times.
4. Lightly spray the air fryer basket with olive oil spray.

5. Divide the batter into 6 equally sized balls; then lightly flatten them and place inside the basket. Repeat until all the fritters are formed.

6. Place the basket in the air fryer and cook for 6 minutes, flip, and then cook another 6 minutes.

7. While the fritters are cooking, in a small bowl, mix the powdered sugar with the milk. Set aside.

8. When the cooking completes, remove the air fryer basket and allow the fritters to cool on a wire rack. Drizzle with the homemade glaze and serve.

# Parmesan Garlic Naan

Servings: 6
Cooking Time: 4 Minutes

**Ingredients:**
- 1 cup bread flour
- 1 teaspoon baking powder
- ⅛ teaspoon salt
- 1 teaspoon garlic powder
- 2 tablespoon shredded parmesan cheese
- 1 cup plain 2% fat Greek yogurt
- 1 tablespoon extra-virgin olive oil

**Directions:**
1. Preheat the air fryer to 400°F.

2. In a medium bowl, mix the flour, baking powder, salt, garlic powder, and cheese. Mix the yogurt into the flour, using your hands to combine if necessary.

3. On a flat surface covered with flour, divide the dough into 6 equal balls and roll each out into a 4-inch-diameter circle.

4. Lightly brush both sides of each naan with olive oil and place one naan at a time into the basket. Cook for 3 to 4 minutes (or until the bread begins to rise and brown on the outside). Remove and repeat for the remaining breads.

5. Serve warm.

# Garlic Parmesan Bread Ring

Servings: 6
Cooking Time: 30 Minutes

**Ingredients:**
- ½ cup unsalted butter, melted
- ¼ teaspoon salt (omit if using salted butter)
- ¾ cup grated Parmesan cheese
- 3 to 4 cloves garlic, minced
- 1 tablespoon chopped fresh parsley
- 1 pound frozen bread dough, defrosted
- olive oil
- 1 egg, beaten

**Directions:**
1. Combine the melted butter, salt, Parmesan cheese, garlic and chopped parsley in a small bowl.

2. Roll the dough out into a rectangle that measures 8 inches by 17 inches. Spread the butter mixture over the dough, leaving a half-inch border un-buttered along one of the long edges. Roll the dough from one long edge to the other, ending with the un-buttered border. Pinch the seam shut tightly. Shape the log into a circle sealing the ends together by pushing one end into the other and stretching the dough around it.

3. Cut out a circle of aluminum foil that is the same size as the air fryer basket. Brush the foil circle with oil and place an oven safe ramekin or glass in the center. Transfer the dough ring to the aluminum foil circle, around the ramekin. This will help you make sure the dough will fit in the basket and maintain its ring shape. Use kitchen shears to cut 8 slits around the outer edge of the dough ring halfway to the center. Brush the dough ring with egg wash.

4. Preheat the air fryer to 400°F for 4 minutes. When it has Preheated, brush the sides of the basket with oil and transfer the dough ring, foil circle and ramekin into the basket. Slide the drawer back into the air fryer, but do not turn the

air fryer on. Let the dough rise inside the warm air fryer for 30 minutes.

5. After the bread has proofed in the air fryer for 30 minutes, set the temperature to 340°F and air-fry the bread ring for 15 minutes. Flip the bread over by inverting it onto a plate or cutting board and sliding it back into the air fryer basket. Air-fry for another 15 minutes. Let the bread cool for a few minutes before slicing the bread ring in between the slits and serving warm.

# Crispy Bacon

Servings: 6
Cooking Time: 20 Minutes

**Ingredients:**
- 12 ounces bacon

**Directions:**
1. Preheat the air fryer to 350°F for 3 minutes.
2. Lay out the bacon in a single layer, slightly overlapping the strips of bacon.
3. Air fry for 10 minutes or until desired crispness.
4. Repeat until all the bacon has been cooked.

# Bread Boat Eggs

Servings: 4
Cooking Time: 10 Minutes

**Ingredients:**
- 4 pistolette rolls
- 1 teaspoon butter
- ¼ cup diced fresh mushrooms
- ½ teaspoon dried onion flakes
- 4 eggs
- ½ teaspoon salt
- ¼ teaspoon dried dill weed
- ¼ teaspoon dried parsley
- 1 tablespoon milk

**Directions:**

1. Cut a rectangle in the top of each roll and scoop out center, leaving ½-inch shell on the sides and bottom.
2. Place butter, mushrooms, and dried onion in air fryer baking pan and cook for 1 minute. Stir and cook 3 moreminutes.
3. In a medium bowl, beat together the eggs, salt, dill, parsley, and milk. Pour mixture into pan with mushrooms.
4. Cook at 390°F for 2minutes. Stir. Continue cooking for 3 or 4minutes, stirring every minute, until eggs are scrambled to your liking.
5. Remove baking pan from air fryer and fill rolls with scrambled egg mixture.
6. Place filled rolls in air fryer basket and cook at 390°F for 2 to 3minutes or until rolls are lightly browned.

# Blueberry Muffins

Servings: 8
Cooking Time: 14 Minutes

**Ingredients:**
- 1⅓ cups flour
- ½ cup sugar
- 2 teaspoons baking powder
- ¼ teaspoon salt
- ⅓ cup canola oil
- 1 egg
- ½ cup milk
- ⅔ cup blueberries, fresh or frozen and thawed
- 8 foil muffin cups including paper liners

**Directions:**
1. Preheat air fryer to 330°F.
2. In a medium bowl, stir together flour, sugar, baking powder, and salt.
3. In a separate bowl, combine oil, egg, and milk and mix well.
4. Add egg mixture to dry ingredients and stir just until moistened.

5. Gently stir in blueberries.

6. Spoon batter evenly into muffin cups.

7. Place 4 muffin cups in air fryer basket and bake at 330°F for 14 minutes or until tops spring back when touched lightly.

8. Repeat previous step to cook remaining muffins.

# Apple-cinnamon-walnut Muffins

Servings: 8
Cooking Time: 11 Minutes

**Ingredients:**
- 1 cup flour
- ⅓ cup sugar
- 1 teaspoon baking powder
- ¼ teaspoon baking soda
- ¼ teaspoon salt
- 1 teaspoon cinnamon
- ¼ teaspoon ginger
- ¼ teaspoon nutmeg
- 1 egg
- 2 tablespoons pancake syrup, plus 2 teaspoons
- 2 tablespoons melted butter, plus 2 teaspoons
- ¾ cup unsweetened applesauce
- ½ teaspoon vanilla extract
- ¼ cup chopped walnuts
- ¼ cup diced apple
- 8 foil muffin cups, liners removed and sprayed with cooking spray

**Directions:**
1. Preheat air fryer to 330°F.

2. In a large bowl, stir together flour, sugar, baking powder, baking soda, salt, cinnamon, ginger, and nutmeg.

3. In a small bowl, beat egg until frothy. Add syrup, butter, applesauce, and vanilla and mix well.

4. Pour egg mixture into dry ingredients and stir just until moistened.

5. Gently stir in nuts and diced apple.

6. Divide batter among the 8 muffin cups.

7. Place 4 muffin cups in air fryer basket and cook at 330°F for 11minutes.

8. Repeat with remaining 4 muffins or until toothpick inserted in center comes out clean.

# Not-so-english Muffins

Servings: 4
Cooking Time: 10 Minutes

**Ingredients:**
- 2 strips turkey bacon, cut in half crosswise
- 2 whole-grain English muffins, split
- 1 cup fresh baby spinach, long stems removed
- ¼ ripe pear, peeled and thinly sliced
- 4 slices Provolone cheese

**Directions:**
1. Place bacon strips in air fryer basket and cook for 2minutes. Check and separate strips if necessary so they cook evenly. Cook for 4 more minutes, until crispy. Remove and drain on paper towels.

2. Place split muffin halves in air fryer basket and cook at 390°F for 2minutes, just until lightly browned.

3. Open air fryer and top each muffin with a quarter of the baby spinach, several pear slices, a strip of bacon, and a slice of cheese.

4. Cook at 360°F for 2minutes, until cheese completely melts.

# Hush Puffins

Servings: 20
Cooking Time: 8 Minutes

**Ingredients:**
- 1 cup buttermilk
- ¼ cup butter, melted
- 2 eggs
- 1½ cups all-purpose flour

- 1½ cups cornmeal
- ⅓ cup sugar
- 1 teaspoon baking soda
- 1 teaspoon salt
- 4 scallions, minced
- vegetable oil

**Directions:**
1. Combine the buttermilk, butter and eggs in a large mixing bowl. In a second bowl combine the flour, cornmeal, sugar, baking soda and salt. Add the dry ingredients to the wet ingredients, stirring just to combine. Stir in the minced scallions and refrigerate the batter for 30 minutes.
2. Shape the batter into 2-inch balls. Brush or spray the balls with oil.
3. Preheat the air fryer to 360°F.
4. Air-fry the hush puffins in two batches at 360°F for 8 minutes, turning them over after 6 minutes of the cooking process.
5. Serve warm with butter.

# Whole-grain Cornbread

Servings: 6
Cooking Time: 25 Minutes

**Ingredients:**
- 1 cup stoneground cornmeal
- ½ cup brown rice flour
- 1 teaspoon sugar
- 2 teaspoons baking powder
- ¼ teaspoon salt
- 1 cup milk
- 2 tablespoons oil
- 2 eggs
- cooking spray

**Directions:**
1. Preheat the air fryer to 360°F.
2. In a medium mixing bowl, mix cornmeal, brown rice flour, sugar, baking powder, and salt together.

3. Add the remaining ingredients and beat with a spoon until batter is smooth.
4. Spray air fryer baking pan with nonstick cooking spray and add the cornbread batter.
5. Bake at 360°F for 25 minutes, until center is done.

# Cinnamon Biscuit Rolls

Servings: 12
Cooking Time: 5 Minutes

**Ingredients:**
- Dough
- ¼ cup warm water (105–115°F)
- 1 teaspoon active dry yeast
- 1 tablespoon sugar
- ½ cup buttermilk, lukewarm
- 2 cups flour, plus more for dusting
- 1 teaspoon baking powder
- ½ teaspoon salt
- 3 tablespoons cold butter
- Filling
- 1 tablespoon butter, melted
- 1 teaspoon cinnamon
- 2 tablespoons sugar
- Icing
- ⅔ cup powdered sugar
- ¼ teaspoon vanilla
- 2–3 teaspoons milk

**Directions:**
1. Dissolve yeast and sugar in warm water. Add buttermilk, stir, and set aside.
2. In a large bowl, sift together flour, baking powder, and salt. Using knives or a pastry blender, cut in butter until mixture is well combined and crumbly.
3. Pour in buttermilk mixture and stir with fork until a ball of dough forms.
4. Knead dough on a lightly floured surface for 5 minutes. Roll into an 8 x 11-inch rectangle.

5. For the filling, spread the melted butter over the dough.

6. In a small bowl, stir together the cinnamon and sugar, then sprinkle over dough.

7. Starting on a long side, roll up dough so that you have a roll about 11 inches long. Cut into 12 slices with a serrated knife and sawing motion so slices remain round.

8. Place rolls on a plate or cookie sheet about an inch apart and let rise for 30minutes.

9. For icing, mix the powdered sugar, vanilla, and milk. Stir and add additional milk until icing reaches a good spreading consistency.

10. Preheat air fryer to 360°F.

11. Place 6 cinnamon rolls in basket and cook 5 minutes or until top springs back when lightly touched. Repeat to cook remaining 6 rolls.

12. Spread icing over warm rolls and serve.

# Pancake Muffins

Servings: 4
Cooking Time: 8 Minutes

## Ingredients:

- 1 cup flour
- 2 tablespoons sugar (optional)
- ½ teaspoon baking soda
- 1 teaspoon baking powder
- ¼ teaspoon salt
- 1 egg, beaten
- 1 cup buttermilk
- 2 tablespoons melted butter
- 1 teaspoon pure vanilla extract
- 24 foil muffin cups
- cooking spray
- Suggested Fillings
- 1 teaspoon of jelly or fruit preserves
- 1 tablespoon or less fresh blueberries; chopped fresh strawberries; chopped frozen cherries; dark chocolate chips; chopped walnuts, pecans, or other nuts; cooked, crumbled bacon or sausage

## Directions:

1. In a large bowl, stir together flour, optional sugar, baking soda, baking powder, and salt.

2. In a small bowl, combine egg, buttermilk, butter, and vanilla. Mix well.

3. Pour egg mixture into dry ingredients and stir to mix well but don't overbeat.

4. Double up the muffin cups and remove the paper liners from the top cups. Spray the foil cups lightly with cooking spray.

5. Place 6 sets of muffin cups in air fryer basket. Pour just enough batter into each cup to cover the bottom. Sprinkle with desired filling. Pour in more batter to cover the filling and fill the cups about ¾ full.

6. Cook at 330°F for 8minutes.

7. Repeat steps 5 and 6 for the remaining 6 pancake muffins.

# Desserts And Sweets

## Keto Cheesecake Cups

Servings: 6
Cooking Time: 10 Minutes

**Ingredients:**
- 8 ounces cream cheese
- ¼ cup plain whole-milk Greek yogurt
- 1 large egg
- 1 teaspoon pure vanilla extract
- 3 tablespoons monk fruit sweetener
- ¼ teaspoon salt
- ½ cup walnuts, roughly chopped

**Directions:**
1. Preheat the air fryer to 315°F.
2. In a large bowl, use a hand mixer to beat the cream cheese together with the yogurt, egg, vanilla, sweetener, and salt. When combined, fold in the chopped walnuts.
3. Set 6 silicone muffin liners inside an air-fryer-safe pan. Note: This is to allow for an easier time getting the cheesecake bites in and out. If you don't have a pan, you can place them directly in the air fryer basket.
4. Evenly fill the cupcake liners with cheesecake batter.
5. Carefully place the pan into the air fryer basket and cook for about 10 minutes, or until the tops are lightly browned and firm.
6. Carefully remove the pan when done and place in the refrigerator for 3 hours to firm up before serving.

## Air-fried Strawberry Hand Tarts

Servings: 9
Cooking Time: 9 Minutes

**Ingredients:**

- ½ cup butter, softened
- ½ cup sugar
- 2 eggs
- 1 teaspoon vanilla extract
- 2 tablespoons lemon zest
- 2½ cups all-purpose flour
- 1 teaspoon baking powder
- ¼ teaspoon salt
- 1¼ cups strawberry jam, divided
- 1 egg white, beaten
- 1 cup powdered sugar
- 2 teaspoons milk

**Directions:**
1. Combine the butter and sugar in a bowl and beat with an electric mixer until the mixture is light and fluffy. Add the eggs one at a time. Add the vanilla extract and lemon zest and mix well. In a separate bowl, combine the flour, baking powder and salt. Add the dry ingredients to the wet ingredients, mixing just until the dough comes together. Transfer the dough to a floured surface and knead by hand for 10 minutes. Cover with a clean kitchen towel and let the dough rest for 30 minutes. (Alternatively, dough can be mixed and kneaded in a stand mixer.)
2. Divide the dough in half and roll each half out into a ¼-inch thick rectangle that measures 12-inches x 9-inches. Cut each rectangle of dough into nine 4-inch x 3-inch rectangles (a pizza cutter is very helpful for this task). You should have 18 rectangles. Spread two teaspoons of strawberry jam in the center of nine of the rectangles leaving a ¼-inch border around the edges. Brush the egg white around the edges of each rectangle and top with the remaining nine rectangles of dough. Press the back of a fork around the edges to seal the tarts shut. Brush the

top of the tarts with the beaten egg white and pierce the dough three or four times down the center of the tart with a fork.

3. Preheat the air fryer to 350°F.

4. Air-fry the tarts in batches at 350°F for 6 minutes. Flip the tarts over and air-fry for an additional 3 minutes.

5. While the tarts are air-frying, make the icing. Combine the powdered sugar, ¼ cup strawberry preserves and milk in a bowl, whisking until the icing is smooth. Spread the icing over the top of each tart, leaving an empty border around the edges. Decorate with sprinkles if desired.

# Giant Buttery Chocolate Chip Cookie

Servings: 4
Cooking Time: 16 Minutes

**Ingredients:**
- ⅔ cup plus 1 tablespoon All-purpose flour
- ¼ teaspoon Baking soda
- ¼ teaspoon Table salt
- Baking spray (see the headnote)
- 4 tablespoons (¼ cup/½ stick) plus 1 teaspoon Butter, at room temperature
- ¼ cup plus 1 teaspoon Packed dark brown sugar
- 3 tablespoons plus 1 teaspoon Granulated white sugar
- 2½ tablespoons Pasteurized egg substitute, such as Egg Beaters
- ½ teaspoon Vanilla extract
- ¾ cup plus 1 tablespoon Semisweet or bittersweet chocolate chips

**Directions:**
1. Preheat the air fryer to 350°F .
2. Whisk the flour, baking soda, and salt in a bowl until well combined.

3. For a small air fryer, coat the inside of a 6-inch round cake pan with baking spray. For a medium air fryer, coat the inside of a 7-inch round cake pan with baking spray. And for a large air fryer, coat the inside of an 8-inch round cake pan with baking spray.

4. Using a hand electric mixer at medium speed, beat the butter, brown sugar, and granulated white sugar in a bowl until smooth and thick, about 3 minutes, scraping down the inside of the bowl several times.

5. Beat in the pasteurized egg substitute or egg (as applicable) and vanilla until uniform. Scrape down and remove the beaters. Fold in the flour mixture and chocolate chips with a rubber spatula, just until combined. Scrape and gently press this dough into the prepared pan, getting it even across the pan to the perimeter.

6. Set the pan in the basket and air-fry undisturbed for 16 minutes, or until the cookie is puffed, browned, and feels set to the touch.

7. Transfer the pan to a wire rack and cool for 10 minutes. Loosen the cookie from the perimeter with a spatula, then invert the pan onto a cutting board and let the cookie come free. Remove the pan and reinvert the cookie onto the wire rack. Cool for 5 minutes more before slicing into wedges to serve.

# Cherry Hand Pies

Servings: 8
Cooking Time: 8 Minutes

**Ingredients:**
- 4 cups frozen or canned pitted tart cherries (if using canned, drain and pat dry)
- 2 teaspoons lemon juice
- ½ cup sugar
- ¼ cup cornstarch
- 1 teaspoon vanilla extract

- 1 Basic Pie Dough (see the preceding recipe) or store-bought pie dough

**Directions:**
1.  In a medium saucepan, place the cherries and lemon juice and cook over medium heat for 10 minutes, or until the cherries begin to break down.
2.  In a small bowl, stir together the sugar and cornstarch. Pour the sugar mixture into the cherries, stirring constantly. Cook the cherry mixture over low heat for 2 to 3 minutes, or until thickened. Remove from the heat and stir in the vanilla extract. Allow the cherry mixture to cool to room temperature, about 30 minutes.
3.  Meanwhile, bring the pie dough to room temperature. Divide the dough into 8 equal pieces. Roll out the dough to ¼-inch thickness in circles. Place ¼ cup filling in the center of each rolled dough. Fold the dough to create a half-circle. Using a fork, press around the edges to seal the hand pies. Pierce the top of the pie with a fork for steam release while cooking. Continue until 8 hand pies are formed.
4.  Preheat the air fryer to 350°F.
5.  Place a single layer of hand pies in the air fryer basket and spray with cooking spray. Cook for 8 to 10 minutes or until golden brown and cooked through.

# Coconut-custard Pie

Servings: 4
Cooking Time: 20 Minutes

**Ingredients:**
- 1 cup milk
- ¼ cup plus 2 tablespoons sugar
- ¼ cup biscuit baking mix
- 1 teaspoon vanilla
- 2 eggs
- 2 tablespoons melted butter
- cooking spray
- ½ cup shredded, sweetened coconut

**Directions:**
1.  Place all ingredients except coconut in a medium bowl.
2.  Using a hand mixer, beat on high speed for 3minutes.
3.  Let sit for 5minutes.
4.  Preheat air fryer to 330°F.
5.  Spray a 6-inch round or 6 x 6-inch square baking pan with cooking spray and place pan in air fryer basket.
6.  Pour filling into pan and sprinkle coconut over top.
7.  Cook pie at 330°F for 20 minutes or until center sets.

# Sweet Potato Donut Holes

Servings: 18
Cooking Time: 4 Minutes Per Batch

**Ingredients:**
- 1 cup flour
- ⅓ cup sugar
- ¼ teaspoon baking soda
- 1 teaspoon baking powder
- ⅛ teaspoon salt
- ½ cup cooked mashed purple sweet potatoes
- 1 egg, beaten
- 2 tablespoons butter, melted
- 1 teaspoon pure vanilla extract
- oil for misting or cooking spray

**Directions:**
1.  Preheat air fryer to 390°F.
2.  In a large bowl, stir together the flour, sugar, baking soda, baking powder, and salt.
3.  In a separate bowl, combine the potatoes, egg, butter, and vanilla and mix well.
4.  Add potato mixture to dry ingredients and stir into a soft dough.

5. Shape dough into 1½-inch balls. Mist lightly with oil or cooking spray.

6. Place 9 donut holes in air fryer basket, leaving a little space in between. Cook for 4 minutes, until done in center and lightly browned outside.

7. Repeat step 6 to cook remaining donut holes.

## Tortilla Fried Pies

Servings: 12
Cooking Time: 5 Minutes

**Ingredients:**
- 12 small flour tortillas (4-inch diameter)
- ½ cup fig preserves
- ¼ cup sliced almonds
- 2 tablespoons shredded, unsweetened coconut
- oil for misting or cooking spray

**Directions:**
1. Wrap refrigerated tortillas in damp paper towels and heat in microwave 30 seconds to warm.
2. Working with one tortilla at a time, place 2 teaspoons fig preserves, 1 teaspoon sliced almonds, and ½ teaspoon coconut in the center of each.
3. Moisten outer edges of tortilla all around.
4. Fold one side of tortilla over filling to make a half-moon shape and press down lightly on center. Using the tines of a fork, press down firmly on edges of tortilla to seal in filling.
5. Mist both sides with oil or cooking spray.
6. Place hand pies in air fryer basket close but not overlapping. It's fine to lean some against the sides and corners of the basket. You may need to cook in 2 batches.
7. Cook at 390°F for 5minutes or until lightly browned. Serve hot.
8. Refrigerate any leftover pies in a closed container. To serve later, toss them back in the air fryer basket and cook for 2 or 3minutes to reheat.

# Maple Cinnamon Cheesecake

Servings: 4
Cooking Time: 12 Minutes

**Ingredients:**
- 6 sheets of cinnamon graham crackers
- 2 tablespoons butter
- 8 ounces Neufchâtel cream cheese
- 3 tablespoons pure maple syrup
- 1 large egg
- ½ teaspoon ground cinnamon
- ¼ teaspoon salt

**Directions:**
1. Preheat the air fryer to 350°F.
2. Place the graham crackers in a food processor and process until crushed into a flour. Mix with the butter and press into a mini air-fryer-safe pan lined at the bottom with parchment paper. Place in the air fryer and cook for 4 minutes.
3. In a large bowl, place the cream cheese and maple syrup. Use a hand mixer or stand mixer and beat together until smooth. Add in the egg, cinnamon, and salt and mix on medium speed until combined.
4. Remove the graham cracker crust from the air fryer and pour the batter into the pan.
5. Place the pan back in the air fryer, adjusting the temperature to 315°F. Cook for 18 minutes. Carefully remove when cooking completes. The top should be lightly browned and firm.
6. Keep the cheesecake in the pan and place in the refrigerator for 3 or more hours to firm up before serving.

# Struffoli

Servings: X
Cooking Time: 20 Minutes

**Ingredients:**

- ¼ cup butter, softened
- ⅔ cup sugar
- 5 eggs
- 2 teaspoons vanilla extract
- zest of 1 lemon
- 4 cups all-purpose flour
- 2 teaspoons baking soda
- ¼ teaspoon salt
- 16 ounces honey
- 1 teaspoon ground cinnamon
- zest of 1 orange
- 2 tablespoons water
- nonpareils candy sprinkles

**Directions:**

1. Cream the butter and sugar together in a bowl until light and fluffy using a hand mixer (or a stand mixer). Add the eggs, vanilla and lemon zest and mix. In a separate bowl, combine the flour, baking soda and salt. Add the dry ingredients to the wet ingredients and mix until you have a soft dough. Shape the dough into a ball, wrap it in plastic and let it rest for 30 minutes.

2. Divide the dough ball into four pieces. Roll each piece into a long rope. Cut each rope into about 25 (½-inch) pieces. Roll each piece into a tight ball. You should have 100 little balls when finished.

3. Preheat the air fryer to 370°F.

4. In batches of about 20, transfer the dough balls to the air fryer basket, leaving a small space in between them. Air-fry the dough balls at 370°F for 3 to 4 minutes, shaking the basket when one minute of cooking time remains.

5. After all the dough balls are air-fried, make the honey topping. Melt the honey in a small saucepan on the stovetop. Add the cinnamon, orange zest, and water. Simmer for one minute. Place the air-fried dough balls in a large bowl and drizzle the honey mixture over top. Gently toss to coat all the dough balls evenly. Transfer the coated struffoli to a platter and sprinkle the nonpareil candy sprinkles over top. You can dress the presentation up by piling the balls into the shape of a wreath or pile them high in a cone shape to resemble a Christmas tree.

6. Struffoli can be made ahead. Store covered tightly.

# Oreo-coated Peanut Butter Cups

Servings:8
Cooking Time: 4 Minutes

**Ingredients:**

- 8 Standard ¾-ounce peanut butter cups, frozen
- ⅓ cup All-purpose flour
- 2 Large egg white(s), beaten until foamy
- 16 Oreos or other creme-filled chocolate sandwich cookies, ground to crumbs in a food processor
- Vegetable oil spray

**Directions:**

1. Set up and fill three shallow soup plates or small pie plates on your counter: one for the flour, one for the beaten egg white(s), and one for the cookie crumbs.

2. Dip a frozen peanut butter cup in the flour, turning it to coat all sides. Shake off any excess, then set it in the beaten egg white(s). Turn it to coat all sides, then let any excess egg white slip back into the rest. Set the candy bar in the cookie crumbs. Turn to coat on all parts, even the sides. Dip the peanut butter cup back in the egg white(s)

as before, then into the cookie crumbs as before, making sure you have a solid, even coating all around the cup. Set aside while you dip and coat the remaining cups.

3. When all the peanut butter cups are dipped and coated, lightly coat them on all sides with the vegetable oil spray. Set them on a plate and freeze while the air fryer heats.

4. Preheat the air fryer to 400°F.

5. Set the dipped cups wider side up in the basket with as much air space between them as possible. Air-fry undisturbed for 4 minutes, or until they feel soft but the coating is set.

6. Turn off the machine and remove the basket from it. Set aside the basket with the fried cups for 10 minutes. Use a nonstick-safe spatula to transfer the fried cups to a wire rack. Cool for at least another 5 minutes before serving.

# Apple Dumplings

Servings: 4
Cooking Time: 25 Minutes

**Ingredients:**
- 1 Basic Pie Dough (see the following recipe)
- 4 medium Granny Smith or Pink Lady apples, peeled and cored
- 4 tablespoons sugar
- 4 teaspoons cinnamon
- ½ teaspoon ground nutmeg
- 4 tablespoons unsalted butter, melted
- 4 scoops ice cream, for serving

**Directions:**
1. Preheat the air fryer to 330°F.
2. Bring the pie crust recipe to room temperature.
3. Place the pie crust on a floured surface. Divide the dough into 4 equal pieces. Roll out each piece to ¼-inch-thick rounds. Place an apple onto each dough round. Sprinkle 1 tablespoon of

sugar in the core part of each apple; sprinkle 1 teaspoon cinnamon and ⅛ teaspoon nutmeg over each. Place 1 tablespoon of butter into the center of each. Fold up the sides and fully cover the cored apples.

4. Place the dumplings into the air fryer basket and spray with cooking spray. Cook for 25 minutes. Check after 14 minutes cooking; if they're getting too brown, reduce the heat to 320°F and complete the cooking.

5. Serve hot apple dumplings with a scoop of ice cream.

# Orange Gooey Butter Cake

Servings: 6
Cooking Time: 85 Minutes

**Ingredients:**
- Crust Layer:
- ½ cup flour
- ¼ cup sugar
- ½ teaspoon baking powder
- ⅛ teaspoon salt
- 2 ounces (½ stick) unsalted European style butter, melted
- 1 egg
- 1 teaspoon orange extract
- 2 tablespoons orange zest
- Gooey Butter Layer:
- 8 ounces cream cheese, softened
- 4 ounces (1 stick) unsalted European style butter, melted
- 2 eggs
- 2 teaspoons orange extract
- 2 tablespoons orange zest
- 4 cups powdered sugar
- Garnish:
- powdered sugar
- orange slices

**Directions:**

1. Preheat the air fryer to 350°F.

2. Grease a 7-inch cake pan and line the bottom with parchment paper. Combine the flour, sugar, baking powder and salt in a bowl. Add the melted butter, egg, orange extract and orange zest. Mix well and press this mixture into the bottom of the greased cake pan. Lower the pan into the basket using an aluminum foil sling (fold a piece of aluminum foil into a strip about 2-inches wide by 24-inches long). Fold the ends of the aluminum foil over the top of the dish before returning the basket to the air fryer. Air-fry uncovered for 8 minutes.

3. To make the gooey butter layer, beat the cream cheese, melted butter, eggs, orange extract and orange zest in a large bowl using an electric hand mixer. Add the powdered sugar in stages, beat until smooth with each addition. Pour this mixture on top of the baked crust in the cake pan. Wrap the pan with a piece of greased aluminum foil, tenting the top of the foil to leave a little room for the cake to rise.

4. Air-fry for 60 minutes at 350°F. Remove the aluminum foil and air-fry for an additional 17 minutes.

5. Let the cake cool inside the pan for at least 10 minutes. Then, run a butter knife around the cake and let the cake cool completely in the pan. When cooled, run the butter knife around the edges of the cake again and invert it onto a plate and then back onto a serving platter. Sprinkle the powdered sugar over the top of the cake and garnish with orange slices.

## Sea-salted Caramel Cookie Cups

Servings: 12
Cooking Time: 12 Minutes

**Ingredients:**
- ⅓ cup butter
- ¼ cup brown sugar
- 1 teaspoon vanilla extract
- 1 large egg
- 1 cup all-purpose flour
- ½ cup old-fashioned oats
- ½ teaspoon baking soda
- ¼ teaspoon salt
- ⅓ cup sea-salted caramel chips

**Directions:**
1. Preheat the air fryer to 300°F.

2. In a large bowl, cream the butter with the brown sugar and vanilla. Whisk in the egg and set aside.

3. In a separate bowl, mix the flour, oats, baking soda, and salt. Then gently mix the dry ingredients into the wet. Fold in the caramel chips.

4. Divide the batter into 12 silicon muffin liners. Place the cookie cups into the air fryer basket and cook for 12 minutes or until a toothpick inserted in the center comes out clean.

5. Remove and let cool 5 minutes before serving.

## Grilled Pineapple Dessert

Servings: 4
Cooking Time: 12 Minutes

**Ingredients:**
- oil for misting or cooking spray
- 4 ½-inch-thick slices fresh pineapple, core removed
- 1 tablespoon honey
- ¼ teaspoon brandy
- 2 tablespoons slivered almonds, toasted
- vanilla frozen yogurt or coconut sorbet

**Directions:**
1. Spray both sides of pineapple slices with oil or cooking spray. Place on grill plate or directly into air fryer basket.

2. Cook at 390°F for 6minutes. Turn slices over and cook for an additional 6minutes.

3. Mix together the honey and brandy.

4. Remove cooked pineapple slices from air fryer, sprinkle with toasted almonds, and drizzle with honey mixture.

5. Serve with a scoop of frozen yogurt or sorbet on the side.

## Coconut Macaroons

Servings: 12
Cooking Time: 8 Minutes

**Ingredients:**

- 1⅓ cups shredded, sweetened coconut
- 4½ teaspoons flour
- 2 tablespoons sugar
- 1 egg white
- ½ teaspoon almond extract

**Directions:**

1. Preheat air fryer to 330°F.
2. Mix all ingredients together.
3. Shape coconut mixture into 12 balls.
4. Place all 12 macaroons in air fryer basket. They won't expand, so you can place them close together, but they shouldn't touch.
5. Cook at 330°F for 8 minutes, until golden.

## Puff Pastry Apples

Servings: 4
Cooking Time: 10 Minutes

**Ingredients:**

- 3 Rome or Gala apples, peeled
- 2 tablespoons sugar
- 1 teaspoon all-purpose flour
- 1 teaspoon ground cinnamon
- ⅛ teaspoon ground ginger
- pinch ground nutmeg
- 1 sheet puff pastry
- 1 tablespoon butter, cut into 4 pieces
- 1 egg, beaten
- vegetable oil
- vanilla ice cream (optional)
- caramel sauce (optional)

**Directions:**

1. Remove the core from the apple by cutting the four sides off the apple around the core. Slice the pieces of apple into thin half-moons, about ¼-inch thick. Combine the sugar, flour, cinnamon, ginger, and nutmeg in a large bowl. Add the apples to the bowl and gently toss until the apples are evenly coated with the spice mixture. Set aside.

2. Cut the puff pastry sheet into a 12-inch by 12-inch square. Then quarter the sheet into four 6-inch squares. Save any remaining pastry for decorating the apples at the end.

3. Divide the spiced apples between the four puff pastry squares, stacking the apples in the center of each square and placing them flat on top of each other in a circle. Top the apples with a piece of the butter.

4. Brush the four edges of the pastry with the egg wash. Bring the four corners of the pastry together, wrapping them around the apple slices and pinching them together at the top in the style of a "beggars purse" appetizer. Fold the ends of the pastry corners down onto the apple making them look like leaves. Brush the entire apple with the egg wash.

5. Using the leftover dough, make leaves to decorate the apples. Cut out 8 leaf shapes, about 1½-inches long, "drawing" the leaf veins on the pastry leaves with a paring knife. Place 2 leaves on the top of each apple, tucking the ends of the leaves under the pastry in the center of the apples. Brush the top of the leaves with additional egg wash. Sprinkle the entire apple with some granulated sugar.

6. Preheat the air fryer to 350°F.

7. Spray or brush the inside of the air fryer basket with oil. Place the apples in the basket and air-fry for 6 minutes. Carefully turn the apples over – it's easiest to remove one apple, then flip the others over and finally return the last apple to the air fryer. Air-fry for an additional 4 minutes.

8. Serve the puff pastry apples warm with vanilla ice cream and drizzle with some caramel sauce.

# S'mores Pockets

Servings: 6
Cooking Time: 5 Minutes

**Ingredients:**

- 12 sheets phyllo dough, thawed
- 1½ cups butter, melted
- ¾ cup graham cracker crumbs
- 1 (7-ounce) Giant Hershey's® milk chocolate bar
- 12 marshmallows, cut in half

**Directions:**

1. Place one sheet of the phyllo on a large cutting board. Keep the rest of the phyllo sheets covered with a slightly damp, clean kitchen towel. Brush the phyllo sheet generously with some melted butter. Place a second phyllo sheet on top of the first and brush it with more butter. Repeat with one more phyllo sheet until you have a stack of 3 phyllo sheets with butter brushed between the layers. Cover the phyllo sheets with one quarter of the graham cracker crumbs leaving a 1-inch border on one of the short ends of the rectangle. Cut the phyllo sheets lengthwise into 3 strips.

2. Take 2 of the strips and crisscross them to form a cross with the empty borders at the top and to the left. Place 2 of the chocolate rectangles in the center of the cross. Place 4 of the marshmallow halves on top of the chocolate. Now fold the pocket together by folding the bottom phyllo strip up over the chocolate and marshmallows. Then fold the right side over, then the top strip down and finally the left side over. Brush all the edges generously with melted butter to seal shut. Repeat with the next three sheets of phyllo, until all the sheets have been used. You will be able to make 2 pockets with every second batch because you will have an extra graham cracker crumb strip from the previous set of sheets.

3. Preheat the air fryer to 350°F.

4. Transfer 3 pockets at a time to the air fryer basket. Air-fry at 350°F for 4 to 5 minutes, until the phyllo dough is light brown in color. Flip the pockets over halfway through the cooking process. Repeat with the remaining 3 pockets.

5. Serve warm.

# Carrot Cake With Cream Cheese Icing

Servings: 6
Cooking Time: 55 Minutes

**Ingredients:**

- 1¼ cups all-purpose flour
- 1 teaspoon baking powder
- ½ teaspoon baking soda
- 1 teaspoon ground cinnamon
- ¼ teaspoon ground nutmeg
- ¼ teaspoon salt
- 2 cups grated carrot (about 3 to 4 medium carrots or 2 large)
- ¾ cup granulated sugar
- ¼ cup brown sugar
- 2 eggs
- ¾ cup canola or vegetable oil
- For the icing:
- 8 ounces cream cheese, softened at room , Temperature: 8 tablespoons butter (4 ounces or 1

stick), softened at room , Temperature: 1 cup powdered sugar

- 1 teaspoon pure vanilla extract

**Directions:**
1. Grease a 7-inch cake pan.
2. Combine the flour, baking powder, baking soda, cinnamon, nutmeg and salt in a bowl. Add the grated carrots and toss well. In a separate bowl, beat the sugars and eggs together until light and frothy. Drizzle in the oil, beating constantly. Fold the egg mixture into the dry ingredients until everything is just combined and you no longer see any traces of flour. Pour the batter into the cake pan and wrap the pan completely in greased aluminum foil.
3. Preheat the air fryer to 350°F.
4. Lower the cake pan into the air fryer basket using a sling made of aluminum foil (fold a piece of aluminum foil into a strip about 2-inches wide by 24-inches long). Fold the ends of the aluminum foil into the air fryer, letting them rest on top of the cake. Air-fry for 40 minutes. Remove the aluminum foil cover and air-fry for an additional 15 minutes or until a skewer inscrted into the center of the cake comes out clean and the top is nicely browned.
5. While the cake is cooking, beat the cream cheese, butter, powdered sugar and vanilla extract together using a hand mixer, stand mixer or food processor (or a lot of elbow grease!).
6. Remove the cake pan from the air fryer and let the cake cool in the cake pan for 10 minutes or so. Then remove the cake from the pan and let it continue to cool completely. Frost the cake with the cream cheese icing and serve.

# Vanilla Butter Cake

Servings: 6
Cooking Time: 20-24 Minutes

**Ingredients:**
- ¾ cup plus 1 tablespoon All-purpose flour
- 1 teaspoon Baking powder
- ¼ teaspoon Table salt
- 8 tablespoons (½ cup/1 stick) Butter, at room temperature
- ½ cup Granulated white sugar
- 2 Large egg(s)
- 2 tablespoons Whole or low-fat milk (not fat-free)
- ¾ teaspoon Vanilla extract
- Baking spray (see here)

**Directions:**
1. Preheat the air fryer to 325°F (or 330°F, if that's the closest setting).
2. Mix the flour, baking powder, and salt in a small bowl until well combined.
3. Using an electric hand mixer at medium speed, beat the butter and sugar in a medium bowl until creamy and smooth, about 3 minutes, occasionally scraping down the inside of the bowl.
4. Beat in the egg or eggs, as well as the white or a yolk as necessary. Beat in the milk and vanilla until smooth. Turn off the beaters and add the flour mixture. Beat at low speed until thick and smooth.
5. Use the baking spray to generously coat the inside of a 6-inch round cake pan for a small batch, a 7-inch round cake pan for a medium batch, or an 8-inch round cake pan for a large batch. Scrape and spread the batter into the pan, smoothing the batter out to an even layer.
6. Set the pan in the basket and air-fry undisturbcd for 20 minutes for a 6-inch layer, 22 minutes for a 7-inch layer, or 24 minutes for an 8-inch layer, or until a toothpick or cake tester inserted into the center of the cake comes out clean. Start checking it at the 15-minute mark to know where you are.

7. Use hot pads or silicone baking mitts to transfer the cake pan to a wire rack. Cool for 5 minutes. To unmold, set a cutting board over the baking pan and invert both the board and the pan. Lift the still-warm pan off the cake layer. Set the wire rack on top of the cake layer and invert all of it with the cutting board so that the cake layer is now right side up on the wire rack. Remove the cutting board and continue cooling the cake for at least 10 minutes or to room temperature, about 30 minutes, before slicing into wedges.

# Peanut Butter S'mores

Servings:10
Cooking Time: 1 Minute

**Ingredients:**
- 10 Graham crackers (full, double-square cookies as they come out of the package)
- 5 tablespoons Natural-style creamy or crunchy peanut butter
- ½ cup Milk chocolate chips
- 10 Standard-size marshmallows (not minis and not jumbo campfire ones)

**Directions:**
1. Preheat the air fryer to 350°F .
2. Break the graham crackers in half widthwise at the marked place, so the rectangle is now in two squares. Set half of the squares flat side up on your work surface. Spread each with about 1½ teaspoons peanut butter, then set 10 to 12 chocolate chips point side up into the peanut butter on each, pressing gently so the chips stick.
3. Flatten a marshmallow between your clean, dry hands and set it atop the chips. Do the same with the remaining marshmallows on the other coated graham crackers. Do not set the other half of the graham crackers on top of these coated graham crackers.

4. When the machine is at temperature, set the treats graham cracker side down in a single layer in the basket. They may touch, but even a fraction of an inch between them will provide better air flow. Air-fry undisturbed for 45 seconds.
5. Use a nonstick-safe spatula to transfer the topped graham crackers to a wire rack. Set the other graham cracker squares flat side down over the marshmallows. Cool for a couple of minutes before serving.

# Sweet Potato Pie Rolls

Servings:3
Cooking Time: 8 Minutes

**Ingredients:**
- 6 Spring roll wrappers
- 1½ cups Canned yams in syrup, drained
- 2 tablespoons Light brown sugar
- ¼ teaspoon Ground cinnamon
- 1 Large egg(s), well beaten
- Vegetable oil spray

**Directions:**
1. Preheat the air fryer to 400°F.
2. Set a spring roll wrapper on a clean, dry work surface. Scoop up ¼ cup of the pulpy yams and set along one edge of the wrapper, leaving 2 inches on each side of the yams. Top the yams with about 1 teaspoon brown sugar and a pinch of ground cinnamon. Fold the sides of the wrapper perpendicular to the yam filling up and over the filling, partially covering it. Brush beaten egg(s) over the side of the wrapper farthest from the yam. Starting with the yam end, roll the wrapper closed, ending at the part with the beaten egg that you can press gently to seal. Lightly coat the roll on all sides with vegetable oil spray. Set it aside seam side down and continue filling, rolling, and spraying the remaining wrappers in the same way.

3. Set the rolls seam side down in the basket with as much air space between them as possible. Air-fry undisturbed for 8 minutes, or until crisp and golden brown.

4. Use a nonstick-safe spatula and perhaps kitchen tongs for balance to gently transfer the rolls to a wire rack. Cool for at least 5 minutes or up to 30 minutes before serving.

# Baked Apple Crisp

Servings: 4
Cooking Time: 23 Minutes

**Ingredients:**
- 2 large Granny Smith apples, peeled, cored, and chopped
- ¼ cup granulated sugar
- ¼ cup plus 2 teaspoons flour, divided
- 2 teaspoons milk
- ¼ teaspoon cinnamon
- ¼ cup oats
- ¼ cup brown sugar
- 2 tablespoons unsalted butter
- ⅛ teaspoon baking powder
- ⅛ teaspoon salt

**Directions:**
1. Preheat the air fryer to 350°F.
2. In a medium bowl, mix the apples, the granulated sugar, 2 teaspoons of the flour, the milk, and the cinnamon.
3. Spray 4 oven-safe ramekins with cooking spray. Divide the filling among the four ramekins.
4. In a small bowl, mix the oats, the brown sugar, the remaining ¼ cup of flour, the butter, the baking powder, and the salt. Use your fingers or a pastry blender to crumble the butter into pea-size pieces. Divide the topping over the top of the apple filling. Cover the apple crisps with foil.
5. Place the covered apple crisps in the air fryer basket and cook for 20 minutes. Uncover and continue cooking for 3 minutes or until the surface is golden and crunchy.

# Thumbprint Sugar Cookies

Servings: 10
Cooking Time: 8 Minutes

**Ingredients:**
- 2½ tablespoons butter
- ⅓ cup cane sugar
- 1 teaspoon pure vanilla extract
- 1 large egg
- 1 cup all-purpose flour
- ½ teaspoon baking soda
- ¼ teaspoon salt
- 10 chocolate kisses

**Directions:**
1. Preheat the air fryer to 350°F.
2. In a large bowl, cream the butter with the sugar and vanilla. Whisk in the egg and set aside.
3. In a separate bowl, mix the flour, baking soda, and salt. Then gently mix the dry ingredients into the wet. Portion the dough into 10 balls; then press down on each with the bottom of a cup to create a flat cookie.
4. Liberally spray the metal trivet of an air fryer basket with olive oil mist.
5. Place the cookies in the air fryer basket on the trivet and cook for 8 minutes or until the tops begin to lightly brown.
6. Remove and immediately press the chocolate kisses into the tops of the cookies while still warm.
7. Let cool 5 minutes and then enjoy.

# Banana Bread Cake

Servings: 6
Cooking Time: 18-22 Minutes

**Ingredients:**

- ¾ cup plus 2 tablespoons All-purpose flour
- ½ teaspoon Baking powder
- ¼ teaspoon Baking soda
- ¼ teaspoon Table salt
- 4 tablespoons (¼ cup/½ stick) Butter, at room temperature
- ½ cup Granulated white sugar
- 2 Small ripe bananas, peeled
- 5 tablespoons Pasteurized egg substitute, such as Egg Beaters
- ¼ cup Buttermilk
- ¾ teaspoon Vanilla extract
- Baking spray (see here)

**Directions:**

1. Preheat the air fryer to 325°F (or 330°F, if that's the closest setting).
2. Mix the flour, baking powder, baking soda, and salt in a small bowl until well combined.
3. Using an electric hand mixer at medium speed, beat the butter and sugar in a medium bowl until creamy and smooth, about 3 minutes, occasionally scraping down the inside of the bowl.
4. Beat in the bananas until smooth. Then beat in egg substitute or egg, buttermilk, and vanilla until uniform. (The batter may look curdled at this stage. The flour mixture will smooth it out.) Add the flour mixture and beat at low speed until smooth and creamy.
5. Use the baking spray to generously coat the inside of a 6-inch round cake pan for a small batch, a 7-inch round cake pan for a medium batch, or an 8-inch round cake pan for a large batch. Scrape and spread the batter into the pan, smoothing the batter out to an even layer.
6. Set the pan in the basket and air-fry for 18 minutes for a 6-inch layer, 20 minutes for a 7-inch layer, or 22 minutes for an 8-inch layer, or until the cake is well browned and set even if there's a little soft give right at the center. Start checking it at the 16-minute mark to know where you are.
7. Use hot pads or silicone baking mitts to transfer the cake pan to a wire rack. To unmold, set a cutting board over the baking pan and invert both the board and the pan. Lift the still-warm pan off the cake layer. Set the wire rack on top of that layer and invert all of it with the cutting board so that the cake layer is now right side up on the wire rack. Remove the cutting board and continue cooling the cake for at least 10 minutes or to room temperature, about 40 minutes, before slicing into wedges.

# Cheesecake Wontons

Servings:16
Cooking Time: 6 Minutes

**Ingredients:**

- ¼ cup Regular or low-fat cream cheese (not fat-free)
- 2 tablespoons Granulated white sugar
- 1½ tablespoons Egg yolk
- ¼ teaspoon Vanilla extract
- ⅛ teaspoon Table salt
- 1½ tablespoons All-purpose flour
- 16 Wonton wrappers (vegetarian, if a concern)
- Vegetable oil spray

**Directions:**

1. Preheat the air fryer to 400°F.
2. Using a flatware fork, mash the cream cheese, sugar, egg yolk, and vanilla in a small bowl until smooth. Add the salt and flour and continue mashing until evenly combined.

3.  Set a wonton wrapper on a clean, dry work surface so that one corner faces you (so that it looks like a diamond on your work surface). Set 1 teaspoon of the cream cheese mixture in the middle of the wrapper but just above a horizontal line that would divide the wrapper in half. Dip your clean finger in water and run it along the edges of the wrapper. Fold the corner closest to you up and over the filling, lining it up with the corner farthest from you, thereby making a stuffed triangle. Press gently to seal. Wet the two triangle tips nearest you, then fold them up and together over the filling. Gently press together to seal and fuse. Set aside and continue making more stuffed wontons, 11 more for the small batch, 15 more for the medium batch, or 23 more for the large one.

4.  Lightly coat the stuffed wrappers on all sides with vegetable oil spray. Set them with the fused corners up in the basket with as much air space between them as possible. Air-fry undisturbed for 6 minutes, or until golden brown and crisp.

5.  Gently dump the contents of the basket onto a wire rack. Cool for at least 5 minutes before serving.

# Pear And Almond Biscotti Crumble

Servings: 6
Cooking Time: 65 Minutes

**Ingredients:**
- 7-inch cake pan or ceramic dish
- 3 pears, peeled, cored and sliced
- ½ cup brown sugar
- ¼ teaspoon ground ginger
- 1 teaspoon ground cinnamon
- ⅛ teaspoon ground nutmeg
- 2 tablespoons cornstarch
- 1¼ cups (4 to 5) almond biscotti, coarsely crushed
- ¼ cup all-purpose flour
- ¼ cup sliced almonds
- ¼ cup butter, melted

**Directions:**
1.  Combine the pears, brown sugar, ginger, cinnamon, nutmeg and cornstarch in a bowl. Toss to combine and then pour the pear mixture into a greased 7-inch cake pan or ceramic dish.
2.  Combine the crushed biscotti, flour, almonds and melted butter in a medium bowl. Toss with a fork until the mixture resembles large crumbles. Sprinkle the biscotti crumble over the pears and cover the pan with aluminum foil.
3.  Preheat the air fryer to 350°F.
4.  Air-fry at 350°F for 60 minutes. Remove the aluminum foil and air-fry for an additional 5 minutes to brown the crumble layer.
5.  Serve warm.

# Fried Banana S'mores

Servings: 4
Cooking Time: 6 Minutes

**Ingredients:**
- 4 bananas
- 3 tablespoons mini semi-sweet chocolate chips
- 3 tablespoons mini peanut butter chips
- 3 tablespoons mini marshmallows
- 3 tablespoons graham cracker cereal

**Directions:**
1.  Preheat the air fryer to 400°F.
2.  Slice into the un-peeled bananas lengthwise along the inside of the curve, but do not slice through the bottom of the peel. Open the banana slightly to form a pocket.

3. Fill each pocket with chocolate chips, peanut butter chips and marshmallows. Poke the graham cracker cereal into the filling.

4. Place the bananas in the air fryer basket, resting them on the side of the basket and each other to keep them upright with the filling facing up. Air-fry for 6 minutes, or until the bananas are soft to the touch, the peels have blackened and the chocolate and marshmallows have melted and toasted.

5. Let them cool for a couple of minutes and then simply serve with a spoon to scoop out the filling.

## Honey-roasted Mixed Nuts

Servings: 8
Cooking Time: 15 Minutes

**Ingredients:**
- ½ cup raw, shelled pistachios
- ½ cup raw almonds
- 1 cup raw walnuts
- 2 tablespoons filtered water
- 2 tablespoons honey
- 1 tablespoon vegetable oil
- 2 tablespoons sugar
- ½ teaspoon salt

**Directions:**
1. Preheat the air fryer to 300°F.
2. Lightly spray an air-fryer-safe pan with olive oil; then place the pistachios, almonds, and walnuts inside the pan and place the pan inside the air fryer basket.
3. Cook for 15 minutes, shaking the basket every 5 minutes to rotate the nuts.
4. While the nuts are roasting, boil the water in a small pan and stir in the honey and oil. Continue to stir while cooking until the water begins to evaporate and a thick sauce is formed.

Note: The sauce should stick to the back of a wooden spoon when mixed. Turn off the heat.

5. Remove the nuts from the air fryer (cooking should have just completed) and spoon the nuts into the stovetop pan. Use a spatula to coat the nuts with the honey syrup.

6. Line a baking sheet with parchment paper and spoon the nuts onto the sheet. Lightly sprinkle the sugar and salt over the nuts and let cool in the refrigerator for at least 2 hours.

7. When the honey and sugar have hardened, store the nuts in an airtight container in the refrigerator.

## Easy Churros

Servings: 12
Cooking Time: 10 Minutes

**Ingredients:**
- ½ cup Water
- 4 tablespoons (¼ cup/½ stick) Butter
- ¼ teaspoon Table salt
- ½ cup All-purpose flour
- 2 Large egg(s)
- ¼ cup Granulated white sugar
- 2 teaspoons Ground cinnamon

**Directions:**
1. Bring the water, butter, and salt to a boil in a small saucepan set over high heat, stirring occasionally.
2. When the butter has fully melted, reduce the heat to medium and stir in the flour to form a dough. Continue cooking, stirring constantly, to dry out the dough until it coats the bottom and sides of the pan with a film, even a crust. Remove the pan from the heat, scrape the dough into a bowl, and cool for 15 minutes.
3. Using an electric hand mixer at medium speed, beat in the egg, or eggs one at a time, until the

dough is smooth and firm enough to hold its shape.

4. Mix the sugar and cinnamon in a small bowl. Scoop up 1 tablespoon of the dough and roll it in the sugar mixture to form a small, coated tube about ½ inch in diameter and 2 inches long. Set it aside and make 5 more tubes for the small batch or 11 more for the large one.

5. Set the tubes on a plate and freeze for 20 minutes. Meanwhile, Preheat the air fryer to 375°F .

6. Set 3 frozen tubes in the basket for a small batch or 6 for a large one with as much air space between them as possible. Air-fry undisturbed for 10 minutes, or until puffed, brown, and set.

7. Use kitchen tongs to transfer the churros to a wire rack to cool for at least 5 minutes. Meanwhile, air-fry and cool the second batch of churros in the same way.

# Fried Snickers Bars

Servings:8
Cooking Time: 4 Minutes

**Ingredients:**
- ⅓ cup All-purpose flour
- 1 Large egg white(s), beaten until foamy
- 1½ cups (6 ounces) Vanilla wafer cookie crumbs
- 8 Fun-size (0.6-ounce/17-gram) Snickers bars, frozen
- Vegetable oil spray

**Directions:**
1. Preheat the air fryer to 400°F.

2. Set up and fill three shallow soup plates or small pie plates on your counter: one for the flour, one for the beaten egg white(s), and one for the cookie crumbs.

3. Unwrap the frozen candy bars. Dip one in the flour, turning it to coat on all sides. Gently shake off any excess, then set it in the beaten egg white(s). Turn it to coat all sides, even the ends, then let any excess egg white slip back into the rest. Set the candy bar in the cookie crumbs. Turn to coat on all sides, even the ends. Dip the candy bar back in the egg white(s) a second time, then into the cookie crumbs a second time, making sure you have an even coating all around. Coat the covered candy bar all over with vegetable oil spray. Set aside so you can dip and coat the remaining candy bars.

4. Set the coated candy bars in the basket with as much air space between them as possible. Air-fry undisturbed for 4 minutes, or until golden brown.

5. Remove the basket from the machine and let the candy bars cool in the basket for 10 minutes. Use a nonstick-safe spatula to transfer them to a wire rack and cool for 5 minutes more before chowing down.

# Vegetarians Recipes

## Arancini With Marinara

Servings: 6
Cooking Time: 15 Minutes

**Ingredients:**

- 2 cups cooked rice
- 1 cup grated Parmesan cheese
- 1 egg, whisked
- ¼ teaspoon dried thyme
- ½ teaspoon dried oregano
- ½ teaspoon dried basil
- ½ teaspoon dried parsley
- 1 teaspoon salt
- ¼ teaspoon paprika
- 1 cup breadcrumbs
- 4 ounces mozzarella, cut into 24 cubes
- 2 cups marinara sauce

**Directions:**

1. In a large bowl, mix together the rice, Parmesan cheese, and egg.
2. In another bowl, mix together the thyme, oregano, basil, parsley, salt, paprika, and breadcrumbs.
3. Form 24 rice balls with the rice mixture. Use your thumb to make an indentation in the center and stuff 1 cube of mozzarella in the center of the rice; close the ball around the cheese.
4. Roll the rice balls in the seasoned breadcrumbs until all are coated.
5. Preheat the air fryer to 400°F.
6. Place the rice balls in the air fryer basket and coat with cooking spray. Cook for 8 minutes, shake the basket, and cook another 7 minutes.
7. Heat the marinara sauce in a saucepan until warm. Serve sauce as a dip for arancini.

## Spicy Vegetable And Tofu Shake Fry

Servings: 4
Cooking Time: 17 Minutes

**Ingredients:**

- 4 teaspoons canola oil, divided
- 2 tablespoons rice wine vinegar
- 1 tablespoon sriracha chili sauce
- ¼ cup soy sauce*
- ½ teaspoon toasted sesame oil
- 1 teaspoon minced garlic
- 1 tablespoon minced fresh ginger
- 8 ounces extra firm tofu
- ½ cup vegetable stock or water
- 1 tablespoon honey
- 1 tablespoon cornstarch
- ½ red onion, chopped
- 1 red or yellow bell pepper, chopped
- 1 cup green beans, cut into 2-inch lengths
- 4 ounces mushrooms, sliced
- 2 scallions, sliced
- 2 tablespoons fresh cilantro leaves
- 2 teaspoons toasted sesame seeds

**Directions:**

1. Combine 1 tablespoon of the oil, vinegar, sriracha sauce, soy sauce, sesame oil, garlic and ginger in a small bowl. Cut the tofu into bite-sized cubes and toss the tofu in with the marinade while you prepare the other vegetables. When you are ready to start cooking, remove the tofu from the marinade and set it aside. Add the water, honey and cornstarch to the marinade and bring to a simmer on the stovetop, just until the sauce thickens. Set the sauce aside.
2. Preheat the air fryer to 400°F.

3. Toss the onion, pepper, green beans and mushrooms in a bowl with a little canola oil and season with salt. Air-fry at 400°F for 11 minutes, shaking the basket and tossing the vegetables every few minutes. When the vegetables are cooked to your preferred doneness, remove them from the air fryer and set aside.

4. Add the tofu to the air fryer basket and air-fry at 400°F for 6 minutes, shaking the basket a few times during the cooking process. Add the vegetables back to the basket and air-fry for another minute. Transfer the vegetables and tofu to a large bowl, add the scallions and cilantro leaves and toss with the sauce. Serve over rice with sesame seeds sprinkled on top.

# Vegetable Couscous

Servings: 4
Cooking Time: 10 Minutes

**Ingredients:**
- 4 ounces white mushrooms, sliced
- ½ medium green bell pepper, julienned
- 1 cup cubed zucchini
- ¼ small onion, slivered
- 1 stalk celery, thinly sliced
- ¼ teaspoon ground coriander
- ¼ teaspoon ground cumin
- salt and pepper
- 1 tablespoon olive oil
- Couscous
- ¾ cup uncooked couscous
- 1 cup vegetable broth or water
- ½ teaspoon salt (omit if using salted broth)

**Directions:**
1. Combine all vegetables in large bowl. Sprinkle with coriander, cumin, and salt and pepper to taste. Stir well, add olive oil, and stir again to coat vegetables evenly.

2. Place vegetables in air fryer basket and cook at 390°F for 5minutes. Stir and cook for 5 more minutes, until tender.

3. While vegetables are cooking, prepare the couscous: Place broth or water and salt in large saucepan. Heat to boiling, stir in couscous, cover, and remove from heat.

4. Let couscous sit for 5minutes, stir in cooked vegetables, and serve hot.

# Tandoori Paneer Naan Pizza

Servings: 4
Cooking Time: 10 Minutes

**Ingredients:**
- 6 tablespoons plain Greek yogurt, divided
- 1¼ teaspoons garam marsala, divided
- ½ teaspoon turmeric, divided
- ¼ teaspoon garlic powder
- ½ teaspoon paprika, divided
- ½ teaspoon black pepper, divided
- 3 ounces paneer, cut into small cubes
- 1 tablespoon extra-virgin olive oil
- 2 teaspoons minced garlic
- 4 cups baby spinach
- 2 tablespoons marinara sauce
- ¼ teaspoon salt
- 2 plain naan breads (approximately 6 inches in diameter)
- ½ cup shredded part-skim mozzarella cheese

**Directions:**
1. Preheat the air fryer to 350°F.

2. In a small bowl, mix 2 tablespoons of the yogurt, ½ teaspoon of the garam marsala, ¼ teaspoon of the turmeric, the garlic powder, ¼ teaspoon of the paprika, and ¼ teaspoon of the black pepper. Toss the paneer cubes in the mixture and let marinate for at least an hour.

3. Meanwhile, in a pan, heat the olive oil over medium heat. Add in the minced garlic and sauté

for 1 minute. Stir in the spinach and begin to cook until it wilts. Add in the remaining 4 tablespoons of yogurt and the marinara sauce. Stir in the remaining ¾ teaspoon of garam masala, the remaining ¼ teaspoon of turmeric, the remaining ¼ teaspoon of paprika, the remaining ¼ teaspoon of black pepper, and the salt. Let simmer a minute or two, and then remove from the heat.

4. Equally divide the spinach mixture amongst the two naan breads. Place 1½ ounces of the marinated paneer on each naan.

5. Liberally spray the air fryer basket with olive oil mist.

6. Use a spatula to pick up one naan and place it in the air fryer basket.

7. Cook for 4 minutes, open the basket and sprinkle ¼ cup of mozzarella cheese on top, and cook another 4 minutes.

8. Remove from the air fryer and repeat with the remaining naan.

9. Serve warm.

# Rigatoni With Roasted Onions, Fennel, Spinach And Lemon Pepper Ricotta

Servings: 2
Cooking Time: 13 Minutes

**Ingredients:**
- 1 red onion, rough chopped into large chunks
- 2 teaspoons olive oil, divided
- 1 bulb fennel, sliced ¼-inch thick
- ¾ cup ricotta cheese
- 1½ teaspoons finely chopped lemon zest, plus more for garnish
- 1 teaspoon lemon juice
- salt and freshly ground black pepper
- 8 ounces (½ pound) dried rigatoni pasta
- 3 cups baby spinach leaves

**Directions:**
1. Bring a large stockpot of salted water to a boil on the stovetop and Preheat the air fryer to 400°F.
2. While the water is coming to a boil, toss the chopped onion in 1 teaspoon of olive oil and transfer to the air fryer basket. Air-fry at 400°F for 5 minutes. Toss the sliced fennel with 1 teaspoon of olive oil and add this to the air fryer basket with the onions. Continue to air-fry at 400°F for 8 minutes, shaking the basket a few times during the cooking process.
3. Combine the ricotta cheese, lemon zest and juice, ¼ teaspoon of salt and freshly ground black pepper in a bowl and stir until smooth.
4. Add the dried rigatoni to the boiling water and cook according to the package directions. When the pasta is cooked al dente, reserve one cup of the pasta water and drain the pasta into a colander.
5. Place the spinach in a serving bowl and immediately transfer the hot pasta to the bowl, wilting the spinach. Add the roasted onions and fennel and toss together. Add a little pasta water to the dish if it needs moistening. Then, dollop the lemon pepper ricotta cheese on top and nestle it into the hot pasta. Garnish with more lemon zest if desired.

## Roasted Vegetable Lasagna

Servings: 6
Cooking Time: 55 Minutes

**Ingredients:**
- 1 zucchini, sliced
- 1 yellow squash, sliced
- 8 ounces mushrooms, sliced
- 1 red bell pepper, cut into 2-inch strips
- 1 tablespoon olive oil
- 2 cups ricotta cheese
- 2 cups grated mozzarella cheese, divided

- 1 egg
- 1 teaspoon salt
- freshly ground black pepper
- ¼ cup shredded carrots
- ½ cup chopped fresh spinach
- 8 lasagna noodles, cooked
- Béchamel Sauce:
- 3 tablespoons butter
- 3 tablespoons flour
- 2½ cups milk
- ½ cup grated Parmesan cheese
- ½ teaspoon salt
- freshly ground black pepper
- pinch of ground nutmeg

**Directions:**

1. Preheat the air fryer to 400°F.

2. Toss the zucchini, yellow squash, mushrooms and red pepper in a large bowl with the olive oil and season with salt and pepper. Air-fry for 10 minutes, shaking the basket once or twice while the vegetables cook.

3. While the vegetables are cooking, make the béchamel sauce and cheese filling. Melt the butter in a medium saucepan over medium-high heat on the stovetop. Add the flour and whisk, cooking for a couple of minutes. Add the milk and whisk vigorously until smooth. Bring the mixture to a boil and simmer until the sauce thickens. Stir in the Parmesan cheese and season with the salt, pepper and nutmeg. Set the sauce aside.

4. Combine the ricotta cheese, 1¼ cups of the mozzarella cheese, egg, salt and pepper in a large bowl and stir until combined. Fold in the carrots and spinach.

5. When the vegetables have finished cooking, build the lasagna. Use a baking dish that is 6 inches in diameter and 4 inches high. Cover the bottom of the baking dish with a little béchamel sauce. Top with two lasagna noodles, cut to fit the dish and overlapping each other a little.

Spoon a third of the ricotta cheese mixture and then a third of the roasted veggies on top of the noodles. Pour ½ cup of béchamel sauce on top and then repeat these layers two more times: noodles – cheese mixture – vegetables – béchamel sauce. Sprinkle the remaining mozzarella cheese over the top. Cover the dish with aluminum foil, tenting it loosely so the aluminum doesn't touch the cheese.

6. Lower the dish into the air fryer basket using an aluminum foil sling (fold a piece of aluminum foil into a strip about 2-inches wide by 24-inches long). Fold the ends of the aluminum foil over the top of the dish before returning the basket to the air fryer. Air-fry for 45 minutes, removing the foil for the last 2 minutes, to slightly brown the cheese on top.

7. Let the lasagna rest for at least 20 minutes to set up a little before slicing into it and serving.

## Roasted Vegetable Pita Pizza

Servings: 4
Cooking Time: 20 Minutes

**Ingredients:**
- 1 medium red bell pepper, seeded and cut into quarters
- 1 teaspoon extra-virgin olive oil
- ⅛ teaspoon black pepper
- ⅛ teaspoon salt
- Two 6-inch whole-grain pita breads
- 6 tablespoons pesto sauce
- ¼ small red onion, thinly sliced
- ½ cup shredded part-skim mozzarella cheese

**Directions:**

1. Preheat the air fryer to 400°F.

2. In a small bowl, toss the bell peppers with the olive oil, pepper, and salt.

3. Place the bell peppers in the air fryer and cook for 15 minutes, shaking every 5 minutes to prevent burning.

4. Remove the peppers and set aside. Turn the air fryer temperature down to 350°F.

5. Lay the pita bread on a flat surface. Cover each with half the pesto sauce; then top with even portions of the red bell peppers and onions. Sprinkle cheese over the top. Spray the air fryer basket with olive oil mist.

6. Carefully lift the pita bread into the air fryer basket with a spatula.

7. Cook for 5 to 8 minutes, or until the outer edges begin to brown and the cheese is melted.

8. Serve warm with desired sides.

# Veggie Fried Rice

Servings: 4
Cooking Time: 25 Minutes

**Ingredients:**
- 1 cup cooked brown rice
- ⅓ cup chopped onion
- ½ cup chopped carrots
- ½ cup chopped bell peppers
- ½ cup chopped broccoli florets
- 3 tablespoons low-sodium soy sauce
- 1 tablespoon sesame oil
- 1 teaspoon ground ginger
- 1 teaspoon ground garlic powder
- ½ teaspoon black pepper
- ⅛ teaspoon salt
- 2 large eggs

**Directions:**
1. Preheat the air fryer to 370°F.
2. In a large bowl, mix together the brown rice, onions, carrots, bell pepper, and broccoli.
3. In a small bowl, whisk together the soy sauce, sesame oil, ginger, garlic powder, pepper, salt, and eggs.

4. Pour the egg mixture into the rice and vegetable mixture and mix together.

5. Liberally spray a 7-inch springform pan (or compatible air fryer dish) with olive oil. Add the rice mixture to the pan and cover with aluminum foil.

6. Place a metal trivet into the air fryer basket and set the pan on top. Cook for 15 minutes. Carefully remove the pan from basket, discard the foil, and mix the rice. Return the rice to the air fryer basket, turning down the temperature to 350°F and cooking another 10 minutes.

7. Remove and let cool 5 minutes. Serve warm.

# Spaghetti Squash And Kale Fritters With Pomodoro Sauce

Servings: 3
Cooking Time: 45 Minutes

**Ingredients:**
- 1½-pound spaghetti squash (about half a large or a whole small squash)
- olive oil
- ½ onion, diced
- ½ red bell pepper, diced
- 2 cloves garlic, minced
- 4 cups coarsely chopped kale
- salt and freshly ground black pepper
- 1 egg
- ⅓ cup breadcrumbs, divided*
- ⅓ cup grated Parmesan cheese
- ½ teaspoon dried rubbed sage
- pinch nutmeg
- Pomodoro Sauce:
- 2 tablespoons olive oil
- ½ onion, chopped
- 1 to 2 cloves garlic, minced
- 1 (28-ounce) can peeled tomatoes
- ¼ cup red wine
- 1 teaspoon Italian seasoning

- 2 tablespoons chopped fresh basil, plus more for garnish
- salt and freshly ground black pepper
- ½ teaspoon sugar (optional)

**Directions:**

1.  Preheat the air fryer to 370°F.
2.  Cut the spaghetti squash in half lengthwise and remove the seeds. Rub the inside of the squash with olive oil and season with salt and pepper. Place the squash, cut side up, into the air fryer basket and air-fry for 30 minutes, flipping the squash over halfway through the cooking process.
3.  While the squash is cooking, Preheat a large sauté pan over medium heat on the stovetop. Add a little olive oil and sauté the onions for 3 minutes, until they start to soften. Add the red pepper and garlic and continue to sauté for an additional 4 minutes. Add the kale and season with salt and pepper. Cook for 2 more minutes, or until the kale is soft. Transfer the mixture to a large bowl and let it cool.
4.  While the squash continues to cook, make the Pomodoro sauce. Preheat the large sauté pan again over medium heat on the stovetop. Add the olive oil and sauté the onion and garlic for 2 to 3 minutes, until the onion begins to soften. Crush the canned tomatoes with your hands and add them to the pan along with the red wine and Italian seasoning and simmer for 20 minutes. Add the basil and season to taste with salt, pepper and sugar (if using).
5.  When the spaghetti squash has finished cooking, use a fork to scrape the inside flesh of the squash onto a sheet pan. Spread the squash out and let it cool.
6.  Once cool, add the spaghetti squash to the kale mixture, along with the egg, breadcrumbs, Parmesan cheese, sage, nutmeg, salt and freshly ground black pepper. Stir to combine well and then divide the mixture into 6 thick portions. You can shape the portions into patties, but I prefer to keep them a little random and unique in shape. Spray or brush the fritters with olive oil.
7.  Preheat the air fryer to 370°F.
8.  Brush the air fryer basket with a little olive oil and transfer the fritters to the basket. Air-fry the squash and kale fritters at 370°F for 15 minutes, flipping them over halfway through the cooking process.
9.  Serve the fritters warm with the Pomodoro sauce spooned over the top or pooled on your plate. Garnish with the fresh basil leaves.

# Charred Cauliflower Tacos

Servings: 4
Cooking Time: 10 Minutes

**Ingredients:**

- 1 head cauliflower, washed and cut into florets
- 2 tablespoons avocado oil
- 2 teaspoons taco seasoning
- 1 medium avocado
- ½ teaspoon garlic powder
- ¼ teaspoon black pepper
- ¼ teaspoon salt
- 2 tablespoons chopped red onion
- 2 teaspoons fresh squeezed lime juice
- ¼ cup chopped cilantro
- Eight 6-inch corn tortillas
- ½ cup cooked corn
- ½ cup shredded purple cabbage

**Directions:**

1.  Preheat the air fryer to 390°F.
2.  In a large bowl, toss the cauliflower with the avocado oil and taco seasoning. Set the metal trivet inside the air fryer basket and liberally spray with olive oil.

3. Place the cauliflower onto the trivet and cook for 10 minutes, shaking every 3 minutes to allow for an even char.

4. While the cauliflower is cooking, prepare the avocado sauce. In a medium bowl, mash the avocado; then mix in the garlic powder, pepper, salt, and onion. Stir in the lime juice and cilantro; set aside.

5. Remove the cauliflower from the air fryer basket.

6. Place 1 tablespoon of avocado sauce in the middle of a tortilla, and top with corn, cabbage, and charred cauliflower. Repeat with the remaining tortillas. Serve immediately.

# Falafel

Servings: 4
Cooking Time: 10 Minutes

**Ingredients:**
- 1 cup dried chickpeas
- ½ onion, chopped
- 1 clove garlic
- ¼ cup fresh parsley leaves
- 1 teaspoon salt
- ¼ teaspoon crushed red pepper flakes
- 1 teaspoon ground cumin
- ½ teaspoon ground coriander
- 1 to 2 tablespoons flour
- olive oil
- Tomato Salad
- 2 tomatoes, seeds removed and diced
- ½ cucumber, finely diced
- ¼ red onion, finely diced and rinsed with water
- 1 teaspoon red wine vinegar
- 1 tablespoon olive oil
- salt and freshly ground black pepper
- 2 tablespoons chopped fresh parsley

**Directions:**

1. Cover the chickpeas with water and let them soak overnight on the counter. Then drain the chickpeas and put them in a food processor, along with the onion, garlic, parsley, spices and 1 tablespoon of flour. Pulse in the food processor until the mixture has broken down into a coarse paste consistency. The mixture should hold together when you pinch it. Add more flour as needed, until you get this consistency.

2. Scoop portions of the mixture (about 2 tablespoons in size) and shape into balls. Place the balls on a plate and refrigerate for at least 30 minutes. You should have between 12 and 14 balls.

3. Preheat the air fryer to 380°F.

4. Spray the falafel balls with oil and place them in the air fryer. Air-fry for 10 minutes, rolling them over and spraying them with oil again halfway through the cooking time so that they cook and brown evenly.

5. Serve with pita bread, hummus, cucumbers, hot peppers, tomatoes or any other fillings you might like.

# Parmesan Portobello Mushroom Caps

Servings: 2
Cooking Time: 14 Minutes

**Ingredients:**
- ¼ cup flour*
- 1 egg, lightly beaten
- 1 cup seasoned breadcrumbs*
- 2 large portobello mushroom caps, stems and gills removed
- olive oil, in a spray bottle
- ½ cup tomato sauce
- ¾ cup grated mozzarella cheese
- 1 tablespoon grated Parmesan cheese
- 1 tablespoon chopped fresh basil or parsley

**Directions:**

1. Set up a dredging station with three shallow dishes. Place the flour in the first shallow dish, egg in the second dish and breadcrumbs in the last dish. Dredge the mushrooms in flour, then dip them into the egg and finally press them into the breadcrumbs to coat on all sides. Spray both sides of the coated mushrooms with olive oil.

2. Preheat the air fryer to 400°F.

3. Air-fry the mushrooms at 400°F for 10 minutes, turning them over halfway through the cooking process.

4. Fill the underside of the mushrooms with the tomato sauce and then top the sauce with the mozzarella and Parmesan cheeses. Reset the air fryer temperature to 350°F and air-fry for an additional 4 minutes, until the cheese has melted and is slightly browned.

5. Serve the mushrooms with pasta tossed with tomato sauce and garnish with some chopped fresh basil or parsley.

# Quinoa Burgers With Feta Cheese And Dill

Servings: 6
Cooking Time: 10 Minutes

**Ingredients:**
- 1 cup quinoa (red, white or multi-colored)
- 1½ cups water
- 1 teaspoon salt
- freshly ground black pepper
- 1½ cups rolled oats
- 3 eggs, lightly beaten
- ¼ cup minced white onion
- ½ cup crumbled feta cheese
- ¼ cup chopped fresh dill
- salt and freshly ground black pepper
- vegetable or canola oil, in a spray bottle

- whole-wheat hamburger buns (or gluten-free hamburger buns*)
- arugula
- tomato, sliced
- red onion, sliced
- mayonnaise

**Directions:**

1. Make the quinoa: Rinse the quinoa in cold water in a saucepan, swirling it with your hand until any dry husks rise to the surface. Drain the quinoa as well as you can and then put the saucepan on the stovetop to dry and toast the quinoa. Turn the heat to medium-high and shake the pan regularly until you see the quinoa moving easily and can hear the seeds moving in the pan, indicating that they are dry. Add the water, salt and pepper. Bring the liquid to a boil and then reduce the heat to low or medium-low. You should see just a few bubbles, not a boil. Cover with a lid, leaving it askew and simmer for 20 minutes. Turn the heat off and fluff the quinoa with a fork. If there's any liquid left in the bottom of the pot, place it back on the burner for another 3 minutes or so. Spread the cooked quinoa out on a sheet pan to cool.

2. Combine the room temperature quinoa in a large bowl with the oats, eggs, onion, cheese and dill. Season with salt and pepper and mix well (remember that feta cheese is salty). Shape the mixture into 6 patties with flat sides (so they fit more easily into the air fryer). Add a little water or a few more rolled oats if necessary to get the mixture to be the right consistency to make patties.

3. Preheat the air-fryer to 400°F.

4. Spray both sides of the patties generously with oil and transfer them to the air fryer basket in one layer (you will probably have to cook these burgers in batches, depending on the size of your air fryer). Air-fry each batch at 400°F for 10

minutes, flipping the burgers over halfway through the cooking time.

5. Build your burger on the whole-wheat hamburger buns with arugula, tomato, red onion and mayonnaise.

# Basic Fried Tofu

Servings: 4
Cooking Time: 17 Minutes

**Ingredients:**

- 14 ounces extra-firm tofu, drained and pressed
- 1 tablespoon sesame oil
- 2 tablespoons low-sodium soy sauce
- ¼ cup rice vinegar
- 1 tablespoon fresh grated ginger
- 1 clove garlic, minced
- 3 tablespoons cornstarch
- ¼ teaspoon black pepper
- ⅛ teaspoon salt

**Directions:**

1. Cut the tofu into 16 cubes. Set aside in a glass container with a lid.
2. In a medium bowl, mix the sesame oil, soy sauce, rice vinegar, ginger, and garlic. Pour over the tofu and secure the lid. Place in the refrigerator to marinate for an hour.
3. Preheat the air fryer to 350°F.
4. In a small bowl, mix the cornstarch, black pepper, and salt.
5. Transfer the tofu to a large bowl and discard the leftover marinade. Pour the cornstarch mixture over the tofu and toss until all the pieces are coated.
6. Liberally spray the air fryer basket with olive oil mist and set the tofu pieces inside. Allow space between the tofu so it can cook evenly. Cook in batches if necessary.

7. Cook 15 to 17 minutes, shaking the basket every 5 minutes to allow the tofu to cook evenly on all sides. When it's done cooking, the tofu will be crisped and browned on all sides.
8. Remove the tofu from the air fryer basket and serve warm.

# Mexican Twice Air-fried Sweet Potatoes

Servings: 2
Cooking Time: 42 Minutes

**Ingredients:**

- 2 large sweet potatoes
- olive oil
- salt and freshly ground black pepper
- ⅓ cup diced red onion
- ⅓ cup diced red bell pepper
- ½ cup canned black beans, drained and rinsed
- ½ cup corn kernels, fresh or frozen
- ½ teaspoon chili powder
- 1½ cups grated pepper jack cheese, divided
- Jalapeño peppers, sliced

**Directions:**

1. Preheat the air fryer to 400°F.
2. Rub the outside of the sweet potatoes with olive oil and season with salt and freshly ground black pepper. Transfer the potatoes into the air fryer basket and air-fry at 400°F for 30 minutes, rotating the potatoes a few times during the cooking process.
3. While the potatoes are air-frying, start the potato filling. Preheat a large sauté pan over medium heat on the stovetop. Add the onion and pepper and sauté for a few minutes, until the vegetables start to soften. Add the black beans, corn, and chili powder and sauté for another 3 minutes. Set the mixture aside.
4. Remove the sweet potatoes from the air fryer and let them rest for 5 minutes. Slice off one inch

of the flattest side of both potatoes. Scrape the potato flesh out of the potatoes, leaving half an inch of potato flesh around the edge of the potato. Place all the potato flesh into a large bowl and mash it with a fork. Add the black bean mixture and 1 cup of the pepper jack cheese to the mashed sweet potatoes. Season with salt and freshly ground black pepper and mix well. Stuff the hollowed out potato shells with the black bean and sweet potato mixture, mounding the filling high in the potatoes.

5. Transfer the stuffed potatoes back into the air fryer basket and air-fry at 370°F for 10 minutes. Sprinkle the remaining cheese on top of each stuffed potato, lower the heat to 340°F and air-fry for an additional 2 minutes to melt the cheese. Top with a couple slices of Jalapeño pepper and serve warm with a green salad.

# Roasted Vegetable Thai Green Curry

Servings: 4
Cooking Time: 16 Minutes

### Ingredients:

- 1 (13-ounce) can coconut milk
- 3 tablespoons green curry paste
- 1 tablespoon soy sauce*
- 1 tablespoon rice wine vinegar
- 1 teaspoon sugar
- 1 teaspoon minced fresh ginger
- ½ onion, chopped
- 3 carrots, sliced
- 1 red bell pepper, chopped
- olive oil
- 10 stalks of asparagus, cut into 2-inch pieces
- 3 cups broccoli florets
- basmati rice for serving
- fresh cilantro
- crushed red pepper flakes (optional)

**Directions:**

1. Combine the coconut milk, green curry paste, soy sauce, rice wine vinegar, sugar and ginger in a medium saucepan and bring to a boil on the stovetop. Reduce the heat and simmer for 20 minutes while you cook the vegetables. Set aside.

2. Preheat the air fryer to 400°F.

3. Toss the onion, carrots, and red pepper together with a little olive oil and transfer the vegetables to the air fryer basket. Air-fry at 400°F for 10 minutes, shaking the basket a few times during the cooking process. Add the asparagus and broccoli florets and air-fry for an additional 6 minutes, again shaking the basket for even cooking.

4. When the vegetables are cooked to your liking, toss them with the green curry sauce and serve in bowls over basmati rice. Garnish with fresh chopped cilantro and crushed red pepper flakes.

# Egg Rolls

Servings: 4
Cooking Time: 8 Minutes

### Ingredients:

- 1 clove garlic, minced
- 1 teaspoon sesame oil
- 1 teaspoon olive oil
- ½ cup chopped celery
- ½ cup grated carrots
- 2 green onions, chopped
- 2 ounces mushrooms, chopped
- 2 cups shredded Napa cabbage
- 1 teaspoon low-sodium soy sauce
- 1 teaspoon cornstarch
- salt
- 1 egg
- 1 tablespoon water
- 4 egg roll wraps
- olive oil for misting or cooking spray

**Directions:**

1. In a large skillet, sauté garlic in sesame and olive oils over medium heat for 1 minute.
2. Add celery, carrots, onions, and mushrooms to skillet. Cook 1 minute, stirring.
3. Stir in cabbage, cover, and cook for 1 minute or just until cabbage slightly wilts.
4. In a small bowl, mix soy sauce and cornstarch. Stir into vegetables to thicken. Remove from heat. Salt to taste if needed.
5. Beat together egg and water in a small bowl.
6. Divide filling into 4 portions and roll up in egg roll wraps. Brush all over with egg wash to seal.
7. Mist egg rolls very lightly with olive oil or cooking spray and place in air fryer basket.
8. Cook at 390°F for 4minutes. Turn over and cook 4 more minutes, until golden brown and crispy.

# Lentil Fritters

Servings: 9
Cooking Time: 12 Minutes

**Ingredients:**

- 1 cup cooked red lentils
- 1 cup riced cauliflower
- ½ medium zucchini, shredded (about 1 cup)
- ¼ cup finely chopped onion
- ¼ teaspoon salt
- ¼ teaspoon black pepper
- ½ teaspoon garlic powder
- ¼ teaspoon paprika
- 1 large egg
- ⅓ cup quinoa flour

**Directions:**

1. Preheat the air fryer to 370°F.
2. In a large bowl, mix the lentils, cauliflower, zucchini, onion, salt, pepper, garlic powder, and paprika. Mix in the egg and flour until a thick dough forms.
3. Using a large spoon, form the dough into 9 large fritters.
4. Liberally spray the air fryer basket with olive oil. Place the fritters into the basket, leaving space around each fritter so you can flip them.
5. Cook for 6 minutes, flip, and cook another 6 minutes.
6. Remove from the air fryer and repeat with the remaining fritters. Serve warm with desired sauce and sides.

# Eggplant Parmesan

Servings: 4
Cooking Time: 8 Minutes Per Batch

**Ingredients:**

- 1 medium eggplant, 6–8 inches long
- salt
- 1 large egg
- 1 tablespoon water
- ⅔ cup panko breadcrumbs
- ⅓ cup grated Parmesan cheese, plus more for serving
- 1 tablespoon Italian seasoning
- ¾ teaspoon oregano
- oil for misting or cooking spray
- 1 24-ounce jar marinara sauce
- 8 ounces spaghetti, cooked
- pepper

**Directions:**

1. Preheat air fryer to 390°F.
2. Leaving peel intact, cut eggplant into 8 round slices about ¾-inch thick. Salt to taste.
3. Beat egg and water in a shallow dish.
4. In another shallow dish, combine panko, Parmesan, Italian seasoning, and oregano.
5. Dip eggplant slices in egg wash and then crumbs, pressing lightly to coat.

6. Mist slices with oil or cooking spray.

7. Place 4 eggplant slices in air fryer basket and cook for 8 minutes, until brown and crispy.

8. While eggplant is cooking, heat marinara sauce.

9. Repeat step 7 to cook remaining eggplant slices.

10. To serve, place cooked spaghetti on plates and top with marinara and eggplant slices. At the table, pass extra Parmesan cheese and freshly ground black pepper.

# Broccoli Cheddar Stuffed Potatoes

Servings: 2
Cooking Time: 42 Minutes

**Ingredients:**
- 2 large russet potatoes, scrubbed
- 1 tablespoon olive oil
- salt and freshly ground black pepper
- 2 tablespoons butter
- ¼ cup sour cream
- 3 tablespoons half-and-half (or milk)
- 1¼ cups grated Cheddar cheese, divided
- ¾ teaspoon salt
- freshly ground black pepper
- 1 cup frozen baby broccoli florets, thawed and drained

**Directions:**
1. Preheat the air fryer to 400°F.

2. Rub the potatoes all over with olive oil and season generously with salt and freshly ground black pepper. Transfer the potatoes into the air fryer basket and air-fry for 30 minutes, turning the potatoes over halfway through the cooking process.

3. Remove the potatoes from the air fryer and let them rest for 5 minutes. Cut a large oval out of the top of both potatoes. Leaving half an inch of potato flesh around the edge of the potato, scoop the inside of the potato out and into a large bowl to prepare the potato filling. Mash the scooped potato filling with a fork and add the butter, sour cream, half-and-half, 1 cup of the grated Cheddar cheese, salt and pepper to taste. Mix well and then fold in the broccoli florets.

4. Stuff the hollowed out potato shells with the potato and broccoli mixture. Mound the filling high in the potatoes – you will have more filling than room in the potato shells.

5. Transfer the stuffed potatoes back to the air fryer basket and air-fry at 360°F for 10 minutes. Sprinkle the remaining Cheddar cheese on top of each stuffed potato, lower the heat to 330°F and air-fry for an additional minute or two to melt cheese.

# Roasted Vegetable, Brown Rice And Black Bean Burrito

Servings: 2
Cooking Time: 20 Minutes

**Ingredients:**
- ½ zucchini, sliced ¼-inch thick
- ½ red onion, sliced
- 1 yellow bell pepper, sliced
- 2 teaspoons olive oil
- salt and freshly ground black pepper
- 2 burrito size flour tortillas
- 1 cup grated pepper jack cheese
- ½ cup cooked brown rice
- ½ cup canned black beans, drained and rinsed
- ¼ teaspoon ground cumin
- 1 tablespoon chopped fresh cilantro
- fresh salsa, guacamole and sour cream, for serving

**Directions:**
1. Preheat the air fryer to 400°F.

2. Toss the vegetables in a bowl with the olive oil, salt and freshly ground black pepper. Air-fry at 400°F for 12 to 15 minutes, shaking the basket a few times during the cooking process. The vegetables are done when they are cooked to your liking.

3. In the meantime, start building the burritos. Lay the tortillas out on the counter. Sprinkle half of the cheese in the center of the tortillas. Combine the rice, beans, cumin and cilantro in a bowl, season to taste with salt and freshly ground black pepper and then divide the mixture between the two tortillas. When the vegetables have finished cooking, transfer them to the two tortillas, placing the vegetables on top of the rice and beans. Sprinkle the remaining cheese on top and then roll the burritos up, tucking in the sides of the tortillas as you roll. Brush or spray the outside of the burritos with olive oil and transfer them to the air fryer.

4. Air-fry at 360°F for 8 minutes, turning them over when there are about 2 minutes left. The burritos will have slightly brown spots, but will still be pliable.

5. Serve with some fresh salsa, guacamole and sour cream.

# Black Bean Empanadas

Servings: 12
Cooking Time: 35 Minutes

**Ingredients:**
- 1½ cups all-purpose flour
- 1 cup whole-wheat flour
- 1 teaspoon salt
- ½ cup cold unsalted butter
- 1 egg
- ½ cup milk
- One 14.5-ounce can black beans, drained and rinsed
- ¼ cup chopped cilantro
- 1 cup shredded purple cabbage
- 1 cup shredded Monterey jack cheese
- ¼ cup salsa

**Directions:**
1. In a food processor, place the all-purpose flour, whole-wheat flour, salt, and butter into processor and process for 2 minutes, scraping down the sides of the food processor every 30 seconds. Add in the egg and blend for 30 seconds. Using the pulse button, add in the milk 1 tablespoon at a time, or until dough is moist enough to handle and be rolled into a ball. Let the dough rest at room temperature for 30 minutes.

2. Meanwhile, in a large bowl, mix together the black beans, cilantro, cabbage, Monterey Jack cheese, and salsa.

3. On a floured surface, cut the dough in half; then form a ball and cut each ball into 6 equal pieces, totaling 12 equal pieces. Work with one piece at a time, and cover the remaining dough with a towel.

4. Roll out a piece of dough into a 6-inch round, much like a tortilla, ¼ inch thick. Place 4 tablespoons of filling in the center of the round, and fold over to form a half-circle. Using a fork, crimp the edges together and pierce the top for air holes. Repeat with the remaining dough and filling.

5. Preheat the air fryer to 350°F.

6. Working in batches, place 3 to 4 empanadas in the air fryer basket and spray with cooking spray. Cook for 4 minutes, flip over the empanadas and spray with cooking spray, and cook another 4 minutes.

# Roasted Vegetable Stromboli

Servings: 2
Cooking Time: 29 Minutes

**Ingredients:**
- ½ onion, thinly sliced
- ½ red pepper, julienned
- ½ yellow pepper, julienned
- olive oil
- 1 small zucchini, thinly sliced
- 1 cup thinly sliced mushrooms
- 1½ cups chopped broccoli
- 1 teaspoon Italian seasoning
- salt and freshly ground black pepper
- ½ recipe of Blue Jean Chef Pizza dough (page 231) OR 1 (14-ounce) tube refrigerated pizza dough
- 2 cups grated mozzarella cheese
- ¼ cup grated Parmesan cheese
- ½ cup sliced black olives, optional
- dried oregano
- pizza or marinara sauce

**Directions:**
1. Preheat the air fryer to 400°F.
2. Toss the onions and peppers with a little olive oil and air-fry the vegetables for 7 minutes, shaking the basket once or twice while the vegetables cook. Add the zucchini, mushrooms, broccoli and Italian seasoning to the basket. Add a little more olive oil and season with salt and freshly ground black pepper. Air-fry for an additional 7 minutes, shaking the basket halfway through. Let the vegetables cool slightly while you roll out the pizza dough.
3. On a lightly floured surface, roll or press the pizza dough out into a 13-inch by 11-inch rectangle, with the long side closest to you. Sprinkle half of the mozzarella and Parmesan cheeses over the dough leaving an empty 1-inch border from the edge farthest away from you.

Spoon the roasted vegetables over the cheese, sprinkle the olives over everything and top with the remaining cheese.
4. Start rolling the stromboli away from you and toward the empty border. Make sure the filling stays tightly tucked inside the roll. Finally, tuck the ends of the dough in and pinch the seam shut. Place the seam side down and shape the stromboli into a U-shape to fit into the air fryer basket. Cut 4 small slits with the tip of a sharp knife evenly in the top of the dough, lightly brush the stromboli with a little oil and sprinkle with some dried oregano.
5. Preheat the air fryer to 360°F.
6. Spray or brush the air fryer basket with oil and transfer the U-shaped stromboli to the air fryer basket. Air-fry for 15 minutes, flipping the stromboli over after the first 10 minutes. (Use a plate to invert the Stromboli out of the air fryer basket and then slide it back into the basket off the plate.)
7. To remove, carefully flip the stromboli over onto a cutting board. Let it rest for a couple of minutes before serving. Cut it into 2-inch slices and serve with pizza or marinara sauce.

# Vegetable Hand Pies

Servings: 8
Cooking Time: 10 Minutes Per Batch

**Ingredients:**
- ¾ cup vegetable broth
- 8 ounces potatoes
- ¾ cup frozen chopped broccoli, thawed
- ¼ cup chopped mushrooms
- 1 tablespoon cornstarch
- 1 tablespoon milk
- 1 can organic flaky biscuits (8 large biscuits)
- oil for misting or cooking spray

**Directions:**

1. Place broth in medium saucepan over low heat.

2. While broth is heating, grate raw potato into a bowl of water to prevent browning. You will need ¾ cup grated potato.

3. Roughly chop the broccoli.

4. Drain potatoes and put them in the broth along with the broccoli and mushrooms. Cook on low for 5 minutes.

5. Dissolve cornstarch in milk, then stir the mixture into the broth. Cook about a minute, until mixture thickens a little. Remove from heat and cool slightly.

6. Separate each biscuit into 2 rounds. Divide vegetable mixture evenly over half the biscuit rounds, mounding filling in the center of each.

7. Top the four rounds with filling, then the other four rounds and crimp the edges together with a fork.

8. Spray both sides with oil or cooking spray and place 4 pies in a single layer in the air fryer basket.

9. Cook at 330°F for approximately 10 minutes.

10. Repeat with the remaining biscuits. The second batch may cook more quickly because the fryer will be hot.

# Thai Peanut Veggie Burgers

Servings: 6
Cooking Time: 14 Minutes

**Ingredients:**
- One 15.5-ounce can cannellini beans
- 1 teaspoon minced garlic
- ¼ cup chopped onion
- 1 Thai chili pepper, sliced
- 2 tablespoons natural peanut butter
- ½ teaspoon black pepper
- ½ teaspoon salt
- ⅓ cup all-purpose flour (optional)
- ½ cup cooked quinoa
- 1 large carrot, grated
- 1 cup shredded red cabbage
- ¼ cup peanut dressing
- ¼ cup chopped cilantro
- 6 Hawaiian rolls
- 6 butterleaf lettuce leaves

**Directions:**
1. Preheat the air fryer to 350°F.

2. To a blender or food processor fitted with a metal blade, add the beans, garlic, onion, chili pepper, peanut butter, pepper, and salt. Pulse for 5 to 10 seconds. Do not over process. The mixture should be coarse, not smooth.

3. Remove from the blender or food processor and spoon into a large bowl. Mix in the cooked quinoa and carrots. At this point, the mixture should begin to hold together to form small patties. If the dough appears to be too sticky (meaning you likely processed a little too long), add the flour to hold the patties together.

4. Using a large spoon, form 8 equal patties out of the batter.

5. Liberally spray a metal trivet with olive oil spray and set in the air fryer basket. Place the patties into the basket, leaving enough space to be able to turn them with a spatula.

6. Cook for 7 minutes, flip, and cook another 7 minutes.

7. Remove from the heat and repeat with additional patties.

8. To serve, place the red cabbage in a bowl and toss with peanut dressing and cilantro. Place the veggie burger on a bun, and top with a slice of lettuce and cabbage slaw.

# Corn And Pepper Jack Chile Rellenos With Roasted Tomato Sauce

Servings: 3
Cooking Time: 30 Minutes

**Ingredients:**
- 3 Poblano peppers
- 1 cup all-purpose flour*
- salt and freshly ground black pepper
- 2 eggs, lightly beaten
- 1 cup plain breadcrumbs*
- olive oil, in a spray bottle
- Sauce
- 2 cups cherry tomatoes
- 1 Jalapeño pepper, halved and seeded
- 1 clove garlic
- ¼ red onion, broken into large pieces
- 1 tablespoon olive oil
- salt, to taste
- 2 tablespoons chopped fresh cilantro
- Filling
- olive oil
- ¼ red onion, finely chopped
- 1 teaspoon minced garlic
- 1 cup corn kernels, fresh or frozen
- 2 cups grated pepper jack cheese

**Directions:**

1. Start by roasting the peppers. Preheat the air fryer to 400°F. Place the peppers into the air fryer basket and air-fry at 400°F for 10 minutes, turning them over halfway through the cooking time. Remove the peppers from the basket and cover loosely with foil.

2. While the peppers are cooling, make the roasted tomato sauce. Place all sauce Ingredients except for the cilantro into the air fryer basket and air-fry at 400°F for 10 minutes, shaking the basket once or twice. When the sauce Ingredients have finished air-frying, transfer everything to a blender or food processor and blend or process to a smooth sauce, adding a little warm water to get the desired consistency. Season to taste with salt, add the cilantro and set aside.

3. While the sauce Ingredients are cooking in the air fryer, make the filling. Heat a skillet on the stovetop over medium heat. Add the olive oil and sauté the red onion and garlic for 4 to 5 minutes. Transfer the onion and garlic to a bowl, stir in the corn and cheese, and set aside.

4. Set up a dredging station with three shallow dishes. Place the flour, seasoned with salt and pepper, in the first shallow dish. Place the eggs in the second dish, and fill the third shallow dish with the breadcrumbs. When the peppers have cooled, carefully slice into one side of the pepper to create an opening. Pull the seeds out of the peppers and peel away the skins, trying not to tear the pepper. Fill each pepper with some of the corn and cheese filling and close the pepper up again by folding one side of the opening over the other. Carefully roll each pepper in the seasoned flour, then into the egg and finally into the breadcrumbs to coat on all sides, trying not to let the pepper fall open. Spray the peppers on all sides with a little olive oil.

5. Air-fry two peppers at a time at 350°F for 6 minutes. Turn the peppers over and air-fry for another 4 minutes. Serve the peppers warm on a bed of the roasted tomato sauce.

# Spicy Sesame Tempeh Slaw With Peanut Dressing

Servings: 2
Cooking Time: 8 Minutes

**Ingredients:**
- 2 cups hot water
- 1 teaspoon salt
- 8 ounces tempeh, sliced into 1-inch-long pieces
- 2 tablespoons low-sodium soy sauce
- 2 tablespoons rice vinegar
- 1 tablespoon filtered water
- 2 teaspoons sesame oil
- ½ teaspoon fresh ginger
- 1 clove garlic, minced
- ¼ teaspoon black pepper
- ½ jalapeño, sliced
- 4 cups cabbage slaw
- 4 tablespoons Peanut Dressing (see the following recipe)
- 2 tablespoons fresh chopped cilantro
- 2 tablespoons chopped peanuts

**Directions:**
1. Mix the hot water with the salt and pour over the tempeh in a glass bowl. Stir and cover with a towel for 10 minutes.
2. Discard the water and leave the tempeh in the bowl.
3. In a medium bowl, mix the soy sauce, rice vinegar, filtered water, sesame oil, ginger, garlic, pepper, and jalapeño. Pour over the tempeh and cover with a towel. Place in the refrigerator to marinate for at least 2 hours.
4. Preheat the air fryer to 370°F. Remove the tempeh from the bowl and discard the remaining marinade.
5. Liberally spray the metal trivet that goes into the air fryer basket and place the tempeh on top of the trivet.
6. Cook for 4 minutes, flip, and cook another 4 minutes.
7. In a large bowl, mix the cabbage slaw with the Peanut Dressing and toss in the cilantro and chopped peanuts.
8. Portion onto 4 plates and place the cooked tempeh on top when cooking completes. Serve immediately.

# Tacos

Servings: 24
Cooking Time: 8 Minutes Per Batch

**Ingredients:**
- 1 24-count package 4-inch corn tortillas
- 1½ cups refried beans (about ¾ of a 15-ounce can)
- 4 ounces sharp Cheddar cheese, grated
- ½ cup salsa
- oil for misting or cooking spray

**Directions:**
1. Preheat air fryer to 390°F.
2. Wrap refrigerated tortillas in damp paper towels and microwave for 30 to 60 seconds to warm. If necessary, rewarm tortillas as you go to keep them soft enough to fold without breaking.
3. Working with one tortilla at a time, top with 1 tablespoon of beans, 1 tablespoon of grated cheese, and 1 teaspoon of salsa. Fold over and press down very gently on the center. Press edges firmly all around to seal. Spray both sides with oil or cooking spray.
4. Cooking in two batches, place half the tacos in the air fryer basket. To cook 12 at a time, you may need to stand them upright and lean some against the sides of basket. It's okay if they're

crowded as long as you leave a little room for air to circulate around them.

5. Cook for 8 minutes or until golden brown and crispy.

6. Repeat steps 4 and 5 to cook remaining tacos.

# Veggie Burgers

Servings: 4
Cooking Time: 15 Minutes

**Ingredients:**

- 2 cans black beans, rinsed and drained
- ½ cup cooked quinoa
- ½ cup shredded raw sweet potato
- ¼ cup diced red onion
- 2 teaspoons ground cumin
- 1 teaspoon coriander powder
- ½ teaspoon salt
- oil for misting or cooking spray
- 8 slices bread
- suggested toppings: lettuce, tomato, red onion, Pepper Jack cheese, guacamole

**Directions:**

1. In a medium bowl, mash the beans with a fork.

2. Add the quinoa, sweet potato, onion, cumin, coriander, and salt and mix well with the fork.

3. Shape into 4 patties, each ¾-inch thick.

4. Mist both sides with oil or cooking spray and also mist the basket.

5. Cook at 390°F for 15minutes.

6. Follow the recipe for Toast, Plain & Simple.

7. Pop the veggie burgers back in the air fryer for a minute or two to reheat if necessary.

8. Serve on the toast with your favorite burger toppings.

# Stuffed Zucchini Boats

Servings: 2
Cooking Time: 20 Minutes

**Ingredients:**

- olive oil
- ½ cup onion, finely chopped
- 1 clove garlic, finely minced
- ½ teaspoon dried oregano
- ¼ teaspoon dried thyme
- ¾ cup couscous
- 1½ cups chicken stock, divided
- 1 tomato, seeds removed and finely chopped
- ½ cup coarsely chopped Kalamata olives
- ½ cup grated Romano cheese
- ¼ cup pine nuts, toasted
- 1 tablespoon chopped fresh parsley
- 1 teaspoon salt
- freshly ground black pepper
- 1 egg, beaten
- 1 cup grated mozzarella cheese, divided
- 2 thick zucchini

**Directions:**

1. Preheat a sauté pan on the stovetop over medium-high heat. Add the olive oil and sauté the onion until it just starts to soften–about 4 minutes. Stir in the garlic, dried oregano and thyme. Add the couscous and sauté for just a minute. Add 1¼ cups of the chicken stock and simmer over low heat for 3 to 5 minutes, until liquid has been absorbed and the couscous is soft. Remove the pan from heat and set it aside to cool slightly.

2. Fluff the couscous and add the tomato, Kalamata olives, Romano cheese, pine nuts, parsley, salt and pepper. Mix well. Add the remaining chicken stock, the egg and ½ cup of the mozzarella cheese. Stir to ensure everything is combined.

3. Cut each zucchini in half lengthwise. Then, trim each half of the zucchini into four 5-inch lengths. (Save the trimmed ends of the zucchini for another use.) Use a spoon to scoop out the center of the zucchini, leaving some flesh around

the sides. Brush both sides of the zucchini with olive oil and season the cut side with salt and pepper.

4. Preheat the air fryer to 380°F.

5. Divide the couscous filling between the four zucchini boats. Use your hands to press the filling together and fill the inside of the zucchini. The filling should be mounded into the boats and rounded on top.

6. Transfer the zucchini boats to the air fryer basket and drizzle the stuffed zucchini boats with olive oil. Air-fry for 19 minutes. Then, sprinkle the remaining mozzarella cheese on top of the zucchini, pressing it down onto the filling lightly to prevent it from blowing around in the air fryer. Air-fry for one more minute to melt the cheese. Transfer the finished zucchini boats to a serving platter and garnish with the chopped parsley.

# Sandwiches And Burgers Recipes

## Best-ever Roast Beef Sandwiches

Servings: 6
Cooking Time: 30-50 Minutes

**Ingredients:**
- 2½ teaspoons Olive oil
- 1½ teaspoons Dried oregano
- 1½ teaspoons Dried thyme
- 1½ teaspoons Onion powder
- 1½ teaspoons Table salt
- 1½ teaspoons Ground black pepper
- 3 pounds Beef eye of round
- 6 Round soft rolls, such as Kaiser rolls or hamburger buns (gluten-free, if a concern), split open lengthwise
- ¾ cup Regular, low-fat, or fat-free mayonnaise (gluten-free, if a concern)
- 6 Romaine lettuce leaves, rinsed
- 6 Round tomato slices (¼ inch thick)

**Directions:**
1. Preheat the air fryer to 350°F .
2. Mix the oil, oregano, thyme, onion powder, salt, and pepper in a small bowl. Spread this mixture all over the eye of round.
3. When the machine is at temperature, set the beef in the basket and air-fry for 30 to 50 minutes (the range depends on the size of the cut), turning the meat twice, until an instant-read meat thermometer inserted into the thickest piece of the meat registers 130°F for rare, 140°F for medium, or 150°F for well-done.
4. Use kitchen tongs to transfer the beef to a cutting board. Cool for 10 minutes. If serving now, carve into ⅛-inch-thick slices. Spread each roll with 2 tablespoons mayonnaise and divide the beef slices between the rolls. Top with a lettuce leaf and a tomato slice and serve. Or set the beef in a container, cover, and refrigerate for up to 3 days to make cold roast beef sandwiches anytime.

## Black Bean Veggie Burgers

Servings: 3
Cooking Time: 10 Minutes

**Ingredients:**
- 1 cup Drained and rinsed canned black beans
- ⅓ cup Pecan pieces
- ⅓ cup Rolled oats (not quick-cooking or steel-cut; gluten-free, if a concern)
- 2 tablespoons (or 1 small egg) Pasteurized egg substitute, such as Egg Beaters (gluten-free, if a concern)
- 2 teaspoons Red ketchup-like chili sauce, such as Heinz
- ¼ teaspoon Ground cumin
- ¼ teaspoon Dried oregano
- ¼ teaspoon Table salt
- ¼ teaspoon Ground black pepper
- Olive oil
- Olive oil spray

**Directions:**
1. Preheat the air fryer to 400°F.
2. Put the beans, pecans, oats, egg substitute or egg, chili sauce, cumin, oregano, salt, and pepper in a food processor. Cover and process to a coarse paste that will hold its shape like sugar-cookie dough, adding olive oil in 1-teaspoon increments to get the mixture to blend smoothly. The amount of olive oil is actually dependent on the internal moisture content of the beans and the oats. Figure on about 1 tablespoon (three 1-teaspoon additions) for the smaller batch, with proportional increases for the other batches. A little too much olive oil can't hurt, but a dry paste

will fall apart as it cooks and a far-too-wet paste will stick to the basket.

3. Scrape down and remove the blade. Using clean, wet hands, form the paste into two 4-inch patties for the small batch, three 4-inch patties for the medium, or four 4-inch patties for the large batch, setting them one by one on a cutting board. Generously coat both sides of the patties with olive oil spray.

4. Set them in the basket in one layer. Air-fry undisturbed for 10 minutes, or until lightly browned and crisp at the edges.

5. Use a nonstick-safe spatula, and perhaps a flatware fork for balance, to transfer the burgers to a wire rack. Cool for 5 minutes before serving.

# Asian Glazed Meatballs

Servings: 4
Cooking Time: 10 Minutes

**Ingredients:**
- 1 large shallot, finely chopped
- 2 cloves garlic, minced
- 1 tablespoon grated fresh ginger
- 2 teaspoons fresh thyme, finely chopped
- 1½ cups brown mushrooms, very finely chopped (a food processor works well here)
- 2 tablespoons soy sauce
- freshly ground black pepper
- 1 pound ground beef
- ½ pound ground pork
- 3 egg yolks
- 1 cup Thai sweet chili sauce (spring roll sauce)
- ¼ cup toasted sesame seeds
- 2 scallions, sliced

**Directions:**
1. Combine the shallot, garlic, ginger, thyme, mushrooms, soy sauce, freshly ground black pepper, ground beef and pork, and egg yolks in a bowl and mix the ingredients together. Gently shape the mixture into 24 balls, about the size of a golf ball.

2. Preheat the air fryer to 380°F.

3. Working in batches, air-fry the meatballs for 8 minutes, turning the meatballs over halfway through the cooking time. Drizzle some of the Thai sweet chili sauce on top of each meatball and return the basket to the air fryer, air-frying for another 2 minutes. Reserve the remaining Thai sweet chili sauce for serving.

4. As soon as the meatballs are done, sprinkle with toasted sesame seeds and transfer them to a serving platter. Scatter the scallions around and serve warm.

# Turkey Burgers

Servings: 3
Cooking Time: 23 Minutes

**Ingredients:**
- 1 pound 2 ounces Ground turkey
- 6 tablespoons Frozen chopped spinach, thawed and squeezed dry
- 3 tablespoons Plain panko bread crumbs (gluten-free, if a concern)
- 1 tablespoon Dijon mustard (gluten-free, if a concern)
- 1½ teaspoons Minced garlic
- ¾ teaspoon Table salt
- ¾ teaspoon Ground black pepper
- Olive oil spray
- 3 Kaiser rolls (gluten-free, if a concern), split open

**Directions:**
1. Preheat the air fryer to 375°F .
2. Gently mix the ground turkey, spinach, bread crumbs, mustard, garlic, salt, and pepper in a large bowl until well combined, trying to keep some of the fibers of the ground turkey intact. Form into two 5-inch-wide patties for the small

batch, three 5-inch patties for the medium batch, or four 5-inch patties for the large. Coat each side of the patties with olive oil spray.

3. Set the patties in in the basket in one layer and air-fry undisturbed for 20 minutes, or until an instant-read meat thermometer inserted into the center of a burger registers 165°F. You may need to add 2 minutes to the cooking time if the air fryer is at 360°F.

4. Use a nonstick-safe spatula, and perhaps a flatware fork for balance, to transfer the burgers to a cutting board. Set the buns cut side down in the basket in one layer (working in batches as necessary) and air-fry for 1 minute, to toast a bit and warm up. Serve the burgers warm in the buns.

# White Bean Veggie Burgers

Servings: 3
Cooking Time: 13 Minutes

**Ingredients:**
- 1⅓ cups Drained and rinsed canned white beans
- 3 tablespoons Rolled oats (not quick-cooking or steel-cut; gluten-free, if a concern)
- 3 tablespoons Chopped walnuts
- 2 teaspoons Olive oil
- 2 teaspoons Lemon juice
- 1½ teaspoons Dijon mustard (gluten-free, if a concern)
- ¾ teaspoon Dried sage leaves
- ¼ teaspoon Table salt
- Olive oil spray
- 3 Whole-wheat buns or gluten-free whole-grain buns (if a concern), split open

**Directions:**
1. Preheat the air fryer to 400°F.
2. Place the beans, oats, walnuts, oil, lemon juice, mustard, sage, and salt in a food processor. Cover and process to make a coarse paste that will hold

its shape, about like wet sugar-cookie dough, stopping the machine to scrape down the inside of the canister at least once.

3. Scrape down and remove the blade. With clean and wet hands, form the bean paste into two 4-inch patties for the small batch, three 4-inch patties for the medium, or four 4-inch patties for the large batch. Generously coat the patties on both sides with olive oil spray.

4. Set them in the basket with some space between them and air-fry undisturbed for 12 minutes, or until lightly brown and crisp at the edges. The tops of the burgers will feel firm to the touch.

5. Use a nonstick-safe spatula, and perhaps a flatware fork for balance, to transfer the burgers to a cutting board. Set the buns cut side down in the basket in one layer (working in batches as necessary) and air-fry undisturbed for 1 minute, to toast a bit and warm up. Serve the burgers warm in the buns.

# Chicken Apple Brie Melt

Servings: 3
Cooking Time: 13 Minutes

**Ingredients:**
- 3 5- to 6-ounce boneless skinless chicken breasts
- Vegetable oil spray
- 1½ teaspoons Dried herbes de Provence
- 3 ounces Brie, rind removed, thinly sliced
- 6 Thin cored apple slices
- 3 French rolls (gluten-free, if a concern)
- 2 tablespoons Dijon mustard (gluten-free, if a concern)

**Directions:**
1. Preheat the air fryer to 375°F .

2. Lightly coat all sides of the chicken breasts with vegetable oil spray. Sprinkle the breasts evenly with the herbes de Provence.

3. When the machine is at temperature, set the breasts in the basket and air-fry undisturbed for 10 minutes.

4. Top the chicken breasts with the apple slices, then the cheese. Air-fry undisturbed for 2 minutes, or until the cheese is melty and bubbling.

5. Use a nonstick-safe spatula and kitchen tongs, for balance, to transfer the breasts to a cutting board. Set the rolls in the basket and air-fry for 1 minute to warm through. (Putting them in the machine without splitting them keeps the insides very soft while the outside gets a little crunchy.)

6. Transfer the rolls to the cutting board. Split them open lengthwise, then spread 1 teaspoon mustard on each cut side. Set a prepared chicken breast on the bottom of a roll and close with its top, repeating as necessary to make additional sandwiches. Serve warm.

# Chicken Spiedies

Servings: 3
Cooking Time: 12 Minutes

**Ingredients:**
- 1¼ pounds Boneless skinless chicken thighs, trimmed of any fat blobs and cut into 2-inch pieces
- 3 tablespoons Red wine vinegar
- 2 tablespoons Olive oil
- 2 tablespoons Minced fresh mint leaves
- 2 tablespoons Minced fresh parsley leaves
- 2 teaspoons Minced fresh dill fronds
- ¾ teaspoon Fennel seeds
- ¾ teaspoon Table salt
- Up to a ¼ teaspoon Red pepper flakes
- 3 Long soft rolls, such as hero, hoagie, or Italian sub rolls (gluten-free, if a concern), split open lengthwise
- 4½ tablespoons Regular or low-fat mayonnaise (not fat-free; gluten-free, if a concern)
- 1½ tablespoons Distilled white vinegar
- 1½ teaspoons Ground black pepper

**Directions:**
1. Mix the chicken, vinegar, oil, mint, parsley, dill, fennel seeds, salt, and red pepper flakes in a zip-closed plastic bag. Seal, gently massage the marinade ingredients into the meat, and refrigerate for at least 2 hours or up to 6 hours. (Longer than that and the meat can turn rubbery.)

2. Set the plastic bag out on the counter (to make the contents a little less frigid). Preheat the air fryer to 400°F.

3. When the machine is at temperature, use kitchen tongs to set the chicken thighs in the basket (discard any remaining marinade) and air-fry undisturbed for 6 minutes. Turn the thighs over and continue air-frying undisturbed for 6 minutes more, until well browned, cooked through, and even a little crunchy.

4. Dump the contents of the basket onto a wire rack and cool for 2 or 3 minutes. Divide the chicken evenly between the rolls. Whisk the mayonnaise, vinegar, and black pepper in a small bowl until smooth. Drizzle this sauce over the chicken pieces in the rolls.

# Thai-style Pork Sliders

Servings: 4
Cooking Time: 15 Minutes

**Ingredients:**
- 11 ounces Ground pork
- 2½ tablespoons Very thinly sliced scallions, white and green parts
- 4 teaspoons Minced peeled fresh ginger
- 2½ teaspoons Fish sauce (gluten-free, if a concern)
- 2 teaspoons Thai curry paste (see the headnote; gluten-free, if a concern)
- 2 teaspoons Light brown sugar
- ¾ teaspoon Ground black pepper
- 4 Slider buns (gluten-free, if a concern)

**Directions:**
1. Preheat the air fryer to 375°F .
2. Gently mix the pork, scallions, ginger, fish sauce, curry paste, brown sugar, and black pepper in a bowl until well combined. With clean, wet hands, form about ⅓ cup of the pork mixture into a slider about 2½ inches in diameter. Repeat until you use up all the meat—3 sliders for the small batch, 4 for the medium, and 6 for the large. (Keep wetting your hands to help the patties adhere.)
3. When the machine is at temperature, set the sliders in the basket in one layer. Air-fry undisturbed for 14 minutes, or until the sliders are golden brown and caramelized at their edges and an instant-read meat thermometer inserted into the center of a slider registers 160°F.
4. Use a nonstick-safe spatula, and perhaps a flatware fork for balance, to transfer the sliders to a cutting board. Set the buns cut side down in the basket in one layer (working in batches as necessary) and air-fry undisturbed for 1 minute, to toast a bit and warm up. Serve the sliders warm in the buns.

# Perfect Burgers

Servings: 3
Cooking Time: 13 Minutes

**Ingredients:**
- 1 pound 2 ounces 90% lean ground beef
- 1½ tablespoons Worcestershire sauce (gluten-free, if a concern)
- ½ teaspoon Ground black pepper
- 3 Hamburger buns (gluten-free if a concern), split open

**Directions:**
1. Preheat the air fryer to 375°F .
2. Gently mix the ground beef, Worcestershire sauce, and pepper in a bowl until well combined but preserving as much of the meat's fibers as possible. Divide this mixture into two 5-inch patties for the small batch, three 5-inch patties for the medium, or four 5-inch patties for the large. Make a thumbprint indentation in the center of each patty, about halfway through the meat.
3. Set the patties in the basket in one layer with some space between them. Air-fry undisturbed for 10 minutes, or until an instant-read meat thermometer inserted into the center of a burger registers 160°F (a medium-well burger). You may need to add 2 minutes cooking time if the air fryer is at 360°F.
4. Use a nonstick-safe spatula, and perhaps a flatware fork for balance, to transfer the burgers to a cutting board. Set the buns cut side down in the basket in one layer (working in batches as necessary) and air-fry undisturbed for 1 minute, to toast a bit and warm up. Serve the burgers in the warm buns.

# Sausage And Pepper Heros

Servings: 3
Cooking Time: 11 Minutes

**Ingredients:**
- 3 links (about 9 ounces total) Sweet Italian sausages (gluten-free, if a concern)
- 1½ Medium red or green bell pepper(s), stemmed, cored, and cut into ½-inch-wide strips
- 1 medium Yellow or white onion(s), peeled, halved, and sliced into thin half-moons
- 3 Long soft rolls, such as hero, hoagie, or Italian sub rolls (gluten-free, if a concern), split open lengthwise
- For garnishing Balsamic vinegar
- For garnishing Fresh basil leaves

**Directions:**
1. Preheat the air fryer to 400°F.
2. When the machine is at temperature, set the sausage links in the basket in one layer and air-fry undisturbed for 5 minutes.
3. Add the pepper strips and onions. Continue air-frying, tossing and rearranging everything about once every minute, for 5 minutes, or until the sausages are browned and an instant-read meat thermometer inserted into one of the links registers 160°F.
4. Use a nonstick-safe spatula and kitchen tongs to transfer the sausages and vegetables to a cutting board. Set the rolls cut side down in the basket in one layer (working in batches as necessary) and air-fry undisturbed for 1 minute, to toast the rolls a bit and warm them up. Set 1 sausage with some pepper strips and onions in each warm roll, sprinkle balsamic vinegar over the sandwich fillings, and garnish with basil leaves.

# Dijon Thyme Burgers

Servings: 3
Cooking Time: 18 Minutes

**Ingredients:**
- 1 pound lean ground beef
- ⅓ cup panko breadcrumbs
- ¼ cup finely chopped onion
- 3 tablespoons Dijon mustard
- 1 tablespoon chopped fresh thyme
- 4 teaspoons Worcestershire sauce
- 1 teaspoon salt
- freshly ground black pepper
- Topping (optional):
- 2 tablespoons Dijon mustard
- 1 tablespoon dark brown sugar
- 1 teaspoon Worcestershire sauce
- 4 ounces sliced Swiss cheese, optional

**Directions:**
1. Combine all the burger ingredients together in a large bowl and mix well. Divide the meat into 4 equal portions and then form the burgers, being careful not to over-handle the meat. One good way to do this is to throw the meat back and forth from one hand to another, packing the meat each time you catch it. Flatten the balls into patties, making an indentation in the center of each patty with your thumb (this will help it stay flat as it cooks) and flattening the sides of the burgers so that they will fit nicely into the air fryer basket.
2. Preheat the air fryer to 370°F.
3. If you don't have room for all four burgers, air-fry two or three burgers at a time for 8 minutes. Flip the burgers over and air-fry for another 6 minutes.
4. While the burgers are cooking combine the Dijon mustard, dark brown sugar, and Worcestershire sauce in a small bowl and mix well. This optional topping to the burgers really

adds a boost of flavor at the end. Spread the Dijon topping evenly on each burger. If you cooked the burgers in batches, return the first batch to the cooker at this time – it's ok to place the fourth burger on top of the others in the center of the basket. Air-fry the burgers for another 3 minutes.

5. Finally, if desired, top each burger with a slice of Swiss cheese. Lower the air fryer temperature to 330°F and air-fry for another minute to melt the cheese. Serve the burgers on toasted brioche buns, dressed the way you like them.

# Thanksgiving Turkey Sandwiches

Servings: 3
Cooking Time: 10 Minutes

**Ingredients:**

- 1½ cups Herb-seasoned stuffing mix (not cornbread-style; gluten-free, if a concern)
- 1 Large egg white(s)
- 2 tablespoons Water
- 3 5- to 6-ounce turkey breast cutlets
- Vegetable oil spray
- 4½ tablespoons Purchased cranberry sauce, preferably whole berry
- ⅛ teaspoon Ground cinnamon
- ⅛ teaspoon Ground dried ginger
- 4½ tablespoons Regular, low-fat, or fat-free mayonnaise (gluten-free, if a concern)
- 6 tablespoons Shredded Brussels sprouts
- 3 Kaiser rolls (gluten-free, if a concern), split open

**Directions:**

1. Preheat the air fryer to 375°F .
2. Put the stuffing mix in a heavy zip-closed bag, seal it, lay it flat on your counter, and roll a rolling pin over the bag to crush the stuffing mix to the consistency of rough sand. (Or you can pulse the stuffing mix to the desired consistency in a food processor.)
3. Set up and fill two shallow soup plates or small pie plates on your counter: one for the egg white(s), whisked with the water until foamy; and one for the ground stuffing mix.
4. Dip a cutlet in the egg white mixture, coating both sides and letting any excess egg white slip back into the rest. Set the cutlet in the ground stuffing mix and coat it evenly on both sides, pressing gently to coat well on both sides. Lightly coat the cutlet on both sides with vegetable oil spray, set it aside, and continue dipping and coating the remaining cutlets in the same way.
5. Set the cutlets in the basket and air-fry undisturbed for 10 minutes, or until crisp and brown. Use kitchen tongs to transfer the cutlets to a wire rack to cool for a few minutes.
6. Meanwhile, stir the cranberry sauce with the cinnamon and ginger in a small bowl. Mix the shredded Brussels sprouts and mayonnaise in a second bowl until the vegetable is evenly coated.
7. Build the sandwiches by spreading about 1½ tablespoons of the cranberry mixture on the cut side of the bottom half of each roll. Set a cutlet on top, then spread about 3 tablespoons of the Brussels sprouts mixture evenly over the cutlet. Set the other half of the roll on top and serve warm.

# Lamb Burgers

Servings: 3
Cooking Time: 17 Minutes

**Ingredients:**

- 1 pound 2 ounces Ground lamb
- 3 tablespoons Crumbled feta
- 1 teaspoon Minced garlic
- 1 teaspoon Tomato paste
- ¾ teaspoon Ground coriander

- ¾ teaspoon Ground dried ginger
- Up to ⅛ teaspoon Cayenne
- Up to a ⅛ teaspoon Table salt (optional)
- 3 Kaiser rolls or hamburger buns (gluten-free, if a concern), split open

**Directions:**
1. Preheat the air fryer to 375°F .
2. Gently mix the ground lamb, feta, garlic, tomato paste, coriander, ginger, cayenne, and salt (if using) in a bowl until well combined, trying to keep the bits of cheese intact. Form this mixture into two 5-inch patties for the small batch, three 5-inch patties for the medium, or four 5-inch patties for the large.
3. Set the patties in the basket in one layer and air-fry undisturbed for 16 minutes, or until an instant-read meat thermometer inserted into one burger registers 160°F. (The cheese is not an issue with the temperature probe in this recipe as it was for the Inside-Out Cheeseburgers, because the feta is so well mixed into the ground meat.)
4. Use a nonstick-safe spatula, and perhaps a flatware fork for balance, to transfer the burgers to a cutting board. Set the buns cut side down in the basket in one layer (working in batches as necessary) and air-fry undisturbed for 1 minute, to toast a bit and warm up. Serve the burgers warm in the buns.

## Chicken Club Sandwiches

Servings: 3
Cooking Time: 15 Minutes

**Ingredients:**
- 3 5- to 6-ounce boneless skinless chicken breasts
- 6 Thick-cut bacon strips (gluten-free, if a concern)
- 3 Long soft rolls, such as hero, hoagie, or Italian sub rolls (gluten-free, if a concern)
- 3 tablespoons Regular, low-fat, or fat-free mayonnaise (gluten-free, if a concern)
- 3 Lettuce leaves, preferably romaine or iceberg
- 6 ¼-inch-thick tomato slices

**Directions:**
1. Preheat the air fryer to 375°F .
2. Wrap each chicken breast with 2 strips of bacon, spiraling the bacon around the meat, slightly overlapping the strips on each revolution. Start the second strip of bacon farther down the breast but on a line with the start of the first strip so they both end at a lined-up point on the chicken breast.
3. When the machine is at temperature, set the wrapped breasts bacon-seam side down in the basket with space between them. Air-fry undisturbed for 12 minutes, until the bacon is browned, crisp, and cooked through and an instant-read meat thermometer inserted into the center of a breast registers 165°F. You may need to add 2 minutes in the air fryer if the temperature is at 360°F.
4. Use kitchen tongs to transfer the breasts to a wire rack. Split the rolls open lengthwise and set them cut side down in the basket. Air-fry for 1 minute, or until warmed through.
5. Use kitchen tongs to transfer the rolls to a cutting board. Spread 1 tablespoon mayonnaise on the cut side of one half of each roll. Top with a chicken breast, lettuce leaf, and tomato slice. Serve warm.

## Inside-out Cheeseburgers

Servings: 3
Cooking Time: 9-11 Minutes

**Ingredients:**
- 1 pound 2 ounces 90% lean ground beef
- ¾ teaspoon Dried oregano

- ¾ teaspoon Table salt
- ¾ teaspoon Ground black pepper
- ¼ teaspoon Garlic powder
- 6 tablespoons (about 1½ ounces) Shredded Cheddar, Swiss, or other semi-firm cheese, or a purchased blend of shredded cheeses
- 3 Hamburger buns (gluten-free, if a concern), split open

**Directions:**

1. Preheat the air fryer to 375°F .
2. Gently mix the ground beef, oregano, salt, pepper, and garlic powder in a bowl until well combined without turning the mixture to mush. Form it into two 6-inch patties for the small batch, three for the medium, or four for the large.
3. Place 2 tablespoons of the shredded cheese in the center of each patty. With clean hands, fold the sides of the patty up to cover the cheese, then pick it up and roll it gently into a ball to seal the cheese inside. Gently press it back into a 5-inch burger without letting any cheese squish out. Continue filling and preparing more burgers, as needed.
4. Place the burgers in the basket in one layer and air-fry undisturbed for 8 minutes for medium or 10 minutes for well-done. (An instant-read meat thermometer won't work for these burgers because it will hit the mostly melted cheese inside and offer a hotter temperature than the surrounding meat.)
5. Use a nonstick-safe spatula, and perhaps a flatware fork for balance, to transfer the burgers to a cutting board. Set the buns cut side down in the basket in one layer (working in batches as necessary) and air-fry undisturbed for 1 minute, to toast a bit and warm up. Cool the burgers a few minutes more, then serve them warm in the buns.

# Provolone Stuffed Meatballs

Servings: 4
Cooking Time: 12 Minutes

**Ingredients:**

- 1 tablespoon olive oil
- 1 small onion, very finely chopped
- 1 to 2 cloves garlic, minced
- ¾ pound ground beef
- ¾ pound ground pork
- ¾ cup breadcrumbs
- ¼ cup grated Parmesan cheese
- ¼ cup finely chopped fresh parsley (or 1 tablespoon dried parsley)
- ½ teaspoon dried oregano
- 1½ teaspoons salt
- freshly ground black pepper
- 2 eggs, lightly beaten
- 5 ounces sharp or aged provolone cheese, cut into 1-inch cubes

**Directions:**

1. Preheat a skillet over medium-high heat. Add the oil and cook the onion and garlic until tender, but not browned.
2. Transfer the onion and garlic to a large bowl and add the beef, pork, breadcrumbs, Parmesan cheese, parsley, oregano, salt, pepper and eggs. Mix well until all the ingredients are combined. Divide the mixture into 12 evenly sized balls. Make one meatball at a time, by pressing a hole in the meatball mixture with your finger and pushing a piece of provolone cheese into the hole. Mold the meat back into a ball, enclosing the cheese.
3. Preheat the air fryer to 380°F.
4. Working in two batches, transfer six of the meatballs to the air fryer basket and air-fry for 12 minutes, shaking the basket and turning the meatballs a couple of times during the cooking process. Repeat with the remaining six meatballs.

You can pop the first batch of meatballs into the air fryer for the last two minutes of cooking to reheat them. Serve warm.

# Salmon Burgers

Servings: 3
Cooking Time: 8 Minutes

**Ingredients:**

- 1 pound 2 ounces Skinless salmon fillet, preferably fattier Atlantic salmon
- 1½ tablespoons Minced chives or the green part of a scallion
- ½ cup Plain panko bread crumbs (gluten-free, if a concern)
- 1½ teaspoons Dijon mustard (gluten-free, if a concern)
- 1½ teaspoons Drained and rinsed capers, minced
- 1½ teaspoons Lemon juice
- ¼ teaspoon Table salt
- ¼ teaspoon Ground black pepper
- Vegetable oil spray

**Directions:**

1. Preheat the air fryer to 375°F .
2. Cut the salmon into pieces that will fit in a food processor. Cover and pulse until coarsely chopped. Add the chives and pulse to combine, until the fish is ground but not a paste. Scrape down and remove the blade. Scrape the salmon mixture into a bowl. Add the bread crumbs, mustard, capers, lemon juice, salt, and pepper. Stir gently until well combined.
3. Use clean and dry hands to form the mixture into two 5-inch patties for a small batch, three 5-inch patties for a medium batch, or four 5-inch patties for a large one.
4. Coat both sides of each patty with vegetable oil spray. Set them in the basket in one layer and air-fry undisturbed for 8 minutes, or until browned and an instant-read meat thermometer inserted into the center of a burger registers 145°F.
5. Use a nonstick-safe spatula, and perhaps a flatware fork for balance, to transfer the burgers to a wire rack. Cool for 2 or 3 minutes before serving.

# Crunchy Falafel Balls

Servings: 8
Cooking Time: 16 Minutes

**Ingredients:**

- 2½ cups Drained and rinsed canned chickpeas
- ¼ cup Olive oil
- 3 tablespoons All-purpose flour
- 1½ teaspoons Dried oregano
- 1½ teaspoons Dried sage leaves
- 1½ teaspoons Dried thyme
- ¾ teaspoon Table salt
- Olive oil spray

**Directions:**

1. Preheat the air fryer to 400°F.
2. Place the chickpeas, olive oil, flour, oregano, sage, thyme, and salt in a food processor. Cover and process into a paste, stopping the machine at least once to scrape down the inside of the canister.
3. Scrape down and remove the blade. Using clean, wet hands, form 2 tablespoons of the paste into a ball, then continue making 9 more balls for a small batch, 15 more for a medium one, and 19 more for a large batch. Generously coat the balls in olive oil spray.
4. Set the balls in the basket in one layer with a little space between them and air-fry undisturbed for 16 minutes, or until well browned and crisp.
5. Dump the contents of the basket onto a wire rack. Cool for 5 minutes before serving.

# Chicken Saltimbocca Sandwiches

Servings: 3
Cooking Time: 11 Minutes

**Ingredients:**
* 3 5- to 6-ounce boneless skinless chicken breasts
* 6 Thin prosciutto slices
* 6 Provolone cheese slices
* 3 Long soft rolls, such as hero, hoagie, or Italian sub rolls (gluten-free, if a concern), split open lengthwise
* 3 tablespoons Pesto, purchased or homemade (see the headnote)

**Directions:**
1. Preheat the air fryer to 400°F.
2. Wrap each chicken breast with 2 prosciutto slices, spiraling the prosciutto around the breast and overlapping the slices a bit to cover the breast. The prosciutto will stick to the chicken more readily than bacon does.
3. When the machine is at temperature, set the wrapped chicken breasts in the basket and air-fry undisturbed for 10 minutes, or until the prosciutto is frizzled and the chicken is cooked through.
4. Overlap 2 cheese slices on each breast. Air-fry undisturbed for 1 minute, or until melted. Take the basket out of the machine.
5. Smear the insides of the rolls with the pesto, then use kitchen tongs to put a wrapped and cheesy chicken breast in each roll.

# Chili Cheese Dogs

Servings: 3
Cooking Time: 12 Minutes

**Ingredients:**
* ¾ pound Lean ground beef
* 1½ tablespoons Chile powder
* 1 cup plus 2 tablespoons Jarred sofrito
* 3 Hot dogs (gluten-free, if a concern)
* 3 Hot dog buns (gluten-free, if a concern), split open lengthwise
* 3 tablespoons Finely chopped scallion
* 9 tablespoons (a little more than 2 ounces) Shredded Cheddar cheese

**Directions:**
1. Crumble the ground beef into a medium or large saucepan set over medium heat. Brown well, stirring often to break up the clumps. Add the chile powder and cook for 30 seconds, stirring the whole time. Stir in the sofrito and bring to a simmer. Reduce the heat to low and simmer, stirring occasionally, for 5 minutes. Keep warm.
2. Preheat the air fryer to 400°F.
3. When the machine is at temperature, put the hot dogs in the basket and air-fry undisturbed for 10 minutes, or until the hot dogs are bubbling and blistered, even a little crisp.
4. Use kitchen tongs to put the hot dogs in the buns. Top each with a ½ cup of the ground beef mixture, 1 tablespoon of the minced scallion, and 3 tablespoons of the cheese. (The scallion should go under the cheese so it superheats and wilts a bit.) Set the filled hot dog buns in the basket and air-fry undisturbed for 2 minutes, or until the cheese has melted.
5. Remove the basket from the machine. Cool the chili cheese dogs in the basket for 5 minutes before serving.

# Fish And Seafood Recipes

## Easy Scallops With Lemon Butter

Servings:3
Cooking Time: 4 Minutes

**Ingredients:**
- 1 tablespoon Olive oil
- 2 teaspoons Minced garlic
- 1 teaspoon Finely grated lemon zest
- ½ teaspoon Red pepper flakes
- ¼ teaspoon Table salt
- 1 pound Sea scallops
- 3 tablespoons Butter, melted
- 1½ tablespoons Lemon juice

**Directions:**
1. Preheat the air fryer to 400°F.
2. Gently stir the olive oil, garlic, lemon zest, red pepper flakes, and salt in a bowl. Add the scallops and stir very gently until they are evenly and well coated.
3. When the machine is at temperature, arrange the scallops in a single layer in the basket. Some may touch. Air-fry undisturbed for 4 minutes, or until the scallops are opaque and firm.
4. While the scallops cook, stir the melted butter and lemon juice in a serving bowl. When the scallops are ready, pour them from the basket into this bowl. Toss well before serving.

## Shrimp, Chorizo And Fingerling Potatoes

Servings: 4
Cooking Time: 16 Minutes

**Ingredients:**
- ½ red onion, chopped into 1-inch chunks
- 8 fingerling potatoes, sliced into 1-inch slices or halved lengthwise
- 1 teaspoon olive oil
- salt and freshly ground black pepper
- 8 ounces raw chorizo sausage, sliced into 1-inch chunks
- 16 raw large shrimp, peeled, deveined and tails removed
- 1 lime
- ¼ cup chopped fresh cilantro
- chopped orange zest (optional)

**Directions:**
1. Preheat the air fryer to 380°F.
2. Combine the red onion and potato chunks in a bowl and toss with the olive oil, salt and freshly ground black pepper.
3. Transfer the vegetables to the air fryer basket and air-fry for 6 minutes, shaking the basket a few times during the cooking process.
4. Add the chorizo chunks and continue to air-fry for another 5 minutes.
5. Add the shrimp, season with salt and continue to air-fry, shaking the basket every once in a while, for another 5 minutes.
6. Transfer the tossed shrimp, chorizo and potato to a bowl and squeeze some lime juice over the top to taste. Toss in the fresh cilantro, orange zest and a drizzle of olive oil, and season again to taste.
7. Serve with a fresh green salad.

# Crabmeat-stuffed Flounder

Servings:3
Cooking Time: 12 Minutes

**Ingredients:**
* 4½ ounces Purchased backfin or claw crabmeat, picked over for bits of shell and cartilage
* 6 Saltine crackers, crushed into fine crumbs
* 2 tablespoons plus 1 teaspoon Regular or low-fat mayonnaise (not fat-free)
* ¾ teaspoon Yellow prepared mustard
* 1½ teaspoons Worcestershire sauce
* ⅛ teaspoon Celery salt
* 3 5- to 6-ounce skinless flounder fillets
* Vegetable oil spray
* Mild paprika

**Directions:**
1. Preheat the air fryer to 400°F.
2. Gently mix the crabmeat, crushed saltines, mayonnaise, mustard, Worcestershire sauce, and celery salt in a bowl until well combined.
3. Generously coat the flat side of a fillet with vegetable oil spray. Set the fillet sprayed side down on your work surface. Cut the fillet in half widthwise, then cut one of the halves in half lengthwise. Set a scant ⅓ cup of the crabmeat mixture on top of the undivided half of the fish fillet, mounding the mixture to make an oval that somewhat fits the shape of the fillet with at least a ¼-inch border of fillet beyond the filling all around.
4. Take the two thin divided quarters (that is, the halves of the half) and lay them lengthwise over the filling, overlapping at each end and leaving a little space in the middle where the filling peeks through. Coat the top of the stuffed flounder piece with vegetable oil spray, then sprinkle paprika over the stuffed flounder fillet. Set aside and use the remaining fillet(s) to make more stuffed flounder "packets," repeating steps 3 and
5. Use a nonstick-safe spatula to transfer the stuffed flounder fillets to the basket. Leave as much space between them as possible. Air-fry undisturbed for 12 minutes, or until lightly brown and firm (but not hard).
6. Use that same spatula, plus perhaps another one, to transfer the fillets to a serving platter or plates. Cool for a minute or two, then serve hot.

# Sea Scallops

Servings: 4
Cooking Time: 8 Minutes

**Ingredients:**
* 1½ pounds sea scallops
* salt and pepper
* 2 eggs
* ½ cup flour
* ½ cup plain breadcrumbs
* oil for misting or cooking spray

**Directions:**
1. Rinse scallops and remove the tough side muscle. Sprinkle to taste with salt and pepper.
2. Beat eggs together in a shallow dish. Place flour in a second shallow dish and breadcrumbs in a third.
3. Preheat air fryer to 390°F.
4. Dip scallops in flour, then eggs, and then roll in breadcrumbs. Mist with oil or cooking spray.
5. Place scallops in air fryer basket in a single layer, leaving some space between. You should be able to cook about a dozen at a time.
6. Cook at 390°F for 8 minutes, watching carefully so as not to overcook. Scallops are done when they turn opaque all the way through. They will feel slightly firm when pressed with tines of a fork.
7. Repeat step 6 to cook remaining scallops.

# Almond-crusted Fish

Servings: 4
Cooking Time: 10 Minutes

**Ingredients:**
- 4 4-ounce fish fillets
- ¾ cup breadcrumbs
- ¼ cup sliced almonds, crushed
- 2 tablespoons lemon juice
- ⅛ teaspoon cayenne
- salt and pepper
- ¾ cup flour
- 1 egg, beaten with 1 tablespoon water
- oil for misting or cooking spray

**Directions:**
1. Split fish fillets lengthwise down the center to create 8 pieces.
2. Mix breadcrumbs and almonds together and set aside.
3. Mix the lemon juice and cayenne together. Brush on all sides of fish.
4. Season fish to taste with salt and pepper.
5. Place the flour on a sheet of wax paper.
6. Roll fillets in flour, dip in egg wash, and roll in the crumb mixture.
7. Mist both sides of fish with oil or cooking spray.
8. Spray air fryer basket and lay fillets inside.
9. Cook at 390°F for 5minutes, turn fish over, and cook for an additional 5minutes or until fish is done and flakes easily.

# Maple-crusted Salmon

Servings: 2
Cooking Time: 8 Minutes

**Ingredients:**
- 12 ounces salmon filets
- ⅓ cup maple syrup
- 1 teaspoon Worcestershire sauce
- 2 teaspoons Dijon mustard or brown mustard
- ½ cup finely chopped walnuts
- ½ teaspoon sea salt
- ½ lemon
- 1 tablespoon chopped parsley, for garnish

**Directions:**
1. Place the salmon in a shallow baking dish. Top with maple syrup, Worcestershire sauce, and mustard. Refrigerate for 30 minutes.
2. Preheat the air fryer to 350°F.
3. Remove the salmon from the marinade and discard the marinade.
4. Place the chopped nuts on top of the salmon filets, and sprinkle salt on top of the nuts. Place the salmon, skin side down, in the air fryer basket. Cook for 6 to 8 minutes or until the fish flakes in the center.
5. Remove the salmon and plate on a serving platter. Squeeze fresh lemon over the top of the salmon and top with chopped parsley. Serve immediately.

# Flounder Fillets

Servings: 4
Cooking Time: 8 Minutes

**Ingredients:**
- 1 egg white
- 1 tablespoon water
- 1 cup panko breadcrumbs
- 2 tablespoons extra-light virgin olive oil
- 4 4-ounce flounder fillets
- salt and pepper
- oil for misting or cooking spray

**Directions:**
1. Preheat air fryer to 390°F.
2. Beat together egg white and water in shallow dish.

3. In another shallow dish, mix panko crumbs and oil until well combined and crumbly (best done by hand).

4. Season flounder fillets with salt and pepper to taste. Dip each fillet into egg mixture and then roll in panko crumbs, pressing in crumbs so that fish is nicely coated.

5. Spray air fryer basket with nonstick cooking spray and add fillets. Cook at 390°F for 3minutes.

6. Spray fish fillets but do not turn. Cook 5 minutes longer or until golden brown and crispy. Using a spatula, carefully remove fish from basket and serve.

# Tuna Patties With Dill Sauce

Servings: 6
Cooking Time: 10 Minutes

**Ingredients:**
- Two 5-ounce cans albacore tuna, drained
- ½ teaspoon garlic powder
- 2 teaspoons dried dill, divided
- ½ teaspoon black pepper
- ½ teaspoon salt, divided
- ¼ cup minced onion
- 1 large egg
- 7 tablespoons mayonnaise, divided
- ¼ cup panko breadcrumbs
- 1 teaspoon fresh lemon juice
- ¼ teaspoon fresh lemon zest
- 6 pieces butterleaf lettuce
- 1 cup diced tomatoes

**Directions:**
1. In a large bowl, mix the tuna with the garlic powder, 1 teaspoon of the dried dill, the black pepper, ¼ teaspoon of the salt, and the onion. Make sure to use the back of a fork to really break up the tuna so there are no large chunks.

2. Mix in the egg and 1 tablespoon of the mayonnaise; then fold in the breadcrumbs so the tuna begins to form a thick batter that holds together.

3. Portion the tuna mixture into 6 equal patties and place on a plate lined with parchment paper in the refrigerator for at least 30 minutes. This will help the patties hold together in the air fryer.

4. When ready to cook, preheat the air fryer to 350°F.

5. Liberally spray the metal trivet that sits inside the air fryer basket with olive oil mist and place the patties onto the trivet.

6. Cook for 5 minutes, flip, and cook another 5 minutes.

7. While the patties are cooking, make the dill sauce by combining the remaining 6 tablespoons of mayonnaise with the remaining 1 teaspoon of dill, the lemon juice, the lemon zest, and the remaining ¼ teaspoon of salt. Set aside.

8. Remove the patties from the air fryer.

9. Place 1 slice of lettuce on a plate and top with the tuna patty and a tomato slice. Repeat to form the remaining servings. Drizzle the dill dressing over the top. Serve immediately.

# Maple Balsamic Glazed Salmon

Servings: 4
Cooking Time: 10 Minutes

**Ingredients:**
- 4 (6-ounce) fillets of salmon
- salt and freshly ground black pepper
- vegetable oil
- ¼ cup pure maple syrup
- 3 tablespoons balsamic vinegar
- 1 teaspoon Dijon mustard

**Directions:**
1. Preheat the air fryer to 400°F.

2. Season the salmon well with salt and freshly ground black pepper. Spray or brush the bottom of the air fryer basket with vegetable oil and place

the salmon fillets inside. Air-fry the salmon for 5 minutes.

3. While the salmon is air-frying, combine the maple syrup, balsamic vinegar and Dijon mustard in a small saucepan over medium heat and stir to blend well. Let the mixture simmer while the fish is cooking. It should start to thicken slightly, but keep your eye on it so it doesn't burn.

4. Brush the glaze on the salmon fillets and air-fry for an additional 5 minutes. The salmon should feel firm to the touch when finished and the glaze should be nicely browned on top. Brush a little more glaze on top before removing and serving with rice and vegetables, or a nice green salad.

# Tilapia Teriyaki

Servings: 3
Cooking Time: 10 Minutes

**Ingredients:**
- 4 tablespoons teriyaki sauce
- 1 tablespoon pineapple juice
- 1 pound tilapia fillets
- cooking spray
- 6 ounces frozen mixed peppers with onions, thawed and drained
- 2 cups cooked rice

**Directions:**
1. Mix the teriyaki sauce and pineapple juice together in a small bowl.
2. Split tilapia fillets down the center lengthwise.
3. Brush all sides of fish with the sauce, spray air fryer basket with nonstick cooking spray, and place fish in the basket.
4. Stir the peppers and onions into the remaining sauce and spoon over the fish. Save any leftover sauce for drizzling over the fish when serving.

5. Cook at 360°F for 10 minutes, until fish flakes easily with a fork and is done in center.
6. Divide into 3 or 4 servings and serve each with approximately ½ cup cooked rice.

# Classic Crab Cakes

Servings:4
Cooking Time: 10 Minutes

**Ingredients:**
- 10 ounces Lump crabmeat, picked over for shell and cartilage
- 6 tablespoons Plain panko bread crumbs (gluten-free, if a concern)
- 6 tablespoons Chopped drained jarred roasted red peppers
- 4 Medium scallions, trimmed and thinly sliced
- ¼ cup Regular or low-fat mayonnaise (not fat-free; gluten-free, if a concern)
- ¼ teaspoon Dried dill
- ¼ teaspoon Dried thyme
- ¼ teaspoon Onion powder
- ¼ teaspoon Table salt
- ⅛ teaspoon Celery seeds
- Up to ⅛ teaspoon Cayenne
- Vegetable oil spray

**Directions:**
1. Preheat the air fryer to 400°F.
2. Gently mix the crabmeat, bread crumbs, red pepper, scallion, mayonnaise, dill, thyme, onion powder, salt, celery seeds, and cayenne in a bowl until well combined.
3. Use clean and dry hands to form ½ cup of this mixture into a tightly packed 1-inch-thick, 3- to 4-inch-wide patty. Coat the top and bottom of the patty with vegetable oil spray and set it aside. Continue making 1 more patty for a small batch, 3 more for a medium batch, or 5 more for a larger

one, coating them with vegetable oil spray on both sides.

4. Set the patties in one layer in the basket and air-fry undisturbed for 10 minutes, or until lightly browned and cooked through.

5. Use a nonstick-safe spatula to transfer the crab cakes to a serving platter or plates. Wait a couple of minutes before serving.

## Salmon Croquettes

Servings: 4
Cooking Time: 8 Minutes

**Ingredients:**
- 1 tablespoon oil
- ½ cup breadcrumbs
- 1 14.75-ounce can salmon, drained and all skin and fat removed
- 1 egg, beaten
- ⅓ cup coarsely crushed saltine crackers (about 8 crackers)
- ½ teaspoon Old Bay Seasoning
- ½ teaspoon onion powder
- ½ teaspoon Worcestershire sauce

**Directions:**
1. Preheat air fryer to 390°F.
2. In a shallow dish, mix oil and breadcrumbs until crumbly.
3. In a large bowl, combine the salmon, egg, cracker crumbs, Old Bay, onion powder, and Worcestershire. Mix well and shape into 8 small patties about ½-inch thick.
4. Gently dip each patty into breadcrumb mixture and turn to coat well on all sides.
5. Cook at 390°F for 8minutes or until outside is crispy and browned.

## Crispy Sweet-and-sour Cod Fillets

Servings:3
Cooking Time: 12 Minutes

**Ingredients:**
- 1½ cups Plain panko bread crumbs (gluten-free, if a concern)
- 2 tablespoons Regular or low-fat mayonnaise (not fat-free; gluten-free, if a concern)
- ¼ cup Sweet pickle relish
- 3 4- to 5-ounce skinless cod fillets

**Directions:**
1. Preheat the air fryer to 400°F.
2. Pour the bread crumbs into a shallow soup plate or a small pie plate. Mix the mayonnaise and relish in a small bowl until well combined. Smear this mixture all over the cod fillets. Set them in the crumbs and turn until evenly coated on all sides, even on the ends.
3. Set the coated cod fillets in the basket with as much air space between them as possible. They should not touch. Air-fry undisturbed for 12 minutes, or until browned and crisp.
4. Use a nonstick-safe spatula to transfer the cod pieces to a wire rack. Cool for only a minute or two before serving hot.

## Beer-breaded Halibut Fish Tacos

Servings: 4
Cooking Time: 10 Minutes

**Ingredients:**
- 1 pound halibut, cut into 1-inch strips
- 1 cup light beer
- 1 jalapeño, minced and divided
- 1 clove garlic, minced
- ¼ teaspoon ground cumin
- ½ cup cornmeal
- ¼ cup all-purpose flour

- 1¼ teaspoons sea salt, divided
- 2 cups shredded cabbage
- 1 lime, juiced and divided
- ¼ cup Greek yogurt
- ¼ cup mayonnaise
- 1 cup grape tomatoes, quartered
- ½ cup chopped cilantro
- ¼ cup chopped onion
- 1 egg, whisked
- 8 corn tortillas

**Directions:**

1. In a shallow baking dish, place the fish, the beer, 1 teaspoon of the minced jalapeño, the garlic, and the cumin. Cover and refrigerate for 30 minutes.

2. Meanwhile, in a medium bowl, mix together the cornmeal, flour, and ½ teaspoon of the salt.

3. In large bowl, mix together the shredded cabbage, 1 tablespoon of the lime juice, the Greek yogurt, the mayonnaise, and ½ teaspoon of the salt.

4. In a small bowl, make the pico de gallo by mixing together the tomatoes, cilantro, onion, ¼ teaspoon of the salt, the remaining jalapeño, and the remaining lime juice.

5. Remove the fish from the refrigerator and discard the marinade. Dredge the fish in the whisked egg; then dredge the fish in the cornmeal flour mixture, until all pieces of fish have been breaded.

6. Preheat the air fryer to 350°F.

7. Place the fish in the air fryer basket and spray liberally with cooking spray. Cook for 6 minutes, flip and shake the fish, and cook another 4 minutes.

8. While the fish is cooking, heat the tortillas in a heavy skillet for 1 to 2 minutes over high heat.

9. To assemble the tacos, place the battered fish on the heated tortillas, and top with slaw and pico de gallo. Serve immediately.

# Firecracker Popcorn Shrimp

Servings: 6
Cooking Time: 8 Minutes

**Ingredients:**

- ½ cup all-purpose flour
- 2 teaspoons ground paprika
- 1 teaspoon garlic powder
- ½ teaspoon black pepper
- ¼ teaspoon salt
- 2 eggs, whisked
- 1½ cups panko breadcrumbs
- 1 pound small shrimp, peeled and deveined

**Directions:**

1. Preheat the air fryer to 360°F.

2. In a medium bowl, place the flour and mix in the paprika, garlic powder, pepper, and salt.

3. In a shallow dish, place the eggs.

4. In a third dish, place the breadcrumbs.

5. Assemble the shrimp by covering them in the flour, then dipping them into the egg, and then coating them with the breadcrumbs. Repeat until all the shrimp are covered in the breading.

6. Liberally spray the metal trivet that fits in the air fryer basket with olive oil mist. Place the shrimp onto the trivet, leaving space between the shrimp to flip. Cook for 4 minutes, flip the shrimp, and cook another 4 minutes. Repeat until all the shrimp are cooked.

7. Serve warm with desired dipping sauce.

# Black Cod With Grapes, Fennel, Pecans And Kale

Servings: 2
Cooking Time: 15 Minutes

**Ingredients:**

- 2 (6- to 8-ounce) fillets of black cod (or sablefish)
- salt and freshly ground black pepper

- olive oil
- 1 cup grapes, halved
- 1 small bulb fennel, sliced ¼-inch thick
- ½ cup pecans
- 3 cups shredded kale
- 2 teaspoons white balsamic vinegar or white wine vinegar
- 2 tablespoons extra virgin olive oil

**Directions:**
1. Preheat the air fryer to 400°F.
2. Season the cod fillets with salt and pepper and drizzle, brush or spray a little olive oil on top. Place the fish, presentation side up (skin side down), into the air fryer basket. Air-fry for 10 minutes.
3. When the fish has finished cooking, remove the fillets to a side plate and loosely tent with foil to rest.
4. Toss the grapes, fennel and pecans in a bowl with a drizzle of olive oil and season with salt and pepper. Add the grapes, fennel and pecans to the air fryer basket and air-fry for 5 minutes at 400°F, shaking the basket once during the cooking time.
5. Transfer the grapes, fennel and pecans to a bowl with the kale. Dress the kale with the balsamic vinegar and olive oil, season to taste with salt and pepper and serve along side the cooked fish.

# Coconut Jerk Shrimp

Servings:3
Cooking Time: 8 Minutes

**Ingredients:**
- 1 Large egg white(s)
- 1 teaspoon Purchased or homemade jerk dried seasoning blend (see the headnote)
- ¾ cup Plain panko bread crumbs (gluten-free, if a concern)
- ¾ cup Unsweetened shredded coconut

- 12 Large shrimp (20–25 per pound), peeled and deveined
- Coconut oil spray

**Directions:**
1. Preheat the air fryer to 375°F .
2. Whisk the egg white(s) and seasoning blend in a bowl until foamy. Add the shrimp and toss well to coat evenly.
3. Mix the bread crumbs and coconut on a dinner plate until well combined. Use kitchen tongs to pick up a shrimp, letting the excess egg white mixture slip back into the rest. Set the shrimp in the bread-crumb mixture. Turn several times to coat evenly and thoroughly. Set on a cutting board and continue coating the remainder of the shrimp.
4. Lightly coat all the shrimp on both sides with the coconut oil spray. Set them in the basket in one layer with as much space between them as possible. (You can even stand some up along the basket's wall in some models.) Air-fry undisturbed for 6 minutes, or until the coating is lightly browned. If the air fryer is at 360°F, you may need to add 2 minutes to the cooking time.
5. Use clean kitchen tongs to transfer the shrimp to a wire rack. Cool for only a minute or two before serving.

# Bacon-wrapped Scallops

Servings: 4
Cooking Time: 8 Minutes

**Ingredients:**
- 16 large scallops
- 8 bacon strips
- ½ teaspoon black pepper
- ¼ teaspoon smoked paprika

**Directions:**
1. Pat the scallops dry with a paper towel. Slice each of the bacon strips in half. Wrap 1 bacon

strip around 1 scallop and secure with a toothpick. Repeat with the remaining scallops. Season the scallops with pepper and paprika.

2. Preheat the air fryer to 350°F.

3. Place the bacon-wrapped scallops in the air fryer basket and cook for 4 minutes, shake the basket, cook another 3 minutes, shake the basket, and cook another 1 to 3 to minutes. When the bacon is crispy, the scallops should be cooked through and slightly firm, but not rubbery. Serve immediately.

# Butternut Squash–wrapped Halibut Fillets

Servings:3
Cooking Time: 11 Minutes

**Ingredients:**
- 15 Long spiralized peeled and seeded butternut squash strands
- 3 5- to 6-ounce skinless halibut fillets
- 3 tablespoons Butter, melted
- ¾ teaspoon Mild paprika
- ¾ teaspoon Table salt
- ¾ teaspoon Ground black pepper

**Directions:**
1. Preheat the air fryer to 375°F .
2. Hold 5 long butternut squash strands together and wrap them around a fillet. Set it aside and wrap any remaining fillet(s).
3. Mix the melted butter, paprika, salt, and pepper in a small bowl. Brush this mixture over the squash-wrapped fillets on all sides.
4. When the machine is at temperature, set the fillets in the basket with as much air space between them as possible. Air-fry undisturbed for 10 minutes, or until the squash strands have browned but not burned. If the machine is at 360°F, you may need to add 1 minute to the cooking time. In any event, watch the fish carefully after the 8-minute mark.

5. Use a nonstick-safe spatula to gently transfer the fillets to a serving platter or plates. Cool for only a minute or so before serving.

# Fish Sticks For Grown-ups

Servings: 4
Cooking Time: 6 Minutes

**Ingredients:**
- 1 pound fish fillets
- ½ teaspoon hot sauce
- 1 tablespoon coarse brown mustard
- 1 teaspoon Worcestershire sauce
- salt
- Crumb Coating
- ¾ cup panko breadcrumbs
- ¼ cup stone-ground cornmeal
- ¼ teaspoon salt
- oil for misting or cooking spray

**Directions:**
1. Cut fish fillets crosswise into slices 1-inch wide.
2. Mix the hot sauce, mustard, and Worcestershire sauce together to make a paste and rub on all sides of the fish. Season to taste with salt.
3. Mix crumb coating ingredients together and spread on a sheet of wax paper.
4. Roll the fish fillets in the crumb mixture.
5. Spray all sides with olive oil or cooking spray and place in air fryer basket in a single layer.
6. Cook at 390°F for 6 minutes, until fish flakes easily.

# Shrimp Patties

Servings: 4
Cooking Time: 10 Minutes

**Ingredients:**
- ½ pound shelled and deveined raw shrimp
- ¼ cup chopped red bell pepper
- ¼ cup chopped green onion
- ¼ cup chopped celery
- 2 cups cooked sushi rice
- ½ teaspoon garlic powder
- ½ teaspoon Old Bay Seasoning
- ½ teaspoon salt
- 2 teaspoons Worcestershire sauce
- ½ cup plain breadcrumbs
- oil for misting or cooking spray

**Directions:**
1. Finely chop the shrimp. You can do this in a food processor, but it takes only a few pulses. Be careful not to overprocess into mush.
2. Place shrimp in a large bowl and add all other ingredients except the breadcrumbs and oil. Stir until well combined.
3. Preheat air fryer to 390°F.
4. Shape shrimp mixture into 8 patties, no more than ½-inch thick. Roll patties in breadcrumbs and mist with oil or cooking spray.
5. Place 4 shrimp patties in air fryer basket and cook at 390°F for 10 minutes, until shrimp cooks through and outside is crispy.
6. Repeat step 5 to cook remaining shrimp patties.

# Horseradish-crusted Salmon Fillets

Servings:3
Cooking Time: 8 Minutes

**Ingredients:**
- ½ cup Fresh bread crumbs (see the headnote)
- 4 tablespoons (¼ cup/½ stick) Butter, melted and cooled
- ¼ cup Jarred prepared white horseradish
- Vegetable oil spray
- 4 6-ounce skin-on salmon fillets (for more information, see here)

**Directions:**
1. Preheat the air fryer to 400°F.
2. Mix the bread crumbs, butter, and horseradish in a bowl until well combined.
3. Take the basket out of the machine. Generously spray the skin side of each fillet. Pick them up one by one with a nonstick-safe spatula and set them in the basket skin side down with as much air space between them as possible. Divide the bread-crumb mixture between the fillets, coating the top of each fillet with an even layer. Generously coat the bread-crumb mixture with vegetable oil spray.
4. Return the basket to the machine and air-fry undisturbed for 8 minutes, or until the topping has lightly browned and the fish is firm but not hard.
5. Use a nonstick-safe spatula to transfer the salmon fillets to serving plates. Cool for 5 minutes before serving. Because of the butter in the topping, it will stay very hot for quite a while. Take care, especially if you're serving these fillets to children.

# Fried Shrimp

Servings:3
Cooking Time: 7 Minutes

**Ingredients:**
- 1 Large egg white
- 2 tablespoons Water
- 1 cup Plain dried bread crumbs (gluten-free, if a concern)
- ¼ cup All-purpose flour or almond flour

- ¼ cup Yellow cornmeal
- 1 teaspoon Celery salt
- 1 teaspoon Mild paprika
- Up to ½ teaspoon Cayenne (optional)
- ¾ pound Large shrimp (20–25 per pound), peeled and deveined
- Vegetable oil spray

**Directions:**

1. Preheat the air fryer to 400°F.

2. Set two medium or large bowls on your counter. In the first, whisk the egg white and water until foamy. In the second, stir the bread crumbs, flour, cornmeal, celery salt, paprika, and cayenne (if using) until well combined.

3. Pour all the shrimp into the egg white mixture and stir gently until all the shrimp are coated. Use kitchen tongs to pick them up one by one and transfer them to the bread-crumb mixture. Turn each in the bread-crumb mixture to coat it evenly and thoroughly on all sides before setting it on a cutting board. When you're done coating the shrimp, coat them all on both sides with the vegetable oil spray.

4. Set the shrimp in as close to one layer in the basket as you can. Some may overlap. Air-fry for 7 minutes, gently rearranging the shrimp at the 4-minute mark to get covered surfaces exposed, until golden brown and firm but not hard.

5. Use kitchen tongs to gently transfer the shrimp to a wire rack. Cool for only a minute or two before serving.

# Coconut Shrimp

Servings: 4
Cooking Time: 12 Minutes

**Ingredients:**

- 1 pound large shrimp (about 16 to 20), peeled and de-veined
- ½ cup flour
- salt and freshly ground black pepper
- 2 egg whites
- ½ cup fine breadcrumbs
- ½ cup shredded unsweetened coconut
- zest of one lime
- ½ teaspoon salt
- ⅛ to ¼ teaspoon ground cayenne pepper
- vegetable or canola oil
- sweet chili sauce or duck sauce (for serving)

**Directions:**

1. Set up a dredging station. Place the flour in a shallow dish and season well with salt and freshly ground black pepper. Whisk the egg whites in a second shallow dish. In a third shallow dish, combine the breadcrumbs, coconut, lime zest, salt and cayenne pepper.

2. Preheat the air fryer to 400°F.

3. Dredge each shrimp first in the flour, then dip it in the egg mixture, and finally press it into the breadcrumb-coconut mixture to coat all sides. Place the breaded shrimp on a plate or baking sheet and spray both sides with vegetable oil.

4. Air-fry the shrimp in two batches, being sure not to over-crowd the basket. Air-fry for 5 minutes, turning the shrimp over for the last minute or two. Repeat with the second batch of shrimp.

5. Lower the temperature of the air fryer to 340°F. Return the first batch of shrimp to the air fryer basket with the second batch and air-fry for an additional 2 minutes, just to re-heat everything.

6. Serve with sweet chili sauce, duck sauce or just eat them plain!

# Italian Tuna Roast

Servings: 8
Cooking Time: 21 Minutes

**Ingredients:**
- cooking spray
- 1 tablespoon Italian seasoning
- ⅛ teaspoon ground black pepper
- 1 tablespoon extra-light olive oil
- 1 teaspoon lemon juice
- 1 tuna loin (approximately 2 pounds, 3 to 4 inches thick, large enough to fill a 6 x 6-inch baking dish)

**Directions:**
1. Spray baking dish with cooking spray and place in air fryer basket. Preheat air fryer to 390°F.
2. Mix together the Italian seasoning, pepper, oil, and lemon juice.
3. Using a dull table knife or butter knife, pierce top of tuna about every half inch: Insert knife into top of tuna roast and pierce almost all the way to the bottom.
4. Spoon oil mixture into each of the holes and use the knife to push seasonings into the tuna as deeply as possible.
5. Spread any remaining oil mixture on all outer surfaces of tuna.
6. Place tuna roast in baking dish and cook at 390°F for 20 minutes. Check temperature with a meat thermometer. Cook for an additional 1 minutes or until temperature reaches 145°F.
7. Remove basket from fryer and let tuna sit in basket for 10minutes.

# Recipe Index

Carrot Chips 34

Carrot Orange Muffins 79

Cauliflower "tater" Tots 31

Charred Cauliflower Tacos 109

Charred Radicchio Salad 66

Cheddar Cheese Biscuits 81

Cheddar-ham-corn Muffins 82

Cheese Straws 30

Cheesecake Wontons 100

Cheesy Potato Pot 64

Cheesy Potato Skins 68

Cheesy Texas Toast 68

Cherry Hand Pies 89

Chicken Adobo 16

Chicken Apple Brie Melt 125

Chicken Chunks 15

Chicken Club Sandwiches 130

Chicken Cutlets With Broccoli Rabe And Roasted Peppers 15

Chicken Eggrolls 69

Chicken Nuggets 21

Chicken Rochambeau 18

Chicken Saltimbocca Sandwiches 133

Chicken Spiedies 126

Chicken Strips 22

Chicken Wellington 22

Chili Cheese Dogs 133

Cinnamon Apple Crisps 32

Cinnamon Biscuit Rolls 86

Cinnamon Rolls With Cream Cheese Glaze 75

Cinnamon-stick Kofta Skewers 55

City "chicken" 52

Classic Crab Cakes 138

Coconut Jerk Shrimp 141

Coconut Macaroons 95

Coconut Shrimp 144

Coconut-custard Pie 90

Corn And Pepper Jack Chile Rellenos With Roasted Tomato Sauce 119

Corn Dog Muffins 32

Corn On The Cob 63

Country Gravy 78

Crabmeat-stuffed Flounder 135

Crispy Bacon 84

Crispy Duck With Cherry Sauce 16

Crispy Sweet-and-sour Cod Fillets 139

Crunchy Falafel Balls 132

Crunchy French Toast Sticks 80

Crunchy Fried Pork Loin Chops 42

Crunchy Lobster Bites 28

**D**

Dijon Thyme Burgers 128

**E**

Easy Churros 102

Easy Scallops With Lemon Butter 134

Egg Rolls 113

Eggplant Parmesan 114

Extra Crispy Country-style Pork Riblets 54

**F**

Falafel 110

Printed by Libri Plureos GmbH in Hamburg,
Germany